PAC POWER

Other Books by Larry J. Sabato

The Rise of Political Consultants: New Ways of Winning Elections (1981)
Goodbye to Good-Time Charlie: The American Governorship Transformed (revised, 1983)
The Democratic Party Primary: Tantamount to Election No Longer (1977)

PAC POWER

Inside the World of Political Action Committees

Larry J. Sabato

With a New Afterword

W·W· NORTON & COMPANY
NEW YORK LONDON

For my students,
who know that
politics is a good thing

Published simultaneously in Canada by
Penguin Books Canada Ltd.,
2801 John Street, Markham, Ontario L3R 1B4

Printed in the United States of America.

First published as a Norton paperback 1985

Library of Congress Cataloging in Publication Data
Sabato, Larry J.
PAC power.
Bibliography: p.
Includes index.
1. Campaign funds–United States. 2. Political
action committees–United States. I. Title
[JK1991.S23 1985] 324.7'0973 85-13916

ISBN 0-393-30257-1

W.W. Norton & Company, Inc.,
500 Fifth Avenue, New York, N. Y. 10110
W. W. Norton & Company Ltd.,
27 Great Russell Street, London WC1B 3NU

4 5 6 7 8 9

Contents

Acknowledgments

An author of a book about political action committees (PACs) learns many things in the course of his research, including how to endure waves of awful puns about the videogame of the same name. (I have resolved to spare the reader all of them.) One of my early discoveries was that despite the best efforts of scholars and journalists, most Americans know far more about PAC-Man than about PACs. What little is known, alas, is often wrong or oversimplified. This study, I hope, will help correct false impressions and inform those who have wondered what is behind every election season's bold headlines about PACs.

My investigation of political action committees rests on a series of more than sixty lengthy interviews with PAC and political party officials (listed at the back of this book) as well as an extensive random-sample survey of 399 PACs (see Introduction, note 16, for details). I am enormously grateful to those who took time to speak with me, for many hours on occasion, and to fill out a torturously long questionnare. Despite ample provocation, only a few respondents took the course of the Minnesota Truck Operators PAC recipient who returned an uncompleted survey with a note that read "I'm sorry but I really don't care to go thru this crap so you can get a raise or write a book." His frankness was refreshing but unilluminating, and I am thankful that most of his peers were more cooperative. All surveys and interview tapes have been preserved, of course. Occasionally interviewees requested that quotations be unattributed, and their wishes have been respected. Incidentally, unfootnoted quotations in this study have been drawn from my personal or telephone interviews, and quoted individuals are cited as holding the position they had when I talked with them. (The PAC world is entered through a constantly revolving door, and many of its leaders appear to change jobs frequently.)

Financial assistance for this work was provided by the American Philosophical Society (Penrose Fund), the Earhart Foundation, and the University of Virginia Research Policy Council, and I acknowledge their generosity. While this monetary aid was vital, the study would not have been begun or completed without the "PAC Team," as my student staff associates were affectionately dubbed. Their energy, enthusiasm, dedication, and skill were truly exceptional, and their friendship and companionship I shall never forget. To Lewis Shepherd, the project administrator who expertly supervised every aspect of the study; to Mark Bowles, who coordinated the interviews with amazing dexterity and produced surveys and transcripts by the dozens; to Steven Bayne, who ever so diligently and meticulously compiled the research cards and footnotes; and to Deborah Pfeiffer, who conquered both the computer and Federal Election Commission data in producing tables and survey programming—I offer inadequate but heartfelt gratitude.

I also want to thank my editor, Steven Forman of W. W. Norton, who has greatly improved this manuscript and been a delight to work with; those who were kind enough to review all or portions of the manuscript, including Herbert Alexander, Staige D. Blackford, Larry Boyle, Kent Cooper, Jeremy Gaunt, Margaret Latus, Michael Malbin, H. Richard Mayberry, Jr., and Clifton McCleskey; the many scholars in the field who freely shared their research with me and who are acknowledged in the selected bibliography; Weldon and Mildred Cooper, for their valued advice and sustenance; Robert H. Evans and the staff of the University of Virginia Department of Government and Foreign Affairs, for their many favors and allowances; Martha Sites and her associates at the University of Virginia's Academic Computing Center; Pierce McCleskey for skillfully making the index; and my typists, Mary Ann Armstrong, Sharon Byrd, Christopher Cherry, and Nancy Hasler, all of whom have obviously studied hieroglyphics.

One final matter must be disclosed. Future researchers will find yet another new PAC listed on the Federal Election Commission's roster: the Higher Education Lovers at the University of Virginia PAC (HELUVA-PAC). It may constitute a conflict of interest to form a PAC while investigating PACs, but we simply could not resist. For that possible error, and all others that exist in this volume, I take the customary responsibility.

L. J. S.

List of Tables

Introduction

I think it is time to declare that the government of the United States is not up for sale. . . . Let's plan controls on these PACs.

—Former Vice-President Walter Mondale[1]

I'm a little amused that suddenly our opponents have developed a real conscience about political action committees. I don't remember them being that aroused when the only ones that you knew about were on their side. Now they're on our side and they want to do away with them. Well, they're not going to do away with [them].

—President Ronald Reagan[2]

Alarming. Outrageous. Downright dangerous. That's the only way to begin to describe the threat posed by the torrents of special interest campaign cash being offered up to our Representatives and Senators by the special interest political action committees. . . . This democracy-threatening trend must be stopped.

—Fred Wertheimer, President of Common Cause[3]

The fact is that the Political Action Committee movement is a *reform movement itself.* It is a straightforward way in which many individuals make small contributions and work in concert to achieve ends in which they believe. It is the antithesis of back-room politics.

—U.S. Sen. Richard Lugar (R–Ind.)[4]

The role of the PACs in our system of campaign finance has become nothing short of scandalous. . . . I'm talking about the dangerous and corrupting influence of the outrageous sums of money—campaign contributions—which have become a paralyzing *obscenity.*

—U.S. Rep. Morris K. Udall (D–Ariz.)[5]

> Excuse me, but this campaign to kill the PACs is snobbish, elitist, antidemocratic and un-American. . . .
>
> Destroy the PACs and you constrict the voice of small business, and restrict the political access of the millions who support them—enhancing the clout of Big Media, Big Business, Big Labor and their ilk who can afford to maintain permanent lobbying representation in [Washington].
>
> —Patrick J. Buchanan, conservative columnist[6]

> When these political action committees give money, they expect something in return other than good government. It is making it difficult to legislate. We may reach a point where everybody is buying something with PAC money. We cannot get anything done.
>
> —U.S. Sen. Robert Dole (R–Kans.)[7]

> The PACs and the people's support of them is a vital part of our political process.
>
> —U.S. Sen. John Glenn (D–Ohio)[8]

The debate about political action committees—the PACs that raise and spend vast sums on behalf of interest groups in American elections—has been raging in Washington and across the country. The rhetoric on both sides has been white hot, and the charges and countercharges have filled the airwaves and enlivened campaigns from coast to coast in recent years.

The focus on PACs is hardly surprising, given the "Golden Rule of Politics": "He who has the gold, rules." PACs have become the new goldmine of American politics, and they are eagerly solicited by contribution-hungry candidates and parties. But money rarely comes without strings attached, PAC opponents hasten to point out. In fact, they claim, PAC gifts are directly buying votes in the Congress of the United States. A "Special Interest State" is being created, they say, in which interest groups with sufficient organization and financing secure favored pieces of legislation in exchange for contributions to influential congressmen at campaign time. Moreover, they insist, PACs, especially the ones formed by corporations and trade associations, abuse the democratic system by coordinating their gifts to maximize their influence, rivaling the parties for the loyalty of elected officials, often soliciting contributions by coercing employees, organizing internally in an undemocratic and unaccountable fashion, encouraging the growth of negative, single-issue politics, and becoming increasingly dominant in elections at all levels.

Nonsense, say the PAC defenders. First of all, they note, political action committees are nothing new: interest-group money has always flowed freely in American politics, and PACs are merely the modern manifestation of an electoral fact of life. The thousands of PACs now in existence are very diverse, they insist, and adequately represent most major segments of American life. Most important, they believe, PACs offer hundreds of thousands of Americans an outlet for political participation and an opportunity to exercise the basic rights of free expression and association. Finally, PAC advocates argue strenuously that political action committees do not dominate the electoral realm. They claim that PACs have supplemented, not replaced, the parties, and that the new corporate and trade PACs have simply restored balance in areas where labor union PACs had gone unchecked and unchallenged for too long.

Not content with genteel discussions of PAC rights and wrongs on newspapers' editorial pages, PAC advocates and opponents alike have taken to organizing extensive efforts to sway public opinion. PAC opponents, led by the citizens' lobbying group Common Cause, have been particularly aggressive. In early February 1983 Common Cause ran a full-page advertisement in the *New York Times* which declared "war on PACs." The ad launched a grassroots "People Against PACs" campaign that included petition drives to Congress, reams of "special reports" on the correlations between PAC gifts and congressional votes on legislation, and even television commercials produced by the Democratic political consultant Michael Kaye which were aired in key primary and caucus states in 1984.[9] The Common Cause programs were supplemented, ironically enough, by the activities of two PACs—which styled themselves as "anti-PAC" PACs. Democratic U.S. Rep. Morris K. Udall's "Independent Action" committee announced its intention to press for commitments from 1984 presidential and congressional candidates to seek legislative limitations on PACs.[10] And a new political action committee called LAST-PAC (Let the American System Triumph), founded by an unsuccessful 1982 Democratic congressional candidate, pledged to raise money to lobby for campaign reform legislation and to monitor PAC activities.[11]

The PAC community was slow at first to respond to the onslaught. "We're not armwavers," explained one PAC leader, while others cited the decentralized nature of the PAC world. But gradually PACs were roused to collective action—not so much by Common Cause (which the pro-PAC Public Affairs Council president Richard A. Armstrong scornfully derided as composed of "the kind of people who come in after the battle and shoot the wounded") as by its anti-PAC allies in the news media. Media criticism of PACs became a steady drumbeat after 1982—from Bill Moyers's series on the "CBS Evening News"[12] to a *Time* cover story[13] to Elizabeth Drew's articles in the *New Yorker*[14] and much more. In response the Public Affairs Council, an organization of Washington, D.C.–based corporate executives, launched a $100,000 public relations counteroffensive which included films, monographs, and pamphlets designed to make "the case for PACs." The Council joined with other PAC-oriented business groups (the U.S. Chamber of Commerce, the National Association of Manufacturers, the National Association of Business PACs, and the Business-Industry PAC) to set up a speakers bureau of corporate PAC officers who could "tell the PAC story" in public forums and on television. The Business-Industry PAC (or BIPAC) issued a videotaped defense of PACs called *The Truth about Political Action Committees.* Individual industries added their public salvos from time to time; Mobil Corporation, for instance, took its stand on the issue in national newspaper advertisements.

The "great PAC debate" is generating not only heat but light. Both PAC defenders and PAC opponents are raising fundamental questions about the operation of American politics and government. Their views are for the most part antithetical, and their facts are often conflicting, but their battle is an enlightening one for any student of politics. My aim has been to evaluate the controversy over PACs, to consider their place in the political landscape, and to suggest ways to remedy abuses in the area of campaign finance.*

Our investigation of the PAC world begins in the first chapter with a review of campaign finance practices *before* PACs and an explanation of the post-Watergate system that spurred the growth of PACs. The second chapter shows how PACs work by examining their organizational, fundraising, and "networking" apparatus. Chapter 3 explains how PACs select candidates to support (and how candidates select PACs), and in what ways PACs spend their huge war chests. Chapter 4 explores the influence PACs have *after* the election, when PAC gifts may affect the fate of congressional legislation and may even buy congressional votes. The sometimes cooperative, sometimes contentious relationship between the PACs and the political parties is the subject of Chapter 5. The concluding chapter assesses the future of PACs and offers proposals for campaign finance reform.

*The substance of this study is derived from two original sets of data: (1) a series of more than sixty personal interviews with PAC and party leaders,[15] and (2) the results of an extensive random-sample mail survey of 399 PACs, conducted in the summer and autumn of 1983.[16]

CHAPTER 1

The Growth of Political Action Committees

> Money has always been an influence on the process. It's not like all of a sudden this great "evil" developed in the last four or five years because business PACs were formed.
>
> —A business PAC organizer[1]

PACS AMERICANA

The prominence of interest groups has been a staple of American life since the earliest days of the Republic. In 1835 Alexis de Tocqueville, after observing firsthand the character of the new country, was moved to write that "Americans of all ages, all conditions and all dispositions constantly form associations. Wherever at the head of some new undertaking you see the government in France, or a man of rank in England, in the United States you will be sure to find an association."[2] Since much of what associations do is affected by legislation and public directives, it is hardly surprising to discover that interest groups in a democracy attempt to influence the government not only by lobbying public officials but also by attempting to elect friends and defeat foes. Throughout American history interest groups have supplied candidates and campaigns with cash, and lots of it.

We can begin at the end of the nineteenth century, when Mark Hanna, the Republican party's national chairman, filled the war chests of the GOP and its presidential candidate, William McKinley, with enormous sums from wealthy businessmen and corporations. Most of McKinley's six to seven million dollars in expenditures during the 1896 campaign came from the "assessments" Hanna levied on major businesses.[3] These brazen machinations, continued by Hanna's successors, became an issue in the 1904 presidential campaign. The Republican president, Theodore Roosevelt, a beneficiary of the largesse but reform minded, pushed for change. Congress responded by passing the Tillman Act of 1907[4] that prohibited direct corporate contributions to federal campaigns.

But the Tillman Act and the subsequent Federal Corrupt Practices Act of 1925,[5] the last basic campaign finance reform until the 1970s, would have relatively little effect on campaign financing.[6] Some corporate executives merely gave themselves or their employees "raises" which were then contributed by these individuals to favored candidates. Corporations often extended to candidates free use of company goods, office equipment, or travel in company automobiles and airplanes. Some employees were loaned full time to a campaign while remaining on the company payroll. And throughout the twentieth century millions in corporate funds continued to flow directly to candidates despite any legal prohibition. Corporations frequently laundered this money through "petty cash" funds, trade associations, legal fees, and public relations firms on retainer.[7] "Under the old system, I bagged a lot of money, everybody did," reported Lloyd Hackler, a former aide to Lyndon B. Johnson who now heads the American Retail Federation. "Nowadays these good government groups put out these lists that say this guy got $5,000 from this PAC and that's why he voted this way. . . . Makes me laugh. We didn't mess around with just $5,000."[8] Russell Hemenway, executive director of the National Committee for an Effective Congress, a liberal PAC, also recalled a system of campaign finance that existed for most of this century: "When I first came to Washington, Sen. Bob Kerr of Oklahoma was handling the oil money, always [given to congressmen] in plain envelopes, always in cash. There was much more oil money going into politics then than now."

Though subterfuge and lax disclosure laws made it difficult to trace campaign contributions, the research that exists suggests that the same corporate interests that predominated before the Tillman Act were still preeminent long after the legislation was passed. The political scientist Louise Overacker, for instance, determined that in the 1928 presidential election nearly a third of the money raised by each of the parties came in contributions of $5,000 or more from bankers, stockbrokers, manufacturers, and individuals from the mining, oil, railroad, and public utilities businesses.[9] If gifts under $5,000 had been counted, the corporate proportion of the parties' war chests would undoubtedly have been even higher. And of course the laundered corporate funds were not included, though one keen academic observer of campaigns, Alexander Heard, suggested in 1960 that "It is not unusual for corporate funds to make up 10 percent of the campaign fund of a candidate for state or local office, and the percentage has gone higher."[10]

Heard's 10 percent standard was exceeded by a large margin in one modern campaign that was so corrupt it spurred dramatic changes in the system of campaign finance. The 1972 reelection effort for President Richard Nixon included practices bordering on extortion, in which corporations and their executives were, in essence, "shaken down" for cash donations.[11] Up to $30 million was legally and illegally contributed by the business sector to Nixon in 1972, thanks to an ingenious "quota system" devised by the president's fundraisers. The system set as the expected "standard" contribution 1 percent of a wealthy individual's net worth or 1 percent of a company's gross annual sales, though this was thoughtfully scaled down to a miserly $100,000 for large corporations. Eleven major American companies (including American Airlines, Goodyear, the 3M Company, and Gulf Oil) and a number of corporate executives were found guilty of illegal contributions in the wake of the Watergate scandals.[12]

THE ORIGINS OF PACS

Long before the Nixon reelection horrors produced the campaign reforms that unleashed PACs, the forerunners of contemporary political action committees were organizing and developing. While most of the current focus is on business PACs, the concept of a PAC in fact originated with labor. As an AFL-CIO official remarked in 1983, "We know we can't throw stones at PACs generally. We invented them."[13] Labor unions had always been involved in campaigns, but until 1936 their direct financial participation was often minimal. In the 1936 presidential campaign, however, interstate labor organizations mounted a major (and controversial) effort, spending over three quarters of a million dollars.[14] The spark for this explosion of labor activity was the aggressive Committee for Industrial Organization (CIO)—later called the Congress of Industrial Organization —which had been founded in 1935. In July 1943 the CIO went on to form CIO-PAC, the first modern political action committee, to collect and disburse the voluntary political contributions of union members. The following year the CIO also instituted a National Citizen's Political Action Committee (NC-PAC) to solicit funds from progressive individuals outside the labor movement.[15] (There is no little irony that the first NC-PAC was not the present-day, well-known National *Conservative* Political Action Committee, but a group from the opposite end of the ideological spectrum.) The CIO-PAC proved to be a powerful fundraiser for labor; in 1944 CIO-PAC alone raised more than $1.2 million for political purposes.

Labor's new political clout did not go unnoticed in Washington, but it generated as much fear as it did gratitude. In 1943, after a series of wartime strikes caused widespread public resentment against organized labor, Congress passed the Smith-Connally Act[16] over President Roosevelt's veto.[17]

This legislation extended the Tillman Act's prohibition on direct campaign contributions by corporations to labor unions as well. While the Smith-Connally Act specified that the new restriction would be in effect only for the duration of World War II, the Taft-Hartley Act of 1947[18] made the ban permanent, and also barred corporate and union treasury money from primary elections and nominating conventions.

These new legal restrictions were troublesome for labor in some respects, but if their goal was to diminish labor's involvement in election campaigns, they failed completely. The American Federation of Labor (AFL), the other major labor organization in the United States besides the CIO, established a PAC in 1947 called Labor's League for Political Education. In 1955, when the two union federations merged to become the AFL-CIO, their PACs also united into the Committee on Political Education (COPE), which quickly established itself and has become, arguably, the most important and effective PAC of all. Its strength rested, in its formative years as now, not just on the amount of money it could raise but also on the manpower it could provide preferred candidates. COPE enhanced the voter registration and election day get-out-the-vote activities at which labor excels.

Business political action committees began forming somewhat later than their labor counterparts. In August 1963 perhaps the most influential of the business PACs, the Business-Industry Political Action Committee (BIPAC) was established by the National Association of Manufacturers. BIPAC and the American Medical Political Action Committee (AMPAC), founded in 1962, together spent over $600,000 in the 1964 federal elections and more than $1.2 million in the 1968 contests (matching COPE's expenditures almost exactly).[19] BIPAC and AMPAC were the pacesetters, accounting collectively for 61 percent of the total expenditures by national business PACs in 1968, and other businesses and professional associations quickly followed their successful example. From 11 registered business-oriented PACs in 1964 the number increased to 33 in 1968 and 200 by 1972.[20] Almost all of this growth, incidentally, took place before the campaign finance reforms of the 1970s, which are often assigned full responsibility for the PAC phenomenon. In fact PACs had begun to grow well before then, as first labor and then business sought appropriate campaign vehicles for their interests at election time.

For businesses, PACs began as supplements to the less visible contribution methods discussed earlier, and also as replacements for the fundraising schemes used for decades within individual corporations. Two general types of corporate contribution programs were widely used before the advent of PACs: the trustee plan and the pass-through or conduit system.[21] Under the trustee plan, the corporation opened a special bank account and paid all administrative costs for each executive who wished to make political contributions. The executive deposited whatever he or she wished (sometimes through payroll deduction) and designated the candidates to receive the funds. A corporate official then made the donation on behalf of the executive; it was an individual gift, but one that retained a kind of corporate identity. The other type of corporate contribution program, the pass-through system, was more informal, often resembling a political "United Way" charity drive. The chief executive officer, the company lobbyist, or the division directors personally solicited management employees, often asking for specific sums based on salary and providing a list of preferred candidates for employees to choose from. The gifts were again delivered by a company spokesman, perhaps using the "double envelope" technique, whereby each employee's contribution was sealed in one small envelope and all such contributions for a particular candidate were collected together in a large envelope with the company's name emblazoned on the outside. Once again these practices suggest that the purposes and methods of current PACs are not as revolutionary as is frequently claimed. In the survey of major PACs I conducted for this book,[22] close to one-third of the corporations with active PACs reported having some form of pre-PAC political contribution scheme.[23]

PACS AND THE NEW CAMPAIGN FINANCE RULES

While other campaign contribution schemes and a good number of PACs of all political persuasions existed prior to the 1970s, it was during this decade—the decade of campaign reform—that the modern PAC era began. The term "PAC" became if not a household word, at least widely used by campaign professionals, politicians, and reporters to designate those political committees not authorized by candidates or political parties that give money to candidates for public office. "PAC" is actually a colloquial expression; it is found nowhere in the federal statutes.[24] It has been applied to groups formed by labor, business, and trade associations, as well as to independent committees that have no sponsoring organization. For our purposes here the colloquial definition is sufficient: a PAC is either the separate, segregated campaign fund of a sponsoring labor, business, or trade organization, or the campaign fund of a group formed primarily or solely for the purpose of giving money to candidates. Party committees do not qualify as PACs; in this sense all PACs are "nonparty," i.e., they are not formed by or directly connected to a political party even if all their money is contributed to the candidates of a single party.

There is one special kind of PAC to which this book gives particular attention: the multicandidate political action committee. A multicandidate PAC is one that has been registered with the Federal Election Commission

(FEC) for at least six months, has received contributions from more than fifty persons, and has made donations to at least five candidates for federal office. Of the 3,716 PACs existing in the 1981–1982 election cycle (a two-year period covering the calendar year preceding each congressional or presidential election as well as the election year itself), for instance, only 2,205 were multicandidate PACs. Many PACs are merely "paper PACs": having registered with the FEC, they exist legally but contribute little or nothing to candidates. Multicandidate PACs are the workhorses of the PAC world, and the survey I conducted for this book concentrates exclusively on them.[25]

PACs then are not defined by federal law, but a series of statutes passed in the 1970s established rules by which they operate.[26] The first in the series was the Federal Election Campaign Act (FECA) of 1971,[27] which repealed the loophole-ridden Corrupt Practices Act of 1925. It tightened the required disclosure of campaign receipts and expenditures for all federal candidates as of April 7, 1972. (On April 6, 1972, some Washington, D.C., banks reportedly remained open late to accommodate lobbyists and others who wanted to transfer large amounts of cash to favored candidates without fear of disclosure.) Most important, FECA specifically legitimized PACs by explicitly granting to both corporations and labor unions the right to create, administer, and raise funds for their PACs, and to cover all organizational expenses from corporate and union treasuries. Ironically this provision, which later led to a proliferation of corporate PACs, was added to FECA with the help of the unions. At the time, though, union leaders wanted to be certain that their own use of treasury funds was given a congressional stamp of approval. They also were convinced that most corporations would be prohibited from establishing PACs by another provision in the law which prevented government contractors (a group that included most major corporations) from making direct or indirect contributions to federal candidates.[28]

The modest reforms of the 1971 FECA were not left undisturbed for even a single election cycle, thanks to the Watergate scandals. Even though FECA, which did not become effective until late in the 1972 primary season, could hardly be blamed for not revealing the Nixon reelection committee's corruption, Watergate created an irresistible demand for more campaign reforms, whether needed or not. The 1974 amendments to FECA[29] were far more sweeping in their scope than the original statute. Among many other changes, the new law limited to $1,000 the amount individuals could contribute to federal candidates in each separate election (counting the primary, runoff, and general election as three elections); placed a cumulative cap of $25,000 on the amount an individual could contribute to all federal candidates combined in a single year; and limited to $1,000 the amount an individual could spend independently of a candidate or campaign to influence elections. (Such spending is called an "independent expenditure," and will be discussed in detail in Chapter 3.)

While these new rules did not affect PACs directly, their indirect effect was to limit other sources of campaign money and thus to increase candidates' reliance on PAC dollars. The 1974 amendments limited multicandidate PAC gifts to $5,000 per candidate per election[30]—five times the individual cap—and unlike the case for individuals, no cumulative limit was placed on the amount a PAC could give all candidates combined in each year. Furthermore, "public financing"—the use of federal tax revenues to finance presidential campaigns in primaries and general elections—was given sanction and form by the 1974 amendments.[31] This had the effect of concentrating PAC money on congressional campaigns at the federal level, since presidential candidates were funded for the most part from the public treasury (as well as individual contributions in the preconvention period).

As vital as these elements were to the emergence of the PAC phenomenon, still another provision of the 1974 amendments had a greater impact: the authorization for companies and unions with government contracts to establish PACs. Corporations, of course, were especially anxious to strike the FECA prohibition on PAC formation by government contractors,[32] but ironically again, the unions were primarily responsible for removing yet another barrier to corporate PAC creation. Union leaders had secured federal contracts for job training, and they feared that their PACs might be found illegal in court as long as the 1971 prohibition remained law. Deciding to gamble that most corporations would not set up PACs, unions encouraged Democrats loyal to them to team up with business-oriented Republicans to remove the prohibition.[33] The spirited opposition of Common Cause, which did not share the unions' optimism about corporate intentions on PAC formation, was not enough to stop the bill, and it went into effect on January 1, 1975. Whatever doubts companies had about the legality of corporate PACs were dispelled by the newly formed Federal Election Commission on November 18, 1975. The FEC issued an advisory opinion to the Sun Oil Company,[34] holding by a four-to-two majority that the company could form a PAC and solicit contributions to it from both stockholders and company employees, providing there was no coercion to contribute. In just the six months following the SunPAC ruling, over 150 corporations created PACs, doubling the number of business PACs.[35]

Labor was outraged by the SunPAC decision and immediately went to work in Congress to reverse key parts of it. This led to yet another campaign reform act, the 1976 FECA Amendments.[36] These new changes, on balance, did serve labor's interests. First, new restrictions were placed on corporate PAC solicitation of employees. Corporate PACs were permitted to solicit donations from stockholders and "executive or administrative personnel" (the executives, managers, professionals, and supervisors) and their families in an unrestricted fashion, but all other employees and their families could be solicited just twice a year. Unions were given corresponding rights to solicit corporate shareholders and executive personnel twice a year by mail, and to solicit their own membership without restrictions. In addition to these "crossover privileges," labor won the right to use payroll-deduction plans (or "checkoffs") to collect PAC contributions from its members as long as the company itself used payroll deduction for contributions from its shareholders or executive personnel. (Payroll deduction is considered the easiest method of contribution, and the one that encourages the highest level of participation.) The unions also won restrictions on the solicitation practices of trade association PACs, most of which are business related. The 1976 FECA Amendments were the first explicitly to authorize trade associations, cooperatives, and corporations without capital stock to establish PACs, but trade associations were limited to seeking donations from those member corporations which specifically authorized the solicitation of their shareholders and executives. Moreover, corporations were allowed to approve such a solicitation by only one trade association each year.

The frenzy of campaign finance reform in the 1970s continued in 1979 with the passage of still more amendments to FECA,[37] although with one minor exception these did not directly affect PACs.[38] The rules changed so quickly during the 1970s that it was difficult to assess the effects of one set of amendments before another set was added to the statute books, and only now has the dust settled enough for tentative judgments to be made. Clearly, the conduct of election campaigns was dramatically altered by many of FECA's provisions, but in few respects has the change been greater than in the law's promotion of PACs as the natural and legitimate vehicle for financial participation in campaigns by the wide array of American interest groups.

THE PAC DECADE

It is a simple and painless procedure to register a political action committee with the Federal Election Commission, and thousands of groups have discovered this in the past decade (see Table 1–1). When FECA took effect in 1972 there were 113 PACs in existence, and by the beginning of 1975 the number had grown to 608. The SunPAC ruling in 1975 spurred the growth of PACs, particularly corporate committees, which tripled in number in the year following the decision.[39] After 1976, the year of the greatest proportional gain in the PAC ranks, increases averaged about 20 percent annually. The 1980 election brought another disproportionately high jump in PAC numbers, as the total climbed to 2,551. The growth rate of all categories of PACs declined somewhat after 1980, and especially in 1983 when the average increase was a mere 4.6 percent. In all, by the end of 1983, 3,525 PACs were in existence, capping a decade of remarkable growth.

Not all categories of PACs grew equally in the "PAC Decade." The FEC classified each registered nonparty PAC into one of six categories:[40] corporate, labor, trade/membership/health organization, nonconnected (i.e., a PAC created independently and not established or administered by a separate group as with all other PACs), cooperative, and corporate without stock. (The first four categories comprise more than 95 percent of all PACs, and will be my focus in this book.) The most dramatic increase has been among corporate committees, whose total grew from 89 in 1974 to 1,536 in 1983. Compared to the over 1,600 percent increase in corporate PACs over this decade, the total number of labor PACs changed relatively little, from 201 in 1974 to 378 in 1983 (an 88 percent gain). In several years the number of labor PACs actually declined, and while labor comprised nearly a third of all PACs in 1974, it could claim only a tenth of the total in 1983. Trade, membership, and health PACs, many of which are also business related, showed a substantial increase, almost 100 percent during the PAC Decade, mushrooming from 318 to 617.[41] Since 1978 no category of PACs has experienced faster growth than the "nonconnecteds," which numbered 110 in 1977 and 821 by 1983. Somewhat less than half these nonconnecteds can be termed "ideological PACs" with an identifiable political philosophy.[42] Cooperative PACs and PACs sponsored by corporations without stock also grew in number, from a combined total of 28 in 1977 to 173 in 1983.

These "head counts" of PACs, while suggestive, are not as revealing as they might seem. A head count assumes that all PACs are created equal when in fact they differ markedly in size and operation. Many PACs, for instance, are essentially inactive: of the 3,479 PACs registered by the time of the 1982 midterm congressional elections, only 2,124 (or 61 percent) had actually made contributions to candidates. There is a relative handful of large, financially well-endowed PACs. Only about three dozen PACs regularly raise $1 million or more during an election cycle, while about 300 PACs raise more than $100,000 but less than $1 million, about 1,500 PACs raise between $10,000 and $100,000, and 1,000 PACs raise between $1,000 and $10,000. More than a fourth of the total number of registered PACs usually report receipts of less than $1,000—the so-called "paltry PACs."[43] The image of the PAC, of course, is that of the well-heeled, centralized, Washington-based lobby, brimming with staffers, computers, and sophisticated data. In fact this characterization is highly misleading. Most PACs operate on modest budgets, with small staffs, outside Washington, and without access to unpublished data.[44]

More instructive than the growth in sheer numbers of PACs is the

Table 1–1.

Number of Registered PACs, 1974–1983[a]

	1974			1975			1976			1977			1978		
CATEGORY	NO.	% OF TOTAL	% CHANGE FROM PREVIOUS YEAR	NO.	% OF TOTAL	% CHANGE FROM PREVIOUS YEAR	NO.	% OF TOTAL	% CHANGE FROM PREVIOUS YEAR	NO.	% OF TOTAL	% CHANGE FROM PREVIOUS YEAR	NO.	% OF TOTAL	% CHANGE FROM PREVIOUS YEAR
Corporate	89	14.6	—	139	19.3	+56.2	433	37.8	+211.5	550	40.4	+27.0	784	47.4	+42.5
Labor	201	33.1	—	226	31.3	+12.4	224	19.5	−0.9	234	17.2	+4.5	217	13.1	−7.3
Trade/Membership/Health[b]	318	52.3	—	357	49.4	+12.3	489	42.7	+25.7	438	32.2	−10.4	451	27.3	+3.0
Nonconnected	—	—	—	—	—	—	—	—	—	110	8.1	—	165	10.0	+50.0
Cooperative	—	—	—	—	—	—	—	—	—	8	0.6	—	12	0.7	+50.0
Corporate without Stock	—	—	—	—	—	—	—	—	—	20	1.5	—	24	1.5	−20.0
Totals	608			722		+18.8	1146		+58.7	1360		+18.7	1653		+21.5

1979			1980			1981			1982			1983		
NO.	% OF TOTAL	% CHANGE FROM PREVIOUS YEAR	NO.	% OF TOTAL	% CHANGE FROM PREVIOUS YEAR	NO.	% OF TOTAL	% CHANGE FROM PREVIOUS YEAR	NO.	% OF TOTAL	% CHANGE FROM PREVIOUS YEAR	NO.	% OF TOTAL	% CHANGE FROM PREVIOUS YEAR
949	47.5	+21.0	1204	47.2	+26.9	1327	45.7	+10.6	1467	43.5	+11.2	1536	43.6	+4.7
240	12.0	+10.6	297	11.6	+23.8	318	11.0	+7.0	380	11.3	+19.5	378	10.7	−0.5
512	25.6	+13.5	574	22.5	+12.1	608	21.0	+5.9	628	18.6	+3.3	617	17.5	−1.8
250	12.5	+51.6	378	14.8	+51.2	539	18.6	+42.6	746	22.1	+38.4	821	23.3	+10.0
17	0.8	+41.7	42	1.7	+47.0	41	1.4	−2.4	47	1.4	+14.7	51	1.4	+8.3
32	1.6	+33.3	56	2.2	+75.0	68	2.3	+21.4	103	3.1	+51.5	122	3.5	+18.4
2000		+21.0	2551		+27.6	2901		+13.7	3371		+16.2	3525		+4.6

SOURCE: Herbert Alexander, *The Case for PACs* (Washington, D.C.: Public Affairs Council, 1983); Lee Ann Elliott, "Political Action Committees—Precincts of the 80's," *Arizona Law Review* 22, no. 2 (1980): 545; Federal Election Commission Press Release, July 28, 1983.

[a]Data as of December 31 for all years except 1975.

[b]Includes all noncorporate and nonlabor PACs through Dec. 31, 1977. The FEC did not add the additional classification categories of nonconnected, cooperative, and corporate without stock until 1977.

increase in PAC fundraising and expenditure. As Table 1–2 shows, PAC spending has jumped almost 900 percent in a decade, from $19.1 million in 1972 to $190.2 million in 1982. (Even after adjusting for inflation,[45] the gain is a substantial 350 percent.) Every category of PAC has registered a dramatic increase, but nonconnected, corporate, and trade PACs have considerably outdistanced labor in their rate of growth. As for contributions to congressional campaigns,[46] all PACs together have given well over $200 million since 1972 to House and Senate contenders (see Table 1–3). Total PAC gifts of $8.5 million in 1972 grew to $83.6 million by the 1982 midterm congressional election. Again, corporate, trade, and other business-related PACs accounted for the lion's share of the increase, though labor also multiplied its donations more than fivefold. By 1982 business-related PACs were outspending labor in direct contributions to congressional campaigns by nearly three to one.[47] From providing half of all PAC contributions in 1974, labor accounted for less than a quarter (24 percent) in 1980 and 1982. Corporate and trade PACs grew from 38 percent of the total in 1974 to 59 percent by 1982, and nonconnected PACs similarly increased from 11 to 17 percent.[48] It should be noted, however, that only *direct* contributions to campaigns are being tallied here. Labor's indirect spending for communica-

Table 1–2.
Expenditures of PACs by Category, 1972–1982[a]

TYPE OF PAC	1972	1974	1976	1978	1980	1982
Labor	$ 8.5	$ 11.0	$ 17.5	$ 18.6	$ 25.1	$ 34.8
Business-oriented[b]	8.0	8.1	—	—	—	—
Corporate	—	—	5.8	15.2	31.4	43.3
Trade/Membership/Health	—	—	—	23.8	32.0	41.9
Nonconnected[c]	2.6	0.8	—	17.4	38.6	64.3
Cooperatives	—	—	—	2.0	2.7	3.8
Corporations without Stock	—	—	—	0.4	1.2	2.1
Other	—	1.1	29.6	—	—	—
Total	19.1	19.9	52.9	77.4	131.1	190.2

SOURCE: For 1972–1980 data, Joseph E. Cantor, *Political Action Committees: Their Evolution and Growth and Their Implications for the Political System* (Washington, D.C.: Library of Congress Congressional Research Service Report No. 82–92 GOV, Nov. 6, 1981; updated May 7, 1982), pp. 83–84. For 1982 data, Federal Election Commission.

[a]The figures are in millions of dollars, rounded to the nearest tenth.

[b]This category is based on the assumption that the majority of PACs within it have a pro-business orientation. It is roughly comparable to the combined corporate and trade/membership/health categories listed for 1978–1982.

[c]For 1972 and 1974 this represents spending by ideological PACs; after 1976 it corresponds directly to the FEC's nonconnected grouping.

Table 1–3.
Contributions to Congressional Candidates from PACs by Category, 1972–1982[a]

TYPE OF PAC	1972	1974	1976	1978	1980	1982
Labor	$ 3.6	$ 6.3	$ 8.2	$ 10.3	$ 13.2	$ 20.3
Business-oriented[b]	2.7	4.4	10.0	—	—	—
Corporate	—	—	—	9.8	19.2	27.5
Trade/Member-ship/Health	—	—	—	11.3	15.9	21.9
Nonconnected[c]	—	0.7	1.5	2.8	4.9	10.8
Cooperatives and Corporations without Stock[d]	2.2	1.0	2.8	1.0	2.0	3.2
Total	$ 8.5	$ 12.5	$ 22.6	$ 35.2	$ 55.2	$ 83.6

SOURCE: For 1972–1980 data, Joseph E. Cantor, *Political Action Committees: Their Evolution and Growth and Their Implications for the Political System* (Washington, D.C.: Library of Congress Congressional Research Service Report No. 82–92 GOV, Nov. 6, 1981; updated May 7 1982), pp. 87–88. For 1982 data, Federal Election Commission.

[a]The figures are in millions of dollars, rounded to the nearest tenth, and cover a two-year election cycle.

[b]This encompasses the categories for business, health, and, in 1976, for lawyers.

[c]For 1974 and 1976 this represents contributions by ideological PACs. Beginning with 1978 it corresponds directly to the FEC's present nonconnected grouping.

[d]Because of differing classification systems, figures for this category can be compared to each other only for 1978–1982.

tions to its members, voter registration, and get-out-the-vote activities is very substantial, as Chapter 2 will demonstrate, and these additional expenditures enable labor to compete with business on more even—or perhaps superior—terms.

Viewed in the abstract the PAC contribution totals are enormous, and they are no less so when examined from the perspective of the individual candidate. In 1982, 170 incumbent House members each received more than $100,000 from PACs, and 20 congressmen each secured more than $200,000.[49] Winners of the 33 Senate races in 1982 collected almost $15 million from PACs, an average of about $450,000 each.[50] Republican Pete Wilson of California became the nation's first million-dollar PAC recipient in his successful 1982 Senate bid; his war chest brimmed with $1.1 million in PAC gifts.

Yet the growth in PAC contributions must also be seen within the context of American campaign financing as a whole. Not just PAC gifts but every other kind of campaign donation was on the increase through the 1970s and early 1980s. Congressional candidates spent almost $344 million in 1981–1982, a 44 percent increase over the 1979–1980 total and a boost of 80 percent over 1977–1978. Yet well under half the average gain in each election cycle can be traced to the PAC spending boom because contributions by individuals and political parties were also on the upswing. Overall, PAC money has been accounting for an ever-increasing proportion of the funds raised by congressional candidates.[51] From 17 percent of all contributions made to House candidates in 1974, PAC money steadily grew to 31 percent by 1982. Among Senate candidates, PAC money provided an 18 percent share of all gifts in 1982 compared with 11 percent in 1974.[52] By the early 1980s, then, PAC money comprised almost a third of the campaign fund of the average House candidate, and nearly a fifth of the average Senate candidate's kitty.

THE PICK OF THE PACS

Some PACs are more responsible than others for their movement's surge to prominence. Table 1–4 takes a look at the "Top Ten" PAC fundraisers and contributors. Fully eight of the ten champion fundraisers are nonconnected groups, led by the conservative NCPAC (pronounced "Nick-pack") and the National Congressional Club (associated with North Carolina GOP Sen. Jesse Helms). All of the richest nonconnected PACs are either ideological groups or candidate PACs formed to promote a potential presidential candidate. Two trade association PACs, the realtors' R-PAC and the doctors' AMPAC, are also found on the top fundraisers' list.

Table 1–4.
"Top Ten" PAC Fundraisers and Contributors

TOP FUNDRAISERS	PAC CATEGORY	TOTAL MONEY RAISED[a]
1. National Conservative Political Action Committee (NCPAC)	Nonconnected	$ 10.0
2. National Congressional Club	Nonconnected	9.7
3. Realtors Political Action Committee (R-PAC)	Trade	3.0
4. Fund for a Conservative Majority	Nonconnected	2.9
5. American Medical Association Political Action Committee (AMPAC)	Trade	2.5
6. National Committee for an Effective Congress (NCEC)	Nonconnected	2.4
7. Citizens for the Republic (CFTR)	Nonconnected	2.4
8. Committee for the Survival of a Free Congress (CSFC)	Nonconnected	2.4
9. Fund for a Democratic Majority	Nonconnected	2.3
10. Committee for the Future of America, Inc.	Nonconnected	2.2

Table 1–4. *(Continued)*

TOP CONTRIBUTORS TO FEDERAL CANDIDATES	PAC CATEGORY	TOTAL MONEY CONTRIBUTED[a]
1. Realtors Political Action Committee (R-PAC)	Trade	$ 2.1
2. American Medical Association Political Action Committee (AMPAC)	Trade	1.7
3. UAW-V-CAP (United Auto Workers)	Labor	1.6
4. Machinists Non-Partisan Political League (MNPL)	Labor	1.4
5. National Education Association PAC (NEA-PAC)	Labor	1.2
6. Build Political Action Committee of the National Association of Home Builders (Build PAC)	Trade	1.0
7. Committee for Thorough Agricultural Political Education of the Associated Milk Producers (C-TAPE)	Cooperative	1.0
8. American Bankers Association BANKPAC	Trade	0.9
9. Automobile and Truck Dealers Election Action Committee	Trade	0.9
10. AFL-CIO COPE Political Contributions Committee	Labor	0.9

SOURCE: Federal Election Commission.
[a]Figures for 1981–1982, in millions of dollars.

Interestingly, R-PAC and AMPAC are the only carryovers from the "top ten" PAC fundraisers to the "top ten" PAC contributors to federal candidates. The nonconnected PACs spend relatively little of their money on direct contributions—only 17 percent in 1981–1982, compared to 63 percent for corporate PACs, 58 percent for labor PACs, and 52 percent for trade PACs. There is a structural reason for this: nonconnected PACs must pay their own administrative and fundraising costs, which are usually substantial, while other PACs' sponsoring organizations are permitted to absorb these expenses. Nonconnected PACs also engage in a very special type of campaigning called "independent expenditure," which will be discussed in Chapter 3. These expenditures, which are also made by other categories of PACs but to a much lesser degree, are not counted as direct contributions to candidates.

Five labor PACs, four trade PACs, and one cooperative PAC comprise the list of "top ten" contributors, and these few PACs together account for about one-seventh of all PAC gifts to federal candidates in 1981 and 1982. The best known labor PAC, the Committee on Political Education (COPE) of the AFL-CIO, actually places last on this list, and is outranked by three other labor groups representing auto workers, machinists, and teachers. (COPE was top-seeded through 1974, but has fallen steadily since.) Besides realtors and doctors, the builders, bankers, and automobile dealers have especially generous trade PACs. The one cooperative PAC on the list represents another business group, the milk producers.

Table 1–5.
"Top Ten" Labor PACs

TOP FUNDRAISERS	TOTAL MONEY RAISED[a]
1. UAW-V-CAP (United Auto Workers)	$ 2.0
2. Machinists Non-Partisan Political League (MNPL)	1.6
3. Transportation Political Education League	1.5
4. Seafarers Political Activity Donation (SPAD)	1.4
5. National Education Association PAC (NEA-PAC)	1.3
6. Active Ballot Club (United Food and Commercial Workers)	1.2
7. AFL-CIO COPE Political Contributions Committee	1.2
8. ILGWU Campaign Committee (International Ladies Garment Workers Union)	1.1
9. United Steelworkers of America Political Action Fund	1.0
10. Voice of Teachers for Education (American Federation of Teachers)	1.0

TOP CONTRIBUTORS TO FEDERAL CANDIDATES	TOTAL MONEY CONTRIBUTED[a]
1. UAW-V-CAP (United Auto Workers)	$ 1.6
2. Machinists Non-Partisan Political League (MNPL)	1.4
3. National Education Association PAC (NEA-PAC)	1.2
4. AFL-CIO COPE Political Contributions Committee	0.9
5. Seafarers Political Activity Donation "SPAD"	0.8
6. Active Ballot Club (United Food and Commercial Workers)	0.7
7. United Steelworkers of America Political Action Fund	0.7
8. Engineers Political Education Committee (Operating Engineers)	0.7
9. MEBA Political Action Fund (Marine Engineers)	0.7
10. CWA-COPE Political Contributions Committee (Communication Workers of America)	0.6

SOURCE: Federal Election Commission.
[a]Figures for 1981–1982, in millions of dollars.

An examination of the "top ten" PACs in each separate category of political action committee yields a broader sample of the most prominent PACs (see Tables 1–5 through 1–9). Both similarities and differences among the categories are apparent. The largest corporate PACs are, on average, much smaller than their counterparts elsewhere. For example, the collective contributions of the "top ten" corporate committees comprised only 9 percent of the total for all corporate PACs in 1981–1982, while trade and labor's "top ten" accounted, respectively, for 45 percent and 43 percent of their category's total contributions.[53] Like all the other categories, though, the première corporate PACs are a mixture of well-known and obscure committees and sponsoring organizations. Taken together, all the champion PACs are a potpourri of significant interest groups—a fact suggestive of the diversity of the PAC phenomenon.

Table 1–6.
"Top Ten" Corporate PACs

TOP FUNDRAISERS	TOTAL MONEY RAISED[a]
1. Tenneco Employees Good Government Fund (Tenneco, Inc.)	$0.5
2. Amoco Political Action Committee (Standard Oil Company, Indiana)	0.5
3. Sunbelt Good Government Committee of Winn-Dixie Stores (Winn-Dixie Stores, Inc.)	0.4
4. Bear, Stearns & Co. Political Campaign Committee (Bear, Stearns & Co.)	0.4
5. American Family Political Action Committee (American Family Corporation)	0.3
6. Signal Companies, Inc. (Wheelabrator-Frye, Inc.)	0.3
7. Fluor Corporation Public Affairs Committee (Fluor Corporation)	0.3
8. Harris Corporation Federal Political Action Committee (Harris Corporation)	0.3
9. General Dynamics Corporation Voluntary Political Contributions (General Dynamics Corporation)	0.3
10. Grumman Political Action Committee (Grumman Corporation)	0.3

TOP CONTRIBUTORS TO FEDERAL CANDIDATES	TOTAL MONEY CONTRIBUTED[a]
1. Tenneco Employees Good Government Fund (Tenneco, Inc.)	$0.5

Table 1–6. *(Continued)*

TOP CONTRIBUTORS TO FEDERAL CANDIDATES	TOTAL MONEY CONTRIBUTED[a]
2. Sunbelt Good Government Committee of Winn-Dixie Stores (Winn-Dixie Stores, Inc.)	0.3
3. Harris Corporation Federal Political Action Committee (Harris Corporation)	0.2
4. American Family Political Action Committee (American Family Corporation)	0.2
5. Fluor Corporation Public Affairs Committee (Fluor Corporation)	0.2
6. Litton Industries Inc. Employees Political Assistance Committee (Litton Industries, Inc.)	0.2
7. United Technologies Corporation PAC (United Technologies Corporation)	0.2
8. Amoco Political Action Committee (Standard Oil Company, Indiana)	0.2
9. Grumman Political Action Committee (Grumman Corporation)	0.2
10. Philip Morris Political Action Committee (Philip Morris, Inc.)	0.2

SOURCE: Federal Election Commission.
[a]Figures for 1981–1982, in millions of dollars.

Table 1–7.
"Top Ten" Trade PACS

TOP FUNDRAISERS	TOTAL MONEY RAISED[a]
1. Realtors Political Action Committee (R-PAC)	$ 3.0
2. American Medical Association Political Action Committee (AMPAC)	2.5
3. NRA Political Victory Fund (National Rifle Association of America)	2.0
4. Build Political Action Committee of the National Association of Home Builders (Build PAC)	1.3
5. League of Conservation Voters	1.3
6. Automobile and Truck Dealers Election Action Committee	1.2
7. Texas Medical Association PAC (TEXPAC)	1.1
8. California Medical Political Action Committee (CALPAC)	1.1
9. National Association of Life Underwriters PAC	1.1
10. Gun Owners of America Campaign Committee	0.9

Table 1–7. *(Continued)*

TOP CONTRIBUTORS TO FEDERAL CANDIDATES	TOTAL MONEY CONTRIBUTED[a]
1. Realtors Political Action Committee (R-PAC)	$ 2.1
2. American Medical Association Political Action Committee (AMPAC)	1.7
3. Build Political Action Committee of the National Association of Home Builders (Build PAC)	1.0
4. American Bankers Association BANKPAC	0.9
5. Automobile and Truck Dealers Election Action Committee	0.9
6. NRA Political Victory Fund (National Rifle Association of America)	0.7
7. Associated General Contractors Political Action Committee	0.7
8. American Dental Political Action Committee (ADPAC)	0.6
9. National Association of Life Underwriters PAC	0.6
10. National Association of Retired Federal Employees	0.6

SOURCE: Federal Election Commission.
[a]Figures for 1981–1982, in millions of dollars.

Table 1–8.
"Top Ten" Nonconnected PACs

TOP FUNDRAISERS	IDEOLOGICAL/PARTY/ CANDIDATE IDENTIFICATION	TOTAL MONEY RAISED[a]
1. National Conservative Political Action Committee (NCPAC)	Conservative	$ 10.0
2. National Congressional Club	Conservative / Jesse Helms	9.7
3. Fund for a Conservative Majority	Conservative	3.0
4. National Committee for an Effective Congress (NCEC)	Liberal	2.4
5. Citizens for the Republic (CFTR)	Republican / Ronald Reagan	2.4
6. Committee for the Survival of a Free Congress (CSFC)	Conservative	2.3

Table 1–8. *(Continued)*

TOP FUNDRAISERS	IDEOLOGICAL/PARTY/ CANDIDATE IDENTIFICATION	TOTAL MONEY RAISED[a]
7. Fund for a Democratic Majority	Democratic / Edward Kennedy	2.3
8. Committee for the Future of America, Inc.	Democratic / Walter Mondale	2.2
9. Republican Majority Fund	Republican / Howard Baker	2.0
10. Independent Action, Inc.	Liberal	1.2

TOP CONTRIBUTORS TO FEDERAL CANDIDATES	IDEOLOGICAL/PARTY/ CANDIDATE IDENTIFICATION	TOTAL MONEY CONTRIBUTED[a]
1. National PAC	Pro-Israel	$ 0.5
2. Citizens for the Republic (CFTR)	Republican / Ronald Reagan	0.5
3. Republican Majority Fund	Republican / Howard Baker	0.5
4. National Committee for an Effective Congress (NCEC)	Liberal	0.4
5. Democrats for the '80s, Inc.	Liberal	0.4
6. Republican Congressional Boosters Club	National Republican party	0.3
7. National Abortion Rights Action League (NARAL)	Pro-Abortion	0.3
8. National Conservative Political Action Committee (NCPAC)	Conservative	0.3
9. NFIB Political Action Committee (National Federation of Independent Business)	Bipartisan (strong GOP tilt)	0.3
10. Louisiana Energy National Political Action Committee	Republican	0.3

SOURCE: Federal Election Commission.
[a]Figures for 1981–1982, in millions of dollars.

Table 1–9.
"Top Ten" PACS of Cooperatives and Corporations without Stock

TOP FUNDRAISERS	PAC CATEGORY	TOTAL MONEY RAISED[a]
1. Committee for Thorough Agricultural Political Education of Associated Milk Producers, Inc. (C-TAPE)	Cooperative	$ 1.8
2. Commodity Futures Political Fund of the Chicago Mercantile Exchange	Corporation without Stock	1.0
3. Dairymen Inc.—Special Political Agricultural Community Education (DI-SPACE)	Cooperative	0.8
4. Mid-America Dairymen Inc. Agricultural and Dairy Educational Political Trust (ADEPT)	Cooperative	0.7
5. Handgun Control Inc. Political Action Committee	Corporation without Stock	0.2
6. Commodity Exchange, Inc., Political Action Committee	Corporation without Stock	0.2
7. Akin, Gump, Strauss, Hauer & Feld Civic Action Committee	Corporation without Stock	0.1
8. Health & People PAC of Blue Cross / Blue Shield of Michigan	Corporation without Stock	0.1
9. National Good Government Fund	Corporation without Stock	0.1
10. CF Industries, Inc. Political Action Committee	Cooperative	0.1

Table 1–9. *(Continued)*

TOP CONTRIBUTORS TO FEDERAL CANDIDATES	PAC CATEGORY	TOTAL MONEY CONTRIBUTED[a]
1. Committee for Thorough Agricultural Political Education of Associated Milk Producers, Inc. (C-TAPE)	Cooperative	$ 1.0
2. Mid-America Dairymen Inc. Agricultural and Dairy Education Political Trust (ADEPT)	Cooperative	0.5
3. Commodity Futures Political Fund of the Chicago Mercantile Exchange	Corporation without Stock	0.3
4. Dairymen Inc.—Special Political Agricultural Community Education (DI-SPACE)	Cooperative	0.2
5. Handgun Control, Inc., Political Action Committee	Corporation without Stock	0.1
6. Commodity Exchange, Inc., Political Action Committee	Corporation without Stock	0.1
7. National Good Government Fund	Corporation without Stock	0.1
8. California Almond Growers Exchange Political Action Committee	Corporation without Stock	0.1
9. Akin, Gump, Strauss, Hauer & Feld Civic Action Committee	Corporation without Stock	0.1
10. Farmland Industries Political Action Committee	Cooperative	0.1

SOURCE: Federal Election Commission.
[a]Figures for 1981–1982, in millions of dollars.

DIVERSITY IN THE PAC WORLD

Dem PACs, Dem PACs, Dem Wild PACs.
Now feel the pow'r of the PACs.

De doctors lobby get de—*Sick* PAC
'N' Richard Nixon got de—*Trick* PAC.
De right wing shaves you with a—*Nick* PAC.
Now feel the pow'r of the PACs.

De ski lift owners got de—*Snow* PAC.
De bourbon drinkers got Old—*Crow* PAC.
De Postal Service got de—*Slow* PAC.
Now feel the pow'r of the PACs.

—Lyrics (sung to "Dry Bones") from
the 1983 Gridiron Press
Club Presentation
in Washington, D.C.

Scanning the list of over 3,000 PACs, an observer might quickly conclude that every conceivable group has gone PAC crazy. The Peanut Butter and Nut Processers Association has its NUTPAC. The beer distributors have their SixPAC. Whataburger, Inc., operates Whata-PAC. There is a Bread-PAC (American Bakers Association), an EggPAC (United Egg Producers), a FishPAC (National Fisheries Institute), a Food PAC (Food Marketing Institute), and—to wash it all down—a Dr. Pepper PAC. Seemingly every "concern" is represented by a PAC: Concerned Italian Americans for Better Government, Concerned Romanians, Concerned Professionals, Concerned Businessmen, and Concerned Texans.[54]

Just about every classification of Americans has at least one entry. Blacks have the Parker-Coltrane PAC (named after founder U.S. Rep. John Conyers's favorite jazz saxophonists). Hispanics (at least the conservatives among them) have the National Coalition for a Free Cuba, created by a group of wealthy Miami-based Cubans opposed to Castro and communism. Women have several PACs dedicated to assisting their campaigns for public office, including the National Organization for Women PAC, the Women's Campaign Fund, and the National Women's Political Caucus Victory Fund-PAC.[55] Senior Citizens have Senior-PAC.[56] Gay rights supporters have the Human Rights Campaign Fund, a national group, and the more locally based Municipal Elections Committee of Los Angeles (MECLA). Animal protection advocates have ROAR-PAC (Respect Our Animal Rights) to fight laboratory abuse of animals.[57]

Most shades of political opinion find expression in a PAC. Conservative Democrats in Congress formed a Boll Weevil PAC, after the name by which they are known, in 1982. Moderate Republicans, thought by some to be a dying breed in an increasingly conservative party, created MODPAC in 1983 to support candidates of their GOP stripe. Pro-Reagan Republican women in Houston, concerned about the "gender gap" which shows women leaning more toward the Democrats, established a PAC called "American Women Supporting the President" to prepare for the 1984 election. Fundamentalist Christians have had several active political action committees since the late 1970s, including the Christian Voice Moral Government Fund and the Christian Voter's Victory Fund.[58] (The better known Moral Majority PAC of the Rev. Jerry Falwell was in fact relatively inactive, raising only $22,089 in 1979 and 1980, compared to $494,722 for the Christian Voice PAC alone. Falwell has since formed another federal committee, the "I Love America" PAC.)

Most PACs, particularly the single-issue and ideological committees, have spurred the growth of opposition PACs. Conservatives were quickest to organize, and some of their PACs continue to dominate fundraising in the ideological sphere. But the left clearly has stirred itself with the formation of new groups such as Democrats for the '80s and Independent Action to complement the work of the well-established liberal PAC, the National Committee for an Effective Congress. More specialized liberal groups are also bringing a balance to PAC spending. Handgun Control PAC supports gun-control advocates; the anti–gun-control PACs of the National Rifle Association and the Gun Owners of America no longer have the field to themselves. Environmental groups, especially the League of Conservation Voters, the Sierra Club, Friends of the Earth, and Environmental Action, have taken the PAC route to counteract pro-development campaign contributions from corporate interests. Even the generally conservative American Medical Association and American Dental Association have attracted competition from Health USA, a PAC formed by more liberal doctors and dentists. In each case cited here, though, the budget of the new liberal PAC is far smaller than its conservative opposite number. The list of ideological nonconnected PACs in Table 1–8, for example, shows that conservative PACs outraised liberal PACs in 1981–1982 by a margin of 3 1/2 to 1 ($29.4 million to $8.1 million). So diversity and balance are still somewhat limited in the evolving PAC world—a problem that will be taken up again in the concluding chapter.

While there is a long tradition of financial involvement in America's political campaigns by business, labor, and other interest groups, the new campaign finance laws of the 1970s have spurred a significant increase in the tempo of interest-group activity, at least in the public arena, with PACs multiplying rapidly and swelling in size. But before we can evaluate the merits of the PAC system, we must consider the structures and operations of PACs. Too many facile generalizations have been made by PAC friends and foes because too little has been understood about the formation, organization, administration, fundraising techniques, and internal activities of political action committees.

CHAPTER 2

PACs at Work Organization and Fundraising

I could create my own client. I could get rich. On PROPAC, Vic Kamber could get rich. . . . [A]n absolute nobody could go out today and, if they have the technological skills, generate dollars and become a political force.

—Victor Kamber, political consultant and founder of the Progressive Political Action Committee (PROPAC)[1]

Of course [NCPAC] is a little family. The whole [conservative] movement's a little family. We socialize with each other, we sign fund-raising letters for each other. . . . Guilty, we are guilty.

—John "Terry" Dolan, chairman of the National Conservative Political Action Committee (NCPAC)[2]

The ways in which PACs organize, operate, and raise their funds are frequently invisible, occasionally questionable, and always revealing of their nature and predisposition. This chapter will analyze the PAC in its administrative setting, and attempt to answer a series of questions which alternately intrigue and trouble political observers. Why do some groups but not others form PACs? Who governs the PACs, and how well are they run? How do PACs make decisions, and do rank-and-file PAC members have much to say in the decision-making? Do PACs merely consult with each other, or is there outright coordination in their actions? How do PACs raise the huge sums they dispense to campaigns? Finally, and most important, are the donations to PAC treasuries truly voluntary gifts from interested members, or are they the product of coercion?

FORMING A PAC: MOTIVES AND RATIONALES

The growth of PACs in recent years has been remarkable. But what motivates each individual company, union, or association to form a PAC? Of course there are as many reasons as there are PACs, and no two PACs are established as a result of precisely the same motives. But to a certain extent we can generalize about why PACs are organized.

The Federal Election Campaign Act is obviously the foundation of PAC formation. FECA (and subsequent Federal Election Commission rulings) legitimized, institutionalized, and encouraged corporations and other entities to create PACs. Besides conferring a legal blessing on PACs, FECA allowed more leeway to PACs than to individuals in political giving. While an individual can donate up to $1,000 to any single candidate and $25,000 to all candidates per election, a PAC can contribute $5,000 to a candidate and has no aggregate limit on giving. These FECA rules provide powerful incentives to individuals and groups to form PACs, and also encourage candidates to spend more of their time soliciting money from PACs than from individuals.

Some corporations and associations were in a better position than others to take advantage of FECA. Those with some form of pre-PAC contribution program—and those already committed to electoral involvement—were especially likely to form PACs.[3] Companies and groups with large staffs and ample material resources were also quick to take advantage of the PAC option.[4] Firms with a politically active chief executive officer (CEO) often created PACs before competitors with less politically oriented leadership.[5] For corporations, the degree of unionization appears to be another factor. In the random-sample survey of multicandidate PACs conducted for this study,[6] fully 58 percent of the corporate PACs were begun by companies whose employees were unionized to some degree. In 38 percent of the cases in which unions exist in a company, at least one union has formed its own PAC. So PAC formation in some instances may have been an extension of the competition between management and labor.

Within corporations there are sometimes other motivations at work to stimulate the establishment of a PAC. Some corporate executives, claiming harassment by candidates and campaigns soliciting contributions, find a PAC to be a convenient referral: "I gave at the office; apply to our PAC."[7]

Other executives, realizing that their companies' influence will be greater if management employees are active in politics, see a PAC as an effective vehicle for involving their people in campaigns.

In an explanation of why some groups are particularly likely to form PACs, perhaps the most powerful element is that the government concerns some industries more directly than others. If an industry is fundamentally affected by governmental regulation, if it depends heavily on governmental contracts, licenses, subsidies, import limitations, tariffs, or special tax breaks, then the companies in that industry have probably established PACs.[8] In reviewing the list of corporate and trade PACs, certain interests stand out: railroads, shipping, trucking, utilities, banks, oil and energy, savings and loan associations, drug companies, timber and paper companies, and the aerospace industry. Governmental decisions are crucial to the operations of each of these interests—much more so than, say, the consumer product companies and retailers. It should be no surprise, then, that more PACs are found among the former interests than among the latter.[9]

The growth of government and federal regulation since the mid-1960s—and particularly since 1970—has served as a powerful stimulus to PAC growth. For example, the staff size of regulatory agencies in Washington has grown by about two-thirds in the last decade.[10] Few segments of society and industry can claim to be "unregulated" today, and so most have a direct stake in the decisions government makes. Several studies have shown that the stronger a group's legislative interests, the more likely the group is to have a PAC.[11] Usually, those legislative interests are quite narrow. Federal Express's PAC (FEPAC), for instance, was formed in 1976 to aid in lobbying Congress for permission to use larger, more efficient aircraft (circumventing the Civil Aeronautics Board in the process).[12] FEPAC has also assisted its parent company's campaigns to change certain postal regulations hampering the growth of its business.

Not all PACs are begun with specific, narrow legislative goals in mind. Some PACs are broadly ideological, intent on transforming the character of government in a conservative or liberal direction. While one readily thinks of PACs like the National Conservative Political Action Committee (NCPAC) on the right and the National Committee for an Effective Congress (NCEC) on the left, a number of union, trade, and corporate PACs are predominantly ideological too.[13] As one corporate PAC manager commented, "We were set up because management had a strong belief that business has a right and obligation to change the direction of government—and we started when they didn't like the direction of government."[14] Ideological groups that are determined to change the status quo are in fact disproportionately likely to form PACs, while more moderate organizations are disinclined to take the PAC route.[15]

There are still other motives behind PAC formation. Some groups have recognized that with all the press attention showered on the PAC movement in the past few years, establishing a PAC is one sure way to gain notice from journalists, the public, and officeholders. "When we were just a lobby and didn't have a PAC, some members didn't pay attention," said Charles Orasin, executive vice-president of Handgun Control, Inc. "Now that we can hurt the members [of Congress], they listen."[16] Proponents of new political ideas and ignored interests find a rich opportunity for publicity in forming a PAC. Advocates of space-based weapons to protect against a Soviet attack registered an American Space Frontier Committee in 1983 and drew considerable press notice for its proposals while pledging to raise $1 million for "high frontier" candidates. Other groups, some representing unpopular causes, see a PAC as a useful tool to change opinions, especially those of public officials. In an effort to do so, Stephen Endean, treasurer of the Human Rights Campaign Fund (HRCF), which promotes gay rights, explained that the HRCF had conducted a study of congressional candidates who supported gay rights; the study purported to prove that the gay rights issue was not damaging to the candidates' chances. Beyond that, of course, HRCF exists (as do all PACs) to promote the interests of the group by "protecting our friends and defeating our enemies" at election time.

In a number of cases PACs have been formed in response to external pressure. Several PAC managers noted pressure from congressmen themselves; as one reported, "Our lack of presence at some of those Washington receptions and fund-raisers had become noticed. It had been insinuated by some on the Hill that it showed a lack of maturity in our legislative approach."[17] Particularly in the corporate sphere, a desire to "keep up with the Joneses" may also have played a role in PAC formation. John Kochevar of the National Chamber of Commerce's PAC suggested, only slightly facetiously, that some chief executive officers from companies without PACs got the idea from PAC-company CEOs on the golf course. The PAC-less CEO, says Kochevar, would come back to his office saying "Goddammit, we've got to get one of those." Referring to the rapid proliferation of business PACs, Kochevar remarked, "I can't explain how it happened any other way."

Occasionally one PAC will serve as midwife in the birth of another. The conservative National Taxpayers Union's PAC (called the Taxpayers Action Fund) was launched with a loan from NCPAC, for example.[18] More frequently PACs have been formed as a result of encouragement from an "umbrella" PAC organization like the Business-Industry Political Action Committee (BIPAC) or the National Association of Business PACs (NAB-PAC). Other groups active in disseminating information which assists PAC formation include the U.S. Chamber of Commerce, the National Association of Manufacturers, the Public Affairs Council, and even the National Republican party.

THE PAC HOLDOUTS

For all of the growth in the number of registered PACs, a large majority of special-interest groups still do not have PACs. One survey of 564 voluntary associations located in and around Washington, D.C., found that only 17 percent had a PAC by 1980.[19] Even among associations set up for profit, where recent PAC growth has been concentrated, PACs were affiliated with little more than a third (36 percent) of the groups; in the nonprofit, mixed, and citizen association categories, less than 8 percent had PACs.

Most surprising, even among *Fortune* magazine's top 500 industrial corporations, companies are nearly as likely *not* to have a PAC as to have one.[20] A random-sample telephone survey of *Fortune* 500 companies without PACs was conducted for this book[21] in order to determine the reasons behind the firms' decisions not to create political action committees. Once again there appeared to be as many reasons as respondents; but overall, several rationales predominated. First of all, the pall of Watergate has proved surprisingly long-lasting, and the specter of illegal corporate contributions continues to haunt major firms. Irving Shapiro, former chairman and CEO of Dupont, personally opposed forming a PAC in his company, claiming that a PAC is "an invidious thing, it's corrupting, it does pollute the system."[22] (Dupont finally established a PAC in 1983.)

Other corporate leaders have also worried aloud about an anti-business backlash by the public because of the image of "slush funds" conjured up by business PAC growth.[23] Many business PACs had to be developed with constant reassurance to members that nothing untoward was occurring.[24] Gregg Ward, manager of the Sheet Metal and Air Conditioning Contractors PAC, admitted that "In the beginning I had to spend a lot of time visiting and motivating the chapter people. Our biggest hurdle was getting over the premise that this was bribery." In some corporations the worries of powerful legal and accounting divisions about the safety and advisability of forming a PAC have been sufficient to stymie efforts to do so by the company's governmental affairs (lobbying) division.[25] Vocal opposition to PAC formation expressed these same doubts outside the corporate world. When politically active scientists established the Science and Technology PAC (SCITEC-PAC) in 1981 to push for greater congressional funding of basic research, many traditionalists strongly objected. "Many scientists and engineers tend to think PACs are a dirty business," said one leader in the field, while another insisted that "There's no reason for us to compromise ourselves by entering the PAC game."[26]

Beyond the vague scent of corruption, many groups have been reluctant to form a PAC because of an aversion to politics. They may have little political orientation by nature and few, if any, legislative interests; relatively unregulated businesses and many nonprofit organizations are examples.

Typically, these groups have never had any sort of organized contribution program and have no large governmental affairs division. Even many businesses with a strong governmental connection have been reluctant to start a PAC because, as one corporate PAC official suggested, "Some of our people believe business simply shouldn't be involved in government. . . . Business has always been scared of politics; ten or fifteen years ago you couldn't even get a CEO to come and testify on the Hill."[27] When PACs were actually formed by corporations or business associations, the process was frequently slow and in stages.[28] Not uncommonly, the debate about whether to start a PAC stretched over years. At the Singer Corporation, described by one senior employee as "old, staid, and conservative," formation of a PAC was under consideration for five years before one was formed in 1981. "At Singer you don't jump into things like this too easily."[29]

Some groups and corporations have very specialized reasons for avoiding PACs. The Dow Jones Corporation, which publishes the *Wall Street Journal, Barron's,* and nearly two dozen local newspapers, views having a PAC as "unethical and inappropriate since we cover PACs and politics," according to a company spokesperson.[30] Other corporations take a "let George do it" attitude, pointing to their membership in a trade association which operates a PAC or claiming that there are now so many business PACs in existence that, first, the business viewpoint is being adequately represented, and second, one additional PAC (their own) would not likely have much impact or gain much notice. Some companies cite decentralization as a reason for not creating a PAC. As one official of a large corporation put it, "We've given considerable autonomy to our subsidiaries, and we don't want senior management having to referee decisions of the subsidiaries on which congressmen to support. . . . A PAC wouldn't be worth that headache to us."[31]

Still other groups boast that they do not need a PAC to make their voices heard. A spokesperson for North American Phillips Corporation explained that, in his company's view, "the best way to a congressman's heart is not through a PAC, but jobs. Jobs in a congressman's district are far more important, and if you can affect employment in the district, a congressman's ears perk right up. It doesn't matter whether you've given him ten cents."[32] A Times-Mirror Corporation executive, explaining its lack of a PAC, noted that "some of our management are extremely well connected—you know, they can pick up the phone and get anybody from the president on down."[33] Similarly, Irving Shapiro of Dupont was perhaps able to do without a PAC because he was chairman of the Business Roundtable, one of Washington's most influential lobbying organizations. There are also many ways for groups to take part in campaigns without forming a PAC,[34] and a number of corporations and unions are using them. Individual corporate executives (and members of their families) can each give $1,000 per election to a favored candidate, and executives can also sponsor fundraising parties in their homes for candidates. Corporations can use general treasury money to send communications (such as newsletters focused on campaigns) to stockholders and administrative and executive personnel (and their families), and unions can do the same in communicating to their members and families. Both corporations and unions can use treasury funds to conduct "nonpartisan" registration and get-out-the-vote drives, and they can also give money to a party's national committee for the purchase or construction of office facilities. All of this, of course, is possible without a PAC.

PAC FORM AND SUBSTANCE

Those associations and corporations that do form PACs follow no fixed organizational model. By law a PAC only has to have a treasurer and a "statement of organization" filed with the Federal Election Commission at least ten days after its creation.[35] While all PACs necessarily follow this mandate, they otherwise exhibit a variety of structures and modes of operation.

Though individual PACs inevitably differ in some ways, PACs in each major category, like family members, have some organizational characteristics in common. Corporate PACs, for instance, are usually closely tied to the company's chief executive officer (CEO).[36] Most often the CEO is the company official who authorizes the formation of a PAC, determines the composition of the PAC's governing board, appoints some or all of the members, specifies the scope and methods of fundraising, helps to design the criteria the PAC uses in selecting candidates for contributions, and (in a minority of cases) actually directs that donations be sent to certain candidates and officeholders.

While the CEO is crucial to the formation, and sometimes the operation, of a corporate PAC, in most cases the CEO then delegates much of his authority to the public affairs (or governmental affairs) executive in the company, and to the PAC's governing board. The public affairs executive, normally a vice-president in the corporate structure, is the natural coordinator of PAC activity since he or she is usually responsible for the company's lobbying efforts and relations with government at all levels. Many of these executives are being drawn directly from the political world, and a large proportion of those interviewed for this study had served in a major party, a campaign, political consulting, a congressional staff, or even an elected position prior to their selection as a corporate executive.[37] (Not surprisingly, more of these executives came from Republican than Democratic ranks.) In most cases the public affairs officer was the first individual in the company to suggest formation of the PAC; some actively lobbied the CEO for one, realizing its usefulness in the political arena from their own prior experience in the field.

Corporate PACs are directly governed by a board or committee, usually chaired by the public affairs executive and composed of a wide range of individuals chosen from among the PAC's membership, which consists of contributors among the company's administrative personnel, executives, and stockholders. Almost always, representatives of the corporation's legal counsel and financial/accounting division will be found on the PAC board, along with a Washington staff member (if there is a D.C. office), and occasionally even the CEO himself.[38] Also present on just about every PAC board are representatives of the broad group of middle-management contributors to the PAC, distributed in fair proportion to the company's geographical or administrative structure. For national companies this means one or more board seats for each region, corporate division, or plant location. For smaller industries it may simply mean a cross-section of PAC contributors from every level of management. Very few corporate PAC boards include any representatives of the stockholders—a somewhat surprising fact since stockholders are theoretically the owners of stock companies.[39]

A few corporations with many plants and divisions have chosen to reconcile the natural conflicts that arise among their constituents by forming a separate PAC, each with its own governing board, for every plant, division, or region. Under FECA, all political committees formed by the same company, union, or group are subject together as a *unit* to the standard PAC contribution limit ($5,000 per candidate per election)—a provision obviously designed to prevent the proliferation of PACs by a single organization in order to evade the contribution limit.[40] But there are other advantages to multiple PAC formation by a single corporation. Such decentralization has been judged a boon to solicitation drives: employees or members seem to feel more involved and in greater control of the money raised by their own PAC. Moreover, multiple PACs can help to obscure the real extent of a group's financial involvement in politics.[41] American Telephone and Telegraph, for example, appeared on no one's list of "top" PACs in 1980, but in fact the twenty-three individual AT&T committees, if aggregated, would have placed the company as the tenth-largest contributor to federal candidates, with more than $650,000 disbursed. Dow Chemical, with eight PACs, and the LTV Corporation, with six PACs, also have used the multiple PAC system to great advantage.

Many elements of the PAC organizational structure used by corporations are also found in committees formed by trade associations, though there are differences. As the political scientist Michael J. Malbin has pointed out, the association PAC's task is somewhat easier than the corporation's since, theoretically at least, the corporate committee has to satisfy employees, stockholders, and even customers, while the trade group has only to worry about its own members.[42] Trade groups then try to ensure that their memberships are fully represented in PAC deliberations. The California Medical Association's CALPAC, for instance, includes on its board of directors forty physicians representing all state Senate districts and medical specialties. The largest trade PAC, the Realtors' R-PAC, has fifty state PACs and over 1,800 local PAC boards advising its eighteen-member national trustees committee.

Most labor PACs also have a governing PAC board or committee, but union leaders are generally considered to have more direct influence on labor PAC activity than their trade and corporate counterparts have on their PAC committees. In part this is because labor PACs—whether headquartered in the states or in the offices of the international union—have always been closely integrated into the union's operation. (The very first PAC, CIO-PAC, in some ways set the precedent for labor.)[43] Moreover, the average union PAC is supported by a very large group of labor contributors each giving a tiny amount (one or two dollars is the norm); consequently they have little say individually in dispensing the collective fund.[44] Under these conditions, union PAC leaders have considerable autonomy in making political decisions, particularly because the PAC board often consists of, or is dominated by, the key state or national union officers.

Labor, trade, and corporate PACs therefore differ to some degree in their organizational structure. Yet they all are connected to a "parent"—the group that spawned them and remains in charge. The nonconnected PACs have no parent, of course, and that simple administrative fact is responsible for their distinctive behavior. The political scientist Frank J. Sorauf has termed the resultant style of nonconnected PACs as "entrepreneurial": their leaders aggressively seek funds, they follow ideological strategies, they tend to support nonincumbent candidates, and they spend independently, unconstrained by ties to a larger group.[45] This differs from the slower moving "participatory" style of most connected PACs, which often try to achieve consensus or at least to reconcile members' views as much as possible. The nonconnected PACs are accountable only to themselves, for the most part, and some have virtually no internal controls either.[46] The National Conservative Political Action Committee (NCPAC), for example, justifies its actions and expenditures only to a five-member executive committee headed and hand-picked by NCPAC chairman John "Terry" Dolan. Besides himself, the committee consists of two men whose firms do business with NCPAC, Dolan's brother-in-law, and Dolan's former secretary. There is also a board of directors, but it appears to be a paper body that exists only to meet the legal requirements for a nonprofit group like NCPAC. As for the executive committee, "They acted as a ratifying body. I brought them up to date; they basically said 'Fine,' " reported Dolan.[47]

The lack of independent oversight is hardly limited to conservative nonconnected PACs. Victor Kamber, founder of the Progressive Political Action Committee (PROPAC), declined even to create a paper executive committee for PROPAC.[48] Kamber simply made all the basic decisions personally. Not all nonconnected PACs follow the NCPAC and PROPAC models, of course; some have active, involved boards. One such PAC is the conservative Committee for the Survival of a Free Congress (CSFC), whose six-member board includes two congressmen and has had "heated discussions" about CSFC policy, according to its executive director, Paul Weyrich.[49] While use of the board is "a more cumbersome procedure" than that followed by some other PACs, Weyrich insists his method is better:

> I'm a strong believer in checks and balances. I think it's important to have somebody to report to, someone to ask questions. . . . I have to justify what I do. That makes you think things through. If you're not reporting to anyone, you're a dictator.

Another unique aspect of some nonconnected PACs is their establishment of a nonprofit educational and research foundation (authorized by section 501[c][3] of the Internal Revenue Service Code) and a lobbying group (authorized by section 501[c][4]). About a third of the nonconnected PACs in my study's multicandidate PAC survey,[50] ranging from the National Federation of Business and Professional Women's Clubs to the Campaign for United Nations Reform PAC, have, like CSFC, some relation to a research foundation or a lobbying group (the latter is most common). The Free Congress Foundation of the CSFC, for instance, conducts research on issues and campaigns, and publishes essentially scholarly monographs as well as the nonpartisan and highly regarded *Political Report.* The advantages this foundation accrues to CSFC are twofold: the political research helps the PAC make its contribution decisions, and since the material is widely distributed, it enhances the credibility of the organization. There can also be financial and fundraising gains because gifts to the foundation (which are tax deductible as charitable donations for individuals and corporations)[51] can be used to pay such fixed costs as rent, salaries, and upkeep. (Usually the PAC, the research foundation, and the lobby are under one roof and share many of the same staff and officers.) And donors to the foundation or lobby can, of course, be solicited to support the PAC as well.[52]

SELECTING CANDIDATES: THE ADMINISTRATIVE PROCESS

In general, the same committees and boards that govern political action committees are also called upon to make the PACs' most crucial decisions: which candidates to select for contributions.[53] Table 2–1 presents my findings concerning the methods PACs use to select the recipients of their money. Overall, almost three-quarters of all multicandidate PACs use a board or committee to choose the candidates they will support. The Washington office staff is delegated the responsibility of candidate selection 6 percent of the time, and the D.C. staff shares the responsibility with the PAC board in another 10 percent of the cases. In only 4 percent of the PACs does the chief executive officer have the sole authority to pick candidates, although in practice his choices—if known or expressed—will undoubtedly carry great weight with the board.

There are considerable differences in selection practices among the PAC categories. More than eight in ten corporate PACs rely on boards and committees to pick their candidates—the highest proportion of any PAC grouping—and another 11 percent use a board in combination with the Washington office staff. Just 2 percent rely on the D.C. staff alone (the smallest proportion of any category) and the same tiny proportion permit their CEO to select candidates unilaterally.[54] Though corporate PACs have clearly settled on the board or committee method of candidate selection, this generalization masks a great variation in the corporate PAC board structure.[55] Some of the corporate PACs, particularly the less well-endowed ones, tend to have small, informal boards dominated by the public affairs executive and his staff. Other corporate PACs, especially those with large war chests, have elaborate, formal, multitiered committees consisting of twenty or more people, including a number of nonspecialist "amateurs" drawn from the broad body of PAC members.

Corporate and labor PACs tend to diverge not only in the candidates they choose to support, but also in their method of selecting campaign favorites. While 60 percent of the labor PACs also use a board or committee, almost

Table 2–1.
Making PAC Decisions on Which Candidates to Support

	CATEGORY OF MULTICANDIDATE PAC			
Decision-maker	ALL PACS	CORPORATE	LABOR	TRADE
Washington office staff	6%	2%	6%	14%
Chief Executive Officer(s) of company, union, or association	4	2	12	3
PAC board or committee	74	84	60	61
Joint decision of PAC board and Washington office staff	10	11	0	16
Other	7	2	23	7

SOURCE: Survey question "Who makes the decisions as to which candidates or parties will be supported by your PAC?" from the questionnaire for the random-sample survey of multicandidate PACs conducted for this study; see Introduction, note 16.

a fifth delegate the decision either to the top union officers (12 percent) or to the Washington office staff (6 percent). On the other hand almost a quarter of the labor PACs are decentralized to the extent that state or local labor councils, rather than the national PAC, decide the basic endorsement and contribution allocations. Trade PACs rely on their Washington office staffs to a greater extent than labor or any other PAC category (about 14 percent of the trade candidate selections are made there). But once again, the board/committee method is the standard, with 61 percent of the trade PACs utilizing a board alone, and another 16 percent using it in combination with the Washington staff. The large national trade PACs use their Washington staff to coordinate the decisions of boards whose members are scattered around the country. The AMPAC staff, for example, initiates frequent "conference call" meetings of its board. "We have conference calls two or three times a week to make decisions in the latter part of an election season," reported AMPAC's Peter Lauer. Table 2–2 contains a few specific examples of candidate-selection practices chosen from each major PAC category. This sample suggests the wide variety of decision-making methods existing in the PAC world.

Several additional observations about the candidate-selection process can be made from the results of the interviews and survey I conducted. First, while the final decisions on contributions may be made by a board, a

Table 2–2.
A Sampler of PAC Decision-making Methods

POLITICAL ACTION COMMITTEE	PAC CATEGORY	CANDIDATES WHO RECEIVE PAC CONTRIBUTIONS ARE CHOSEN BY . . .
1. Business-Industry Political Action Committee (BIPAC)	Trade	A six-member (three from each party) candidate-review committee based on recommendations from state BIPAC director. Decision to endorse (and on how much to contribute) must be unanimous.
2. Committee for the Survival of a Free Congress (CSFC)	Nonconnected	A six-member board including two congressmen based on recommendations from the executive director and CSFC field staff.

Table 2–2.*(Continued)*

POLITICAL ACTION COMMITTEE	PAC CATEGORY	CANDIDATES WHO RECEIVE PAC CONTRIBUTIONS ARE CHOSEN BY . . .
3. COPE (AFL-CIO)	Labor	Executive Committee of AFL-CIO based on recommendations of COPE staff and internal committees.
4. Honeywell Employees PAC (HEPAC)	Corporate	Steering committee of 11 employee members based on recommendations of a "candidate evaluation" committee composed of 15–20 employee PAC members.
5. Machinists Non-Partisan Political League (MNPL)	Labor	For president: Committee of the three top union officers based on recommendations of PAC director and state union leaders. For Congress: state MNPL councils.
6. National Conservative Political Action Committee (NCPAC)	Nonconnected	National chairman of NCPAC (John T. "Terry" Dolan), and sometimes "ratified" by a five-member executive board.
7. NEA-PAC (National Education Association)	Labor	Majority vote of the National NEA-PAC Council, with the written concurrence of the state NEA affiliate and after local NEA members have interviewed (or secured written questionnaire responses from) congressional candidates.[a]
8. Pennsylvania Dental PAC	Trade	A board composed of 10 dentists, one from each association region in Pennsylvania.
9. Progressive Political Action Committee (PROPAC)	Nonconnected	PROPAC founder Victor Kamber.

Table 2–2.*(Continued)*

POLITICAL ACTION COMMITTEE	PAC CATEGORY	CANDIDATES WHO RECEIVE PAC CONTRIBUTIONS ARE CHOSEN BY . . .
10. Spring Industries PAC	Corporate	Committee of eight middle-management employees plus a corporate officer and one division president, chaired by the director of public affairs.

SOURCE: Personal interviews and the survey of multicandidate PACs conducted for this study (see Introduction, note 16).

[a]The National Education Association has a different selection procedure for presidential candidates. Prior to the nominating conventions, NEA-PAC can recommend that the 125-member NEA Board of Directors "support" a candidate or candidates in one or both parties. The Board can authorize such support by a 58 percent majority vote; each state NEA affiliate must also concur before any activity on behalf of a favored candidate can take place in its state. For the general election, the 7,500-member NEA Representative Assembly must vote any presidential endorsement. NEA-PAC and the NEA Board of Directors can make endorsement recommendations to the Representative Assembly.

committee, or a group's officers, information and suggestions are gathered from many sources: the political parties, officeholders and candidates, political consultants (especially pollsters) and campaign managers, and of course the PAC staff and membership. The larger the PAC, the more vigorous is the effort to secure intelligence internally and externally. Rarely is a formal survey of PAC members taken to determine their opinions about possible recipients,[56] but the contributors' representatives and the amateur political observers, on many selection boards do represent the sentiments of their peers to some degree. While most PAC leaders report that the flow of opinion and suggestion from the ranks to the PAC governing board is minimal, it is nevertheless true that PAC boards keep the views of contributors in mind lest PAC members grow upset with the candidate choices and cease giving.

Second, the PAC staff not only often influences candidate selection, it many times completely determines it. As we have already seen, the Washington office staff is delegated some or all the candidate-selection authority in nearly a quarter of the PACs. Moreover, in almost all cases involving a board or committee, the PAC staff (whether in Washington or in the home office) makes specific recommendations to the board on which candidates should receive money and how much they should be given. Not a single one of the several dozen PAC officers I interviewed reported that even as many as 5 percent of the staff recommendations were denied or significantly altered by the PAC selection boards. Many of the larger PACs, such as CSFC, NCEC, NCPAC, NEA-PAC, R-PAC, and AMPAC, have full-time field workers scattered throughout the country in regional offices or sent to particular states and congressional districts to scout out firsthand the political situation. Field staff decisions seem particularly influential, and normally override information from secondary sources about individual contests. Field staff recommendations are very seldom overturned; most PAC directors had difficulty citing even one or two instances in which they were.

Finally, it appears that most PAC boards strive for unanimity in their deliberations. Although formal votes are rarely taken, one strident voice can sometimes be enough to derail a campaign contribution, even when the reasons are personal. A director of a liberal PAC, for instance, told of a 1982 meeting of his board when one liberal Democratic congressman from a midwestern state vetoed a donation to another liberal Democratic congressman from the same state because the pair had been involved in a scrap over redrawing the boundary lines of their House districts.[57] This particular PAC formally permitted a one-person blackball under its operating rules; it is a less formal but accepted norm of conduct in many other PACs.

THE WASHINGTON OFFICE

One administrative (and physical) structure which has major effects on PAC behavior is a Washington, D.C., office. Whether or not a PAC is headquartered in the capital, or has official, full-time representation there, is an important variable in explaining the differences in strategy and activity among PACs. Only about 14 percent of all PACs are solely based in Washington,[58] but a much higher percentage have at least a branch office in the capital. Of the PACs I surveyed, 42 percent reported the existence of a Washington office.[59] A Washington office affects PAC operations in a number of ways.[60] First of all, a PAC directly influenced or controlled outright by Washington contacts naturally tends to be more pragmatic and more concerned with congressional access. PAC leaders and staff centered in the capital are daily forced to accommodate legislative realities and to embrace the essential element of success on Capitol Hill: compromise. PAC officials located in the hinterlands are more removed from the legislative hurly-burly and the pressures that tend to temper purist ideological urges.

The result of this difference is readily apparent in the candidate preferences expressed by PAC officials. When asked whether an incumbent, a challenger, or an open-seat candidate would be preferred for a PAC contribution "if all else were the same between any two [congressional] candidates," PACs with a D.C. office chose the safe, pragmatic bet, the incumbent, by a much larger margin than PACs without a D.C. office. Fully 61 percent of the Washington-office PACs picked incumbents, compared to 38 percent of non–Washington-office PACs. Those PACs without a D.C. office are somewhat more ideological and willing to take risks, with 10 percent selecting a challenger as the preferred recipient of a campaign contribution, compared to just 6 percent for Washington-office PACs.[61] The Washington-office PACs are probably more incumbent oriented not only because of their proximity to Congress but also because many work closely with their group's Washington lobbyists, whose primary task is to develop influence with sitting congressmen.[62] "The D.C. PAC representative gets a lot more pressure from the lobbyists as well as congressmen themselves," explains Richard Armstrong of the Public Affairs Council. "It's a natural consequence of the Washington networking."

Many other behavioral distinctions between Washington-office PACs and other PACs are apparent.[63] Washington-office PACs are far more likely to contribute to that staple of congressional campaign events, the D.C. fundraiser. Nearly all Washington-office PACs (90 percent) reported giving money at D.C. fundraisers in 1981–1982, while only 49 percent of non–Washington-office PACs did so. Perhaps because there are so many $100- and $250-per-person fundraisers in the capital, Washington-office PACs on average make a greater number of contributions than non–Washington-office PACs, while the size of the contribution tends to be smaller.[64]

PACs with a D.C. office also appear to be more sophisticated in several ways. The Washington-office PACs are somewhat more inclined to use "in-kind" expenditures. As Chapter 3 will explain in more detail, "in-kind" expenditures include the contribution of polling information, telephone banks, and other sorts of campaign services to a candidate as an alternative to simply giving money. Provision for in-kind services by a PAC implies the existence of a technically knowledgeable and politically savvy PAC staff, and 21 percent of the Washington-office PACs provide in-kind services while only 11 percent of PACs without a D.C. office do so. Similarly, Washington-office PACs are more inclined to organize major "political education" programs for their groups' membership or contributors. (Political education programs such as voter registration and get-out-the-vote drives will be discussed later in this chapter.) While just 15 percent of Washington-office PACs have no political education programs, 33 percent of the PACs without a Washington office have none.

Washington office PACs are more focused on national politics as well. Only 19 percent of the D.C.-office PACs have subsidiary or affiliated state PACs around the country. (A state PAC usually contributes only to nonfederal state and local candidates rather than to federal contenders.) By contrast, 40 percent of the non–Washington-office PACs are associated with one or more state PACs. The national orientation of many Washington-office PACs may sometimes mean that PAC contributors in the state and local district offices of the sponsoring company, union, or organization have less influence on the PAC's choice of which candidates to support. The state and local offices often conduct all the fundraising drives, then channel donations to the Washington office. While many PACs (especially trade committees) are required to redistribute much of the total back to the states and localities, and other PACs delegate much of the responsibility for candidate selection to their local divisions, disposal of at least a portion of the locally raised funds is left to the Washington PAC's discretion. Contributors can be expected to have a more direct say on PAC contribution decisions when they go to candidates below the national level.[65]

If the existence of a Washington office has a wide-ranging influence on the performance and outlook of a PAC, it must be said that that influence is not always harmonious. A Washington office often has a discernibly divisive effect: the creation of such tension between the home office and the capital branch that an experienced PAC official termed one instance "a war." In a reference to corporate PACs which could apply as well to the other kinds of political action committees, Bernadette Budde of the Business-Industry Political Action Committee observed, "In the average corporation there is a great deal of jealousy and misunderstanding about the role of the Washington office to begin with, and when you add . . . the appearance of [the Washington office] dictating what happens with PAC money you have a terrible conflict." Not surprisingly, this conflict—rather than purely rational calculation—appears to affect, and occasionally even determine, a PAC's choice of candidate recipients for its largesse.[66]

THE PAC FAMILIES: CONSULTATION AND COORDINATION IN THE PAC COMMUNITY

Even without a Washington office, no PAC has to be an island unto itself. There is active "networking" among the PACs, not just in Washington but throughout the country. PACs share information about candidates and, some charge, coordinate contributions for maximum effect. Whether or not the PACs "run in packs" in selecting candidates, they certainly share information freely with one another and use regular, organized meetings as well as informal consultations to do so. As the National Republican Congressional Committee warned its 1982 House candidates who had come PAC hunting in Washington, "Don't lie, exaggerate, or obfuscate. PAC people talk with one another and have a very effective communications network. Pull a fast one with one PAC and the word will get around to others in no time at all."[67]

Certain PACs matter more than others not simply because they have larger budgets—some of the key PACs have relatively modest war chests, in fact—but because they are considered coordinators and "pricing leaders" for other, less well-informed political action committees. "People talk about 2,000 or more PACs, but the truth is that there are only about 45 corporate PACs, 6 conservative PACs, and 15 to 20 trade association PACs that really count . . . a group of less than 75 people," observed Paul Dietrich of the Fund for a Conservative Majority.[68] Many of the rank-and-file PACs are directly affiliated with a PAC leader or coordinating agency. Fully 61 percent of all multicandidate corporate PACs are affiliated with the Business-Industry Political Action Committee (BIPAC), 59 percent are members of the National Chamber of Commerce, and 41 percent belong to the Public Affairs Council.[69] About a third of all multicandidate trade PACs are also affiliated with BIPAC and the Chamber.[70] An interlocking membership is shared by all these groups: 80 percent of BIPAC's members also are affiliated with the Chamber of Commerce, and 49 percent of BIPAC's members are on the Public Affairs Council list.[71]

BIPAC, the AFL-CIO's COPE, and the political parties are among those groups that are regularly relied on by their PACs for basic information about congressional contests. As Table 2–3 indicates, BIPAC is the most popular overall source of electoral intelligence, especially so for corporate and trade PACs. The Republican (RNC) and Democratic National Committees (DNC) are close behind,[72] though their constituencies differ. The RNC draws more corporate PACs, the DNC more labor committees, with trade PACs splitting their attentions about equally. Labor PACs rely most heavily on COPE, the DNC, and other liberal sources (such as the National Committee for an Effective Congress, or NCEC), but a fair number also obtain information from the Republican party, which usually has the most up-to-date political data. Nonconnected PACs, true to their maverick reputations, are less likely to rely on the nonideological, "establishment" information centers, and disproportionately prefer the NCEC on the left and the Free Congress Foundation on the right.

On the liberal side of the spectrum it is clear that, other than the DNC, COPE is the vital information source and coordinating unit. COPE holds frequent and well-attended political briefings for liberal PACs. A number of directors of other labor PACs, such as William Holayter of the Machinists Non-Partisan Political League, sit on COPE's operating committees. Even the Teamsters, a non–AFL-CIO union, is usually invited to participate in COPE activities. Reported David Sweeney, executive director of the Teamsters' DRIVE PAC, "Sometimes our local guys work hand-in-glove with the COPE operation. In some of the states our people actually participate in the COPE screenings and ratings." The NCEC supplements labor's efforts on the left with monthly meetings during election years that usually

Table 2–3.
Information Exchange in the PAC Community

	CATEGORY OF MULTICANDIDATE PAC				
INFORMATION SOURCE	ALL PACS[a]	CORPORATE[a]	LABOR[a]	TRADE[a]	NONCONNECTED[a]
Business-Industry PAC (BIPAC)	57%	64%	0	71%	8%
COPE (AFL-CIO)	21	10	81	4	25
Democratic National Committee (or other Democratic committees)	44	33	65	57	25
Republican National Committee (or other Republican committees)	47	45	44	64	25
National Committee for an Effective Congress (NCEC)	8	2	6	7	33
Free Congress Foundation[b]	4	2	0	4	17
Other group(s)	10	5	7	17	17

SOURCE: Survey question "Does your PAC or its Washington representative regularly obtain information or attend meetings of any of the following?" from the questionnaire for the random-sample survey of multicandidate PACs conducted for this study; see Introduction, note 16.

[a]Columns do not total 100 percent due to multiple responses.

[b]The Free Congress Foundation is associated with the Committee for the Survival of a Free Congress (CSFC).

draw 100 or more representatives of women's groups, teachers, environmentalists, and peace organizations. Other liberal PACs such as Pamela Harriman's Democrats for the '80s have also held briefing sessions from time to time.

The business side of the PAC community is tied together by even-stronger bonds of communication. A half dozen major groups both inform their professional allies about current races and encourage other corporations and associations to form PACs. The leader in the field is BIPAC, founded in 1963 by the National Association of Manufacturers as its answer to COPE.[73] With about 1,400 members, BIPAC contributes directly to candidates, making gifts of about $200,000 in 1982. More important, it has held monthly briefings during election seasons since 1972 for 100–125 PAC managers, in Washington and in roadshows around the country. In election years BIPAC also operates a recorded telephone service called DIAL that plays daily updates on key congressional races. A BIPAC endorsement is highly prized by candidates since it sends a signal to other PACs that the selected contender is "right" on the issues and has a reasonable chance to win. With a field staff and an extensive nationwide organization, BIPAC is well positioned to identify close races and alert its members by means of a publication it mails every few weeks. BIPAC has enhanced its influence as an early-warning signal with its willingness to get involved in party primaries, to focus on attractive challengers rather than on safe incumbents, and to give "seed money" to favored contenders many months before the general election campaign.

The U.S. Chamber of Commerce's PAC (called the National Chamber Alliance for Politics) is another vital barometer for the business PAC community. While it does not contribute money to candidates, the Chamber PAC issues an "opportunity race" list of its preferred candidates in close races, and its director John Kochevar is not shy in suggesting the impact of being on the Chamber's list: "Congressman Tony Coelho [head of the Democratic Congressional Campaign Committee] has stated that our endorsement is worth $100,000 to a candidate. We know that one U.S. senator [Democrat Jennings Randolph of West Virginia], because we had endorsed his opponent, went out and borrowed $80,000." The Chamber gets the word out about candidates in other ways too. In September 1982, for instance, a four-hour, closed-circuit teleconference called "See How They Run," in which several dozen key congressional races were discussed and handicapped, was beamed to 150–200 PAC managers scattered in seven U.S. cities. The Chamber plans far more extensive and personalized use of teleconferencing, possibly including weekly shows with more two-way interaction, for the future.

The BIPAC and Chamber programs, while the best known, are not alone in the business PAC arena. Four trade association PACs have been established to coordinate and serve as clearinghouses for other corporate and trade PACs: the National Association for Association PACs, the National Federation of Independent Businesses, the Congressional Small Business Campaign Committee, and the National Association of Business Political Action Committees (NABPAC). NABPAC, for example, was formed in 1977 as a service organization to provide research and information to business PAC staffs. It was the initiative of Paul Thornbrugh, an executive with the MAPCO corporation, who created NABPAC after he realized that his own company's new PAC could be helped by the technical expertise and experience of other PACs. With headquarters in Oklahoma City and about 225 PAC members paying $400 annual dues, NABPAC produces evaluations of approximately the top fifty campaigns in each election cycle, and holds workshops around the country. Beyond candidate evaluation, it advises PACs on how to increase their memberships and contributions, and operates a "hot line" to answer questions from PAC administrators.

The Public Affairs Council is yet another business PAC catalyst on the Washington scene. Chartered in 1954, the Council has 430 corporate members, more than half of which are *Fortune* 500 companies with PACs. As far back as 1975, after the FEC's crucial SunPAC decision opened the floodgates for business PACs, the Public Affairs Council (as well as other groups)[74] began to host seminars on organizing and administering PACs. Business PAC promotion rather than candidate endorsement is still the focus of the Council's work. Besides occasional seminars on the mechanics of PAC formation, the Council has produced a twelve-minute color film called *PACs under Fire,* which presents the pro-PAC gospel in a format that can be customized to include each individual PAC's pitch for members. As of 1983 the Council also began publishing a "Corporate PAC Newsmemo" to alert PAC leaders regularly to "new facts and materials they can use to help spread the word about the positive aspects of PACs."[75]

Like the Public Affairs Council, the National Association of Manufacturers does not make contributions to candidates, but the 13,000-member NAM is hardly without influence among business PACs. With BIPAC among its progeny and with 300 of its own members operating PACs, NAM is well positioned to identify good investments for business PACs. This it accomplishes through publication and distribution of *PAC Manager,* which features candidates who have won NAM's favor. The chosen contenders "must have the support of the NAM members in their districts, and their opponents must be people who from a business viewpoint are not representing our philosophy of government," explained Helena Hutton, NAM's director of public affairs. She refused to term a *PAC Manager* feature article an endorsement of the selected candidate, but it is surely tantamount to one —a message not lost on NAM's membership.

Aside from trade and professional groups, several conservative organizations and individuals act as go-betweens and coordinators in the PAC community. The Americans for Constitutional Action (ACA) sponsors fundraising dinners to bring together conservative congressmen and PAC officials.[76] The conservative activist Morton Blackwell organizes an informal luncheon meeting twice a month for traditional conservative and New Right PACs; twenty or more of these PACs trade information at the lunches, and candidates seeking their backing address the gatherings. Finally, the Free Congress Foundation, affiliated with the Committee for the Survival of a Free Congress, publishes the weekly *Political Report* which, while a balanced account of races across the country, is distributed widely in the conservative community and includes the candidate ratings of CSFC and other conservative and liberal groups.

Formal consultation and coordination among PACs then is very substantial, but the informal contacts among the staffs of soulmate PACs are even more frequent. As Bernadette Budde of BIPAC put it, in understated fashion: "We're all very cooperative. Many of our directors are the same." The staffs of PACs on both left and right, for instance, have various "working group" caucuses to supplement the structured programs open to a wider public. The organizations themselves sometimes cosponsor seminars or projects such as the development of a "pro-PAC speakers bureau" (an effort of NABPAC, BIPAC, NAM, and the Public Affairs Council). These ties do not prove that there is a "conspiracy" in the PAC community to channel contributions to candidates as a group in order to maximize their influence. The friendly rivalries (the Chamber and BIPAC feud about whose information is more reliable; the National Committee for an Effective Congress and PROPAC are barely on speaking terms) and the not-so-friendly rivalries (the New Right despises most business PACs for their "sell-out" gifts to liberal Democrats) would probably prevent any wholesale deal-making. Interviews with the major PACs confirm how jealously each one guards its treasury and disbursements from it. As Peter Lauer, AMPAC's director of political affairs, commented: "Sharing information does not automatically mean there is a *quid pro quo.* It's not like Bernadette [Budde] calls me up and says, 'I just gave $2,500 to Snodgrass' and I say 'Oh, good, I'm going to give $2,500 too.' That just doesn't happen." And as Lauer also noted, "Usually it's the candidates, not the PACs, who will put together a list of PACs that are supporting them."

In general, both the interests *and* the research information (about whether a candidate is good and his campaign competitive) of two different PACs must coincide before both will contribute to the same candidate. The open sharing of data in the PAC community obviously helps to fulfill at least the second of these two qualifiers. And the easy flow of information in the PAC world enables groups on the right and left to construct an overall "consensus" roster of ideologically qualified, competitive candidates from which to choose. These rosters become particularly important once a PAC has given money to all of its priority candidates—those contenders selected because they are crucial to the PAC's specific interests—and it begins to search for other less-familiar but worthy recipients of its leftover campaign cash.

THE COSTS OF RUNNING A PAC

In the case of PACs, it takes money to give money, since running a PAC is a very expensive proposition. The political scientist Herbert Alexander found that in the 1980 election cycle almost $57 million (43.5 percent) of the $131 million spent by PACs could be attributed to administrative expenses.[77] Alexander also estimated that corporations and unions incurred an additional $30 million in administrative PAC costs not required to be reported under FECA, yielding a total of $87 million in operating costs for that two-year election cycle. For the individual PAC, the costs of administration can easily exceed the actual contributions it makes to candidates.[78] While most PACs with parent organizations are unsure of their exact costs since salaries, rent, and other administrative expenses may be absorbed directly by the sponsoring group, the multicandidate PACs I surveyed estimated their total operating expenses: the average estimate was slightly under $43,700.

Corporate, trade, and labor PACs have an important advantage over nonconnected political action committees in the way they pay administrative expenses. Corporations and unions are permitted to finance these costs —which include all salaries, legal and accounting services, travel and rent, equipment, postage, printing, and consulting fees—directly from their general treasury funds. More than three-quarters of all corporate and labor PACs have all their expenses paid by their parent company or union, and only about a fifth have no expenses paid.[79] The parent associations of trade PACs are also permitted to cover administrative costs, and under a 1980 advisory opinion[80] of the Federal Election Commission (FEC), trade PACs are allowed to accept as well corporate contributions from member companies to defray administrative expenses. There is no limit on the amount or frequency of these corporate gifts, no reporting to the FEC is required, the money can be used for political education programs as well as administration, and the donation may even be tax deductible.[81] Some trade PACs, such as the Sheet Metal and Air Conditioning Contractors PAC (SMACPAC), have aggressively solicited corporate money for a separate administrative fund. In 1982 alone, for instance, SMACPAC was able to collect over $37,000 from member companies to pay the PAC's expenses (such as the fundraising costs of local chapters), so that its $225,000 in 1982 PAC funds could be devoted almost entirely to campaign contributions.

If trade PACs are at a comparative disadvantage relative to their labor and corporate counterparts, nonconnected PACs are severely penalized in administrative matters because they lack a parent body. With no group to absorb operating costs, the nonconnecteds must pay all expenses from the money they are able to raise—a hardship that partially accounts for the small proportion of their funds (about 17 percent) actually contributed to candidates.[82] There is a tradeoff for the nonconnecteds, though: they are permitted to solicit funds from the general public, whereas the other kinds of PACs can seek donations only from their members, shareholders, and employees. Additionally, some of the ideological nonconnected PACs have related lobby groups or research and educational foundations to absorb some of their expenses.

Because there is no parental body to supervise them, and because their governing committees are often relatively inactive or even nonexistent, the nonconnected PACs (particularly the ideological ones) sometimes appear to be financially unaccountable or corrupt, and administratively uncontrollable as well. The journalist Robert Timberg, in a series of investigative articles for the *Baltimore Sun,*[83] calculated that of $17.7 million raised by NCPAC since its establishment in 1975, about $6.5 million had been channeled to individuals and firms whose owners were closely linked with NCPAC and its national chairman, Terry Dolan. Similarly on the left, PROPAC founder Victor Kamber's political consulting firm, the Kamber Group, seems to have materially benefited in some ways from its in-house operation of PROPAC.[84] Both Dolan and Kamber heatedly deny that anything untoward has occurred; Dolan claims that his friends and patrons are superior to the competition and give NCPAC cut-rate prices (for printing, mailing, and consulting, for instance), while Kamber insists that he has accepted no pay from PROPAC and that his firm has lost money on the proposition.[85]

It is the Federal Election Commission's own disclosure rules that contribute to the appearance of improper behavior by the nonconnected PACs, and a close examination of the groups' (and other nonconnected PACs') budgets do tend to support Dolan's and Kamber's protestations. Not all the principals in the groups appear to have profited handsomely; Dolan's salary is only $33,000, low by Washington's standards for a similar position. Beyond that, as Dolan says, "The FEC divides the world into two parts: contributions to candidates, and everything else is overhead. That's ridiculous."[86] Not only is independent spending (a kind of indirect contribution that nonconnecteds frequently make to candidates) often lumped together with more legitimate overhead costs like office, salaries, and equipment, but direct-mail costs—which alone have consumed well over a quarter of all NCPAC's funds—are classed as overhead too. Nonconnected PACs are virtually forced by FECA's rules to turn for fundraising to direct mail, which can regularly generate a large number of small contributions from a broad base. But direct mail is an enormously expensive operation, requiring a large initial outlay and consuming much of its own profits for a lengthy period.[87] Direct mail necessarily will drive up the size of a PAC's budget, while simultaneously reducing the portion of the budget available for campaign contributions. Moreover, direct mail has persuasive uses; in addition to raising money, it can win converts on a candidate's or ideology's behalf and thus cannot fairly be categorized solely as a noncampaign expense. Finally, the FEC's reporting requirements have encouraged some nonconnected groups to classify political expenditures as operating costs for simplicity's sake.[88] While PAC staff members may allocate large amounts of time to helping certain candidates organize their campaigns, the staff salaries are often reported to the FEC as lump-sum operating expenses rather than, more properly, as in-kind contributions to the assisted campaigns.

But even when all this is said, the appearance of impropriety in some nonconnected PACs remains, heightened by the shockingly few controls on groups like NCPAC and PROPAC. Kamber himself has acknowledged the lack of reasonable safeguards. And as for the contributor who conscientiously sends his dollars to PROPAC, Kamber suggested in frankness, "I guess in the simplest sense . . . they've got to trust, yeah, I guess they do, Vic Kamber."[89]

FUNDRAISING BY THE PACS

Every good advertising man knows that you cannot sell a steak without the sizzle. We learned that you don't just form a political action committee, send around a note on company letterhead announcing its creation, and expect big things to happen. You must *merchandise* the PAC.

—A spokesman for the
Loctite Corporation's PAC[90]

This PAC officer's instincts are widely followed in the PAC community. Aggressive fundraising which utilizes all the technological tricks of the modern campaign is fast becoming standard practice among political action committees. Before PACs can contribute dollars, they must get them, and the solicitation of donors has very rapidly become both an art and a science. Borrowing the political consultants' tools of direct mail, videotape, television, and telephone banks, PAC managers have increasingly and successfully sought to enlarge their committees' bank accounts, and thus their political clout.

The rules of solicitation[91] are best described as a thicket, with somewhat different regulations applied to the different categories of PACs. Generally, as we saw in Chapter 1, a corporate PAC[92] may solicit the parent corporation's administrative, executive, and professional employees, as well as stockholders, at any time and as frequently as it wishes. Additionally, a corporate committee may solicit the corporation's rank-and-file employees twice each year by mail to the employees' homes. In parallel fashion, a labor PAC may solicit its parent union's members without restriction, and twice yearly may solicit nonunion employees and the corporation's administrative, executive, and professional employees and stockholders. Trade association PACs operate under other strictures, and they must secure prior approval from their member corporations each year in order to solicit the executive and administrative personnel of those corporations. A member corporation is free to permit only a single trade PAC to solicit its employees and stockholders in a given year, and it may restrict both the solicitation pool and the number of solicitations made by its chosen trade PAC.[93] Trade PACs have more flexibility in soliciting their noncorporate members—there is no limitation on frequency there—and trade PACs can of course freely solicit their own executive and administrative staffs. They have the same twice-yearly solicitation rights for their own nonexecutive employees as corporate PACs do.[94] Finally, nonconnected PACs have wide latitude in solicitation; essentially, they may solicit the general public as often as they please for contributions.

Within this regulatory framework, how do the PACs go about asking money from those they can contact? The survey results in Table 2–4 suggest the answers.[95] Over two-thirds (67 percent) of the PACs use various forms of direct-mail solicitation, with trade PACs and especially corporate committees wedded to this type of fundraising. Personal, face-to-face solicitation is the second most popular method (54 percent use it), although almost two-thirds of the trade PACs and 79 percent of the labor PACs select this device. Group seminars to promote the PAC are also relatively popular: 37 percent of the PACs choose this alternative. Telephoning is surprisingly rare; only 10 percent of all PACs use it, though close to half of the trade and nonconnected PACs do so. Labor PACs have a distinctive fundraising pattern: they are most likely to employ rallies and special events in addition to personal, face-to-face encounters to fill their coffers. Most notable is the fact that all categories of PACs use most or all of the solicitation methods listed in Table 2–4, and a large majority of individual PACs use two or more of the methods. Often one approach (say, a group seminar) is used to initiate contact, with a different approach (personal, telephone, or direct mail) used as a follow-up. The PACs with the highest response rates tend to use repeated follow-ups; if at first they don't succeed, or get only a pledge, they try, try again. Linking all the methods of solicitation is the consistent emphasis on tax credits for political donations. Each individual taxpayer can claim credit for half the amount of a contribution, up to $50 ($100 for a joint return), and some states offer additional credits or deductions.

The most personalized solicitations are generally agreed to be the most effective. Many PACs, particularly labor but also some corporate committees, completely decentralize their fundraising in the belief that local officers, who know potential contributors on a first-name basis, are in a much better position to secure a donation. These PACs produce all materials for

Table 2–4.
How PACs Raise Money

SOLICITATION METHOD	CATEGORY OF MULTICANDIDATE PAC				
	ALL PACS[a]	CORPO-RATE[a]	LABOR[a]	TRADE[a]	NONCON-NECTED[a]
Personal, face-to-face	54%	45%	79%	65%	56%
Direct mail/letters	67	82	36	73	56
Group seminars	37	40	36	27	22
Telephone	10	7	0	46	44
Other	20	12	46[b]	19	11

SOURCE: Survey question "What solicitation methods do you use?" from questionnaire for the random-sample survey of multicandidate PACs conducted for this study; see Introduction, note 16.
[a]Columns do not total 100 percent due to multiple responses.
[b]For the labor PAC questionnaire only, another solicitation method was listed—"rallies and special events"—which 46 percent of the labor PACs reported using.

the fund drive in their headquarters or Washington office, and then send them to each local union or corporate plant for face-to-face distribution and discussion. The next most personal form of solicitation is the small-group seminar. Both labor unions and corporations hold these, but the format is decidedly different. Labor's usual forum is the traditional local union meeting. As David Sweeney, director of the Teamsters' DRIVE PAC, explained his operation:

> We have a staff of five guys who will attend local meetings and tell them "we need money to help your friends and defeat your enemies." We'll go with [congressional] voting records, legislative reports, and we tailor each local presentation to what their interests are and what their bitches are.

The corporate PACs, by contrast, usually center their pitch around a short videotape presentation filled with praise for the PAC idea from leading politicians and climaxed by patriotic exhortations to get involved. Many of these sessions become PAC pep rallies, with a speech by the chief executive officer encouraging the audience to join up. The CEO is always the favored choice to lead such gatherings, or indeed to sign the direct-mail letters. As a PAC official surmised, "If the CEO plays golf, everyone plays golf. If the CEO is involved in PACs, everyone gets involved in PACs."[96] These seminars can be quite effective. After one such presentation for the Baltimore Gas and Electric PAC, including a showing of *BG&E PAC: Your Shot at Political Action,* a random-sample mail survey of participants indicated dramatic gains in awareness of the PAC and willingness to contribute to it.[97] The organizers' aims were at least partially realized, for the PAC registered an 82 percent increase in contributors during the succeeding months.

Fundraising gimmicks of every stripe have become a PAC staple too. PACs have reported using "casino" nights, rummage sales, Hawaiian luaus, theater outings, and bowling, golf, tennis, and fishing tournaments to raise money—everything but bake sales.[98] NEA-PAC and SMACPAC have raffled away automobiles. The Pennsylvania Dental PAC hired a shapely model to entice potential contributors to its booth at the group's annual association meeting. The National Committee for an Effective Congress secured the Washington comedian Mark Russell for a benefit concert. Television producer Norman Lear's People for the American Way PAC auctioned off Debbie Reynolds's promise to jump out of a birthday cake as she did in the movie *Singin' in the Rain.* Star-studded fundraising dinners are also popular. Sen. Edward Kennedy corraled a bevy of glitterati and all the declared 1984 Democratic presidential candidates for a $1,000-a-plate dinner for his Fund for a Democratic Majority. Tony Randall was featured at a brunch for Pamela Harriman's Democrats for the '80s, and Ginger Rogers performed for a NCPAC reception on the former presidential yacht *Sequoia.*

Adaptations are made for the special needs of each PAC. In addition to large dinners featuring Walter Mondale and Jesse Jackson, the gay-oriented Human Rights Campaign Fund held a series of "low-profile" cocktail parties for closeted gays in Washington, D.C., that netted $30,000. (Mike Farrell of "M*A*S*H" taped a film for HRCF that was shown at each party.) There are many other fundraising gimmicks and tools being adopted by PACs. For instance, rare is the PAC that does not invest its money in interest-bearing accounts, certificates of deposit, or money-market funds.[99] An occasional PAC will even reach beyond the grave by accepting a bequest from the estate of a deceased member.[100]

Another technique fast becoming standard is the creation of "high-donor" clubs and awards. Already more than a third (38 percent) of the multicandidate PACs have at least one such group, with trade PACs leading the way.[101] (Almost half the trade committees have established one or more of them.) A "high-donor" club is a special category reserved for contributors who give over a certain minimum. The Mortgage Bankers Association's PAC has a Capitol Club for $250 givers and a Chairman's Club for donors of $500 and over. The Workover and Well Servicing Action Committee (WOWSAC) has a Wildcatter Club with an admission price of $1,000 or $100 for each oil rig owned by the donor. These clubs are sometimes sold very simply. The National Association of Broadcasters' Television and Radio PAC (TARPAC) issues special colored pins to match the size of the contributions given by their "Red, White, and Blue Club" members. Average gift size increased considerably, according to TAR-

PAC's Steven Stockmeyer, because "at our receptions everybody checks out everybody else to see what color pins they have on." Other PACs sell their high-donor clubs by offering exclusivity and the chance for special favors. SMACPAC, for instance, offers members of its $535-a-year Congressional Insiders Club complimentary tickets to its fundraising events and sweepstakes contests, as well as mention in the "honor roll" published in its PAC Newsletter.

Whether they have donor clubs or not, most PACs establish contribution guidelines which, while never "enforced" and rarely adhered to, suggest to those solicited what they should be giving. Labor and large trade PACs usually just set a certain amount (most often $10) for all members, regardless of rank or salary. Corporate PACs are normally more precise, listing a range of gift levels corresponding to salary or position. In general, corporate PACs seem to hope for a donation of between 0.2 and 1.5 percent of an individual's gross salary.[102] High-donor clubs and contribution guidelines are also useful in efforts to "upgrade" a contributor's donation. Every sophisticated PAC attempts to increase the size of each person's gift at renewal time, and donor's clubs can be a special inducement.

Direct mail,* as Table 2–4 indicates, is by far the most common method of PAC solicitation. PAC mailings range from the most primitive kind of mimeographed, impersonal note to highly sophisticated personalized letters with state-of-the-art enclosures.[103] Labor PACs tend to have technologically the most inferior types of direct mail, although there are numerous exceptions, and COPE has been expanding its direct mail capacity of late. Some labor mailings, even when technologically unimpressive, have had excellent responses, such as the Machinists Non-Partisan League's mailings to its retirees. This rough, offset letter has consistently received a high response rate and a large return in contributions.[104] Much corporate direct mail is not terribly sophisticated either. In part this is because corporations that use direct mail are simply looking for an easy and economical way to solicit, as Donald Cogman of MAPCO suggested: "Most corporate PACs want to do [solicitation] the cheapest way with the least amount of trouble—and that's direct mail." By contrast, trade and nonconnected PACs usually produce the most effective direct-mail packages, possibly because they have fewer opportunities than corporate and labor PACs to convince potential contributors personally; thus they must count on mail to a greater degree to get a donor's attention. Some of these PACs hire prominent political consultants with considerable direct-mail experience to conduct their campaigns. The AMA's AMPAC, for instance, uses Republican consultant Robert Odell. Trade PACs are also likely to spend heavily on the packages they send their member corporations requesting permission to solicit their employees.

*Direct mail is a generic term for mass fundraising through "personalized" letters.

But the most comprehensive and masterful use of direct mail is by the ideological membership and nonconnected PACs, which depend heavily (in some cases, exclusively) on this means of solicitation. Pure emotion, lightning-rod issues, and "hot" names fuel the ideological PACs' search for funds by mail. Former Secretary of the Interior James Watt was a goldmine for environmentalist PACs; prominent mention of his name in a direct-mail piece would usually increase the group's profit.[105] Sen. Edward Kennedy performs the same function for the right-wing PACs. NCPAC is particularly fond of citing Kennedy's "ever-present danger," and it featured him in several of its fundraising letters in the 1982 midterm elections. NCPAC has depended on direct mail since its inception in 1975, when conservative direct-mailer Richard Viguerie mailed NCPAC's first appeal, signed by Republican Sen. Jesse Helms. One of Helms's later letters for NCPAC is testimony to the emotionalism that characterizes ideological direct mail of all hues; the letter read in part: "Your tax dollars are being used to pay for grade school classes that teach our children that CANNIBALISM, WIFE-SWAPPING, and the MURDER of infants and the elderly are acceptable behavior."

Direct-mail packages for right-wing and left-wing PACs are often mirror images of one another. While the liberal National Committee for an Effective Congress was declaring in one of its 1982 letters, "Right wing extremists dominate the Senate. . . . throw the rascals out!" NCPAC was solemnly warning its mail readership that "At this very moment, we're facing a potential nightmare—Liberal domination of the U.S. Senate." The PACs also raise money by using each other as punching bags. NCPAC asked its contributors to dig deeper because of "the millions of dollars [the] new liberal pressure groups will be pouring into the 1982 election." Meanwhile PROPAC asked for donations to "expose groups like NCPAC" and Independent Action pled for money to fight "the NCPAC challenge." Independent Action also employed a novel approach for a PAC: it asked direct-mail recipients to contribute to it in order to "fight special-interest PACs."[106]

Some PACs solicit not just individuals but other PACs, since PACs can give up to $5,000 to one another. PROPAC, under the signature of union president William H. Wynn of the United Food and Commercial Workers, has sent letters to labor union committees requesting the maximum gift. The Congressional Black Caucus's PAC (CBC-PAC) also has sought PAC support.[107] In a 1983 letter to PAC officers, the CBC-PAC's executive director none too subtly wrote, "You have surely noticed that our PAC consists entirely of Congressmen," and portrayed the Black Caucus as a defender of the PAC movement despite the support of various PAC-limitation bills by leading black congressmen.

Other PACs are beginning to experiment with new forms of "direct-response" solicitation that technologically go beyond mail while operating on fundraising principles similar to those underlying direct-mail efforts. For example, People for the American Way, the PAC formed by Norman Lear in part to oppose the Moral Majority, produced a half-hour documentary on the "radical right" titled *Life and Liberty . . . For All Who Believe.* Hosted by Burt Lancaster, the film aired on cable channels and certain network affiliates from early October to December 1982; it concluded with a toll-free "800" number for contributors to call. Not only did the program generate enough pledges to raise most of the $525,000 costs of production and airing, but it added nearly 10,000 supporters to the group's membership rolls—a list ripe for additional direct-mail appeals.[108]

The costs of direct-mail campaigns, especially the personalized, sophisticated variety, are very high, and because of this the nonconnected PACs spend an extraordinarily large portion of their operating budgets on the direct-mail process.[109] Because "prospecting" for new donors—a task essential to building and maintaining a direct-mail contributor list—usually eats up all revenues produced by the mailings, many nonconnected PACs in their early years have virtually no money to spend on direct gifts to candidates.[110] Even well-established PACs with large "house files" of proven direct-mail givers expend a considerable portion of new funds on mailing costs and direct-mail consultants. Through 1982 NCPAC had paid more than $4.7 million (out of a total budget of $17.7 million) to Richard Viguerie's direct-mail businesses;[111] the National Congressional Club (associated with Jesse Helms) spends a minimum of 30 percent of its annual budget on mailing, and a larger percentage whenever prospecting is being done on a large scale.[112] Many of the New Right PACs consider direct mail not merely a form of fundraising but a very useful and persuasive form of advertising, and therefore an investment with important secondary rewards.[113] Liberal PACs tend to discount this theory as excuse-making for low candidate contribution totals ("That's the Viguerie line, and I think it's horseshit," says Russell Hemenway, director of the National Committee for an Effective Congress).

NCEC is one of a number of PACs that have abandoned or reduced their direct mailing because of the financial problems associated with it. "We took a major bath on direct mail; we lost a lot of money," reported Hemenway. Direct-mail fundraising is often only marginally profitable, so PACs that depend on it too heavily can be damaged by even slight shifts of public opinion. As one conservative trade PAC manager ruefully noted, "The election of Reagan and a Republican Senate really did some damage to our direct-mail program. Our letter recipients said, 'What the hell is the problem? There's nothing to worry about now.' We're lacking a good boogeyman. Teddy Kennedy isn't in the [Senate] majority so we can't kick him around anymore."

Direct mail has the lowest response rate (i.e., the proportion of the solicited who actually contribute) of all the forms of PAC solicitation. For the mass-mailing ideological PACs, tiny break-even response rates of 1 or 2 percent (and $10–$15 per donation) on prospecting are the norm, while mailings to the house list show a somewhat better response. The conservative Committee for the Survival of a Free Congress, for instance, posts a 1.5–2 percent return on prospecting, with a 5–8 percent house-list return rate. Handgun Control's PAC fares similarly: 0.9 percent on prospecting and 7–20 percent on the house list. Overall, as Table 2–5 indicates, nonconnected PACs have the lowest average response rate of all PAC categories (just 3 percent) because of their heavy reliance on direct mail. By direct-mail standards the other kinds of PACs do a phenomenally successful fundraising business. Between 23 and 32 percent of those solicited by corporate, trade, and labor PACs actually make a donation. However, their universe is much smaller and many of these PACs are selective about which em-

Table 2–5.
PAC Solicitation: How Much and How Often

	CATEGORY OF MULTICANDIDATE PAC				
	ALL PACS	CORPORATE	LABOR	TRADE	NONCONNECTED[a]
Average donation to PAC (1981–1982)[b]	$100	$160	$14	$81	$65
Number of individual donors (1981–1982)[b]	400	155	2,700	400	1,150
Average response rate[c]	25%	26%	23%	32%	3%
Frequency of solicitation					
More than twice a year	16%	5%	21%	18%	33%
Twice a year	22%	24%	0%	30%	22%
Once a year	47%	56%	50%	48%	22%
Once every two years	10%	12%	0%	4%	22%
Other	5%	2%	29%	0%	0%

SOURCE: Drawn from responses to the random-sample survey of multicandidate PACs conducted for this study; see Introduction, note 16.

[a]Nonconnected PACs were also asked how often they conducted repeat solicitations. The results: 33%—more than once a year; 22%—twice a year; 11%—once a year; 33%—less than once a year.

[b]Figures in this row are medians.

[c]The response rate is the proportion of solicited individuals who make a contribution to the PAC.

ployees or members they solicit even within their permissible group.[114] While the average nonconnected PAC asks 141,000 individuals for money, the typical corporate PAC asks 900, and its labor counterpart PAC contacts 12,000.[115] In a more intimate setting, even direct mail can produce a larger return, and most corporate PACs reported that their letters had between a 15 and 20 percent response rate.[116] No other method could match personal, face-to-face solicitation, however; response rates for PACs utilizing the personal touch were usually well over 35 percent.[117]

Overall, the PACs raised about 41 percent of their funds in the first year of the election cycle and the remaining 59 percent in the second year. They solicit fairly frequently: 38 percent of the PACs try to raise funds twice a year or more, while about half (47 percent) restrict themselves to once a year. The corporate committees are more infrequent in their fundraisers (to avoid irritating their employees, as they see it), while many nonconnected PACs are always on the hustings or in the mailboxes. (Only 5 percent of the corporate PACs solicit more than twice a year, while 33 percent of the nonconnected committees do so.) The amounts actually contributed by PAC givers are, on average, quite small—about $100 per donation. Corporate contributors are the most generous, averaging $160, while the usual labor donor's gift is just $14. Labor's large base and relatively high response rate, of course, enable unions to match the heftier but more infrequent corporate gifts. While, in light of potential membership, relatively few individuals participate in any PAC, PAC donors as a group form a mighty army: fully 7 percent of all adult Americans report contributing to one or more PACs—as many as give to all candidate organizations put together.[118]

BROADENING PAC SOLICITATION

There is considerable room for expansion of PAC solicitation within the current rules and regulations. First, most categories of PACs are permitted to solicit outside their usual constituencies twice a year (as described earlier).[119] Yet 92 percent of the multicandidate PACs make no use at all of the "twice-yearly" provision, and few plan to take advantage of it in the near future.[120] Union PACs are reluctant because of limited resources and underutilization of labor's own membership. According to Dick Warden of the United Auto Workers, "We need to do so much more with our own members through modernization before we think about soliciting from anyone else." The same thinking prevails among corporations, but they also chafe under the FEC's requirement that corporations utilizing the twice-yearly option make available to their unions the same mailing lists and methods of solicitation.[121] One company officer frankly disclosed that his corporation, which had been conducting twice-yearly mailings, ceased the practice when it acquired a unionized company.

If the potential of the twice-yearly rule is unlikely to be realized by PACs in the future, then stockholder solicitation is only a slightly more likely area for expansion in fundraising. Currently, only 17 percent of corporate PACs have any form of shareholder solicitation, and of those PACs that do contact shareholders, few report that the effort brings any appreciable contributions.[122] Shareholder solicitation is, in the eyes of most PAC managers, costly, cumbersome, and of doubtful effectiveness. Shareholders tend to be a diverse group with a variety of political affiliations, and as one PAC official suggested, "The average stockholder is not thinking, 'Gee, I have ten shares of AT&T. I wonder what's happening on the deregulation of the telecommunications industry?' "

On the other hand a few PACs report considerable success in their stockholder solicitations. They have concentrated on large shareholders (as opposed to casual investors), and have built up a rapport with stockholders by communicating frequently with them. One corporate PAC that reports better than a 30 percent response rate from 20,000 stockholders explained that "Our management has always believed in keeping in close touch with our stockholders. Our chairman will give a speech somewhere and he'll send a copy to all of them. There's an established, continuing link between our company and our shareholders, and that's why we get such a good response." Success stories like this have convinced some PACs to place stockholder solicitation on their agenda; 10 percent of the corporate PACs that do not now solicit stockholders see it as a likely course in the future.

A third area of possible expansion for PACs is in the trade associations' bailiwick. Only about 24 percent of corporate PACs presently permit a trade association to solicit their management personnel. Because corporations frequently belong to more than one trade association, and under FECA rules can authorize solicitation from only one of them, some companies refuse all association requests rather than be forced to choose among them. Other corporate PACs simply do not want fundraising competition from a trade association, and decline to authorize solicitation on that basis. Some trade PACs have begun aggressively to seek such authorizations, however. The Sheet Metal and Air Conditioning Contractors' SMACPAC has secured the highest approval rate among corporate members (50 percent) of any trade association. "We conducted a major educational push to achieve that," reported SMACPAC's director Gregg Ward. Newsletters and other missives detailing the rationale for trade solicitation were sent, and members signing up were promised admission to candidate briefing sessions and other special activities. The U.S. Chamber of Commerce has also started to push for solicitation approvals from its membership, particularly from smaller businesses unlikely to form a PAC of their own. "There is a whole untapped market out there," observed the Chamber's John Kochevar, and trade associations seem poised to take better advantage of it. Moreover, many trade PACs are determined to improve on their surprisingly limited record of following through on approvals secured; of the group of corporate PACs that have granted solicitation permission to a trade PAC, only 36 percent indicate that the trade association has actually conducted the solicitation.

Far more than the twice-yearly rule or stockholder solicitation, the method of payroll deduction (also called the "checkoff") is making a significant difference in PACs' levels of fundraising. When a worker or executive agrees to the payroll deduction plan, a PAC contribution is automatically subtracted from his or her paycheck and deposited in the committee's account.[123] Compared to the alternative methods of lump-sum payment by check or monthly pledge payments which must be individually collected from contributors, payroll deduction has numerous advantages. It is considered a more invisible, and therefore less painful, method of giving. The PAC also has some advance notice of how much money to expect, aiding its own planning and that of the candidates it chooses to support. The money flows to the PAC regularly, in off-years as well as election years, and without significant fluctuations, for once an individual has given permission for the deduction to be made, he or she must personally take the initiative to stop it by making a written request to the payroll office or PAC. This in turn conserves PAC resources: no longer does every employee have to be approached repeatedly for a gift. Those resources can then be devoted instead to increasing participation and upgrading contributions. Some PAC critics have objected to payroll deduction because the process is potentially coercive, although this objection has more validity for "negative (or reverse) checkoffs" than positive deductions. The FEC has ruled against negative checkoffs, whereby an individual must *object* to a PAC deduction or it will automatically be made, and instead has insisted that PAC deductions be made only at the voluntary and specific request of a worker. The National Education Association paid a $75,000 civil penalty in 1980 for having such a negative checkoff on its dues statement,[124] and its NEA-PAC was forced to refund $800,000 in contributions collected under the system.[125]

With all the advantages of the payroll deduction system, it is hardly surprising to find an increasing proportion of PACs adopting it. By 1983, 81 percent of the corporate PACs and 50 percent of the labor PACs used payroll deduction. Fully 80 percent of all corporate PAC gifts came by way of the device; labor's proportion, 30 percent, was considerably lower.[126] It seems that every PAC manager has a testimonial to the difference payroll deduction can make. One corporate PAC officer recalled his original organizational meeting for his company's political action committee.[127] One hundred percent of the audience agreed to give an average of several hundred dollars each, and since there was no payroll deduction, they were given the home office's address, where checks were to be sent. Nobody sent a check. By the time of the next meeting, wiser PAC officials had instituted payroll deduction and signed up 90 percent on the spot.

For labor PACs, payroll deduction probably holds even greater promise because of large union memberships. Businesses understand this, and some have been reluctant to make the system available to labor until forced to do so by the FEC.[128] The AFL-CIO has actively encouraged its member unions to bargain for payroll deduction as a provision of new contracts.[129] It points to examples such as one Machinists' local that raised $600 in PAC funds in 1982 without the checkoff, and $30,000 in 1983 with it. The Machinists are a good illustration of payroll deduction's potential for labor: only about 2,000 of its members are currently on checkoff out of a possible 70,000–80,000. The United Auto Workers has assigned one staff person full time to arrange for payroll deductions, and the National Education Association bluntly advises its members:

> No matter which fundraising programs you choose to implement, they will work better if you can use the payroll deduction system. If your state or district has not implemented the payroll deduction system for NEA-PAC contributions, push for it. Work for it. Fight for it. In the long run, it is the only way to keep NEA-PAC strong.[130]

As Bernard Albert of COPE noted, payroll deduction for labor "is just beginning to pick up steam. The big payoff is down the road."[131]

EARMARKING: PURE DEMOCRACY IN THE PACS

One additional kind of solicitation device, earmarking, deserves special mention. Earmarking permits the individual PAC contributor to designate the recipient of his or her donation. There are many forms of earmarking. Some PACs allow the contributor to name specifically the candidate(s) or party to receive the money. Other PACs limit earmarking in various ways: the contributor can choose generically between Democrats and Republicans, or the House and the Senate, but cannot target individual candidates for PAC gifts. Still other PACs, perhaps using the avenue of direct mail, may list several intended congressional recipients, or targets for negative attacks, and permit respondents to pick their favorite hero or villain.[132]

Opinions about earmarking in the PAC world are split. On the one hand it is a marvelous way to enhance a PAC's influence. This is because most earmarked contributions are counted as *individual* gifts, not PAC donations, and thus the amount earmarked does not count against the $5,000 PAC contribution limit; at the same time the PAC gets most of the credit for the gift in the candidate's eyes.[133] (Usual practice calls for a PAC to "bundle" all individual gifts for each candidate and to transmit them with a cover letter from the PAC identifying the donors as PAC members.)[134] Earmarking is also believed to increase a PAC's general appeal and solicitation success. A number of the PAC managers I interviewed claimed that their PACs enroll more members and raise more money thanks to this appealing democratic device. Not only is earmarking attractive to the individual who desires more control over his or her money, but it can be attractive to the corporate PAC for tax purposes as well. Lawyers have been advising corporations to use earmarking as a justification for deducting PAC administrative expenses from their taxes, since the Internal Revenue Service has disapproved such a deduction when PACs were "not politically impartial."[135] Earmarking permits PACs to claim they are nonpartisan conduits of individual gifts.

These arguments have not convinced a majority of PACs, however. They see earmarking as a terribly cumbersome device which complicates already extensive solicitation, accounting, and reporting practices. Earmarking may also lead to embarrassment of a PAC in two respects. Frequently a PAC may have to send money to candidates who do not fit the committee's criteria for selection or who are philosophically out of tune with the PAC's sponsor. Gifts earmarked to both major-party candidates in the same race are not uncommon either, and nothing looks worse in print or smacks more of influence-peddling than giving to both sides. Overall, the multicandidate PACs have opted against earmarking by a margin of 63 percent to 37 percent, and on the average just 4 percent of PAC contributors choose to earmark their gifts when the option is available.[136] Even these figures overstate the extent of earmarking. A number of PACs permitting the practice were frank to admit that they did not publicize the option, allowing it only when a contributor requested it. PAC democracy has clear limits; as one PAC stated its policy: "The PAC is not intended as a substitute for an individual's personal desire to contribute to specific candidates."[137]

COERCION IN PAC GIVING

I know it isn't mandatory to give. But the word around the water cooler is that if you don't give or if you give less than the amount expected based on your salary, you're liable to be called in for a pep talk from the divisional president.

—An employee of a Litton Industries unit.[138]

> It would hit the paper right away if an employee's arm was twisted. It would be the dumbest thing for a business to do.
>
> —An official of the Pennsylvania Chamber of Commerce[139]

When critics of the PAC system suggest that fundraising by political action committees is tinged with coercion, with company employees or union members feeling pressured or forced to ante up lest they lose favor (or worse), most PAC officials respond as did BIPAC's Bernadette Budde: "I'm not going to say [coercion] doesn't exist. All I'm saying is nothing has ever been brought to anybody's attention."[140] In fact there have been a number of publicized examples of PAC coercion in fundraising. The Atlanta division head of Winn-Dixie Stores, Inc., personally awarded $2,000 to $2,500 in bonuses to each of his key management subordinates, coupling the award with a strong suggestion (and a printed request in the same envelope as the check) that a PAC contribution was in order.[141] For a while DartPAC of Dart Industries (now Dart and Kraft, Inc.) had its head, Justin Dart (until his recent death a close friend of President Reagan), personally calling executives who had not given to the PAC, inquiring why their names were absent from the list of contributors.[142] (Widespread criticism led to abandonment of this and other unseemly tactics at DartPAC.) A number of PACs send follow-up letters to employees who have chosen not to give, expressing disappointment and asking them to reconsider.[143] Labor PACs have hardly been immune from the coercion charges; gifts to the very first union committee, CIO-PAC, were thought to be sometimes involuntary,[144] and conservatives have frequently aimed their fire at labor solicitation methods.[145]

Suspicions of coercion are inevitable and legitimate since corporations and unions solicit their own employees and members. "There's no way you can avoid a feeling of pressure on . . . the people who were asked to give," commented John Fishwick, who refused to start a PAC when he was president and CEO of Norfolk and Western Railway.[146] At higher management levels in a company or a union, individuals unavoidably are subject to pressure (at the least, psychological) to make a PAC donation if their superiors enthusiastically endorse the idea. Imagine how an executive must feel when his company's president and chairman of the board says to him and his peers, as one did at a PAC group meeting:

> We need more [money]. Once again I am asking you to contribute at least one percent of your salary to our PAC. I don't believe this is asking too much in view of what's at stake. . . . However, if for some reason you don't feel you can give that much, at least give something. I would like to think that every eligible Mustang [Corporation] employee understands our PAC's importance and wants to get involved. If we could say that 100 percent of our employees, not just 65 percent, were PAC members, we would be telling the anti-business, anti-free enterprise politicians

that we acknowledge our obligation of stewardship to the free market system, and we're going to do something about it.[147]

While some companies and unions attempt to reduce such pressure by keeping all contributions anonymous within the organization,[148] the PAC must send the names of all contributors of $200 and over to the FEC; they are then a matter of public record, open for inspection by anyone.

In a 1979 complaint to the FEC, the International Association of Machinists and Aerospace Workers (IAM) alleged that corporations were concentrating their PAC solicitations on vulnerable middle-management employees whose careers depended on their superiors' goodwill.[149] The proof, said the IAM, was plain for all to see: a high response rate and sizable average donations, especially as compared to the few and tiny gifts received through direct-mail solicitation of the general public. Both the FEC and a federal district court rejected the IAM challenge, and in 1981 the Supreme Court, despite its admission in a 1972 case[150] that some element of coercion was present in PAC solicitation, also denied the IAM claims.

There were good reasons for the failure of the IAM case. Despite the worrisome examples cited in this section, there is little evidence that such coercive tactics are widespread among PACs, and the FEC's stringent rules on the issue are partially responsible.[151] First of all, personal, face-to-face requests for money often come from those of the same or lower rank as the solicited employee, although it is permissible for an employee to be solicited by a direct supervisor.[152] In addition, a contributor must be advised of his right to refuse to give; as a result, many PACs require each donor to attest that a contribution is made freely, and without any threats of job discrimination, physical force, or financial consequences. ("I subscribe freely and voluntarily and not out of fear of reprisal" says the PAC contribution card of the Teamsters, a union not otherwise known for subtle persuasion.) Furthermore, if contribution guidelines are included as a part of the solicitation, it must be stated that they are merely suggestive, and that there is no minimum acceptable gift—indeed, no gift need be made at all. These FEC regulations have moved one observer to suggest that the PAC system puts the average union member or corporate employee under less pressure to donate money than did the old system that prevailed before FECA.[153] PAC supporters also point to response rates to bolster their claim that coercion is not a factor in contributions. Even with an average corporate PAC response rate of about 25 percent, three-quarters of the typical sponsor company's employees choose not to participate; surely if they believed that promotions depended on their joining up, no draft would be necessary. "If there were any coercion, there would be a lot more money," Lee Ann Elliott, a former PAC official and now a member of the FEC, says flatly. Still, the question of coercion in PACs is a serious one, the potential for abuse is never absent, and vigilance will always be required.

POLITICAL EDUCATION AND INTERNAL COMMUNICATIONS

Making contributions to candidates is just one part of many PACs' programs. Common also is a wide range of activities to educate PAC members in the ways and means of politics, to get them involved in campaigns, to make sure they register and vote, and of course, to keep them informed about the PAC itself.

Almost all PACs communicate directly with their membership on a regular basis. As Table 2–6 shows, a newsletter is the preferred instrument: 59 percent of the PACs publish and distribute some kind of newsletter periodically. A large proportion of PACs also issue annual reports, and

Table 2–6.
PAC Internal Communications and Political Education Programs

	CATEGORY OF MULTICANDIDATE PAC				
COMMUNICATIONS METHOD[a]	ALL PACS[b]	CORPO-RATE[b]	LABOR[b]	TRADE[b]	NONCON-NECTED[b]
Newsletter	59%	56%	47%	68%	62%
Meetings or seminars	33	35	27	32	38
Annual report	44	63	20	32	38
Other	16	10	27	21	12
PROGRAM[c]					
Political education	40	23	77	43	N.A.
Citizenship involvement	22	12	17	18	N.A.
Register-to-vote	30	26	62	7	N.A.
Get-out-the-vote	23	21	92	11	N.A.
Publishing issue information	56	49	62	68	N.A.
Publishing economic information	15	14	N.A.	14	N.A.
Other public affairs efforts	33	33	18	46	N.A.
None of these	24	30	12	19	N.A.

SOURCE: Responses to questions drawn from the survey of multicandidate PACs conducted for this study; see Introduction, note 16.
[a]Survey question: "By what means does your PAC regularly communicate with members?" N.A. = not asked.
[b]Columns do not total 100 percent due to multiple responses.
[c]Survey question: "In addition to a PAC, does your corporation/union/association have any of the following programs?"

nearly two-thirds of the corporate committees do so. Frequent meetings and seminars are held as well. Most of the committees use these communications tools to maintain the membership's interest and loyalty, and also to report on the process and results of candidate selection. Fully nine of ten PACs take some steps to inform members about how the PAC's candidates are chosen, and 83 percent of the PACs report to members the names of candidates who have been selected, as well as the PAC's overall win/loss record once the election has passed.[154] Frequently when the win/loss record is favorable, the PAC trumpets it as part of its fundraising appeal, hoping for a bandwagon effect among members who like to identify with a winning team.

Nearly as often, PACs or their parent unions, corporations, or associations undertake one or more "political education" programs.[155] Table 2–6 suggests the variety existing in the PAC community. More than three-quarters of all PACs have adopted at least one of the listed activities. Labor PACs are especially likely to organize these programs, although there are indications that more and more corporations are beginning to follow suit.

About 56 percent of the PACs or their parent bodies publish information on issues or candidates. Under the campaign finance laws, corporations, unions, membership organizations, and trade associations can spend unlimited amounts of their own treasuries (wholly apart from PAC funds) on election-related communications to stockholders, employees, or members. Only those groups for which such expenditures go over $2,000 in a single election are required to report it to the FEC. There are enough additional loopholes[156] that a large portion of the money spent on these publications is never disclosed. Of those groups that do report communications expenses, most are labor unions. In the 1981–1982 election cycle, labor accounted for slightly over half the approximately $2.2 million spent on materials promoting the election or defeat of House and Senate candidates.[157] This $2.2 million total represents a 67 percent increase over 1979–1980 and a 251 percent rise since 1977–1978.[158] Thirteen of the fifteen highest spending groups in this area were labor unions, but the top record holder was the National Rifle Association (NRA), with over $800,000 in reported communication costs. In October 1982, for instance, the NRA's Institute for Legislative Action sent out tens of thousands of copies of its "political preference chart," which contained a "report card" grade on all candidates (A = "solidly pro-gun" through F = "would vote for banning handguns, all firearms, and/or hunting"). The NRA and many of the ideological nonconnected PACs associated with the New Right view their direct mailings and internal communications as an alternative to a liberal-biased mass media and a means to get across their views in an undiluted fashion.[159]

Efforts to complement PAC giving with other demonstrations of political muscle are becoming more prominent among interest groups. Again under the FECA rules, corporations and unions are permitted to use general treasury funds—precious PAC money does not have to be touched—for nonpartisan voter registration and get-out-the-vote drives aimed at stockholders, employees, or union members (as well as their families).[160] As the political scientist Michael J. Malbin has observed, these activities serve the PAC well even if not directly sponsored by it, since employees or members who become politically active in some way are more likely to respond to a PAC fundraising solicitation.[161]

Nowhere is that principle demonstrated more clearly than in the ranks of organized labor. Unions with major political education and campaign-involvement programs include the United Auto Workers, the American Federation of State, County and Municipal Employees, the Communications Workers of America, the United Food and Commercial Workers Union, the National Education Association, and the American Federation of Teachers. More so than any of the others, the political exertions of the AFL-CIO's COPE are consistently impressive. In the 1968 presidential campaign COPE registered 4.6 million voters, distributed 55 million pieces of literature, established 638 major phone bank centers operated by 25,000 volunteers, and produced 72,000 preelection canvassers and 95,000 precinct workers on election day.[162] In 1976 COPE's 120,000 volunteers, 10 million telephone calls, and 80 million pieces of literature on behalf of the Democratic presidential ticket were worth an estimated $8.5 million.[163] By 1984 the AFL-CIO's presidential endorsement of Democrat Walter Mondale was being assigned a pricetag of $5–$8 million just for its prenomination value.[164]

In part because of the business PAC challenge, labor has worked to improve the quality of its political education services. COPE has updated and expanded its telephone and address lists of 13 million affiliate union members and organized them by voting precinct. The Democratic pollster Peter Hart was hired in 1982 to develop an in-house survey capacity for COPE; in the first year alone thirteen polls, mainly "tracking" surveys of union members, were conducted both to measure rank-and-file opinion and to determine members' reactions to labor direct-mail and telephone canvassing. Computer terminals have been installed in the headquarters of some state labor organizations to give them access to COPE data banks of polling information, voting records, and so on. COPE has also stepped up the number and frequency of its leadership workshops, held in Washington and in most of the states, to train labor activists in campaign skills and the election process. With a substantial increase in union dues[165] producing an extra $14 million for the AFL-CIO treasury, a $2-million-a-year Labor Institute for Public Affairs was established in 1982 to fund political education programs for unions, as well as television films and news shows taking a labor perspective.[166] Finally, COPE's direct-mail effort has been personalized and refined: for instance, special messages were sent to each union member in seven occupational groupings residing in key 1982 House districts. Peter Hart's polling showed clear and positive effects from the mailings, said COPE's director John Perkins, save for one area where the glittering new campaign technology was foiled by an uncooperative Republican postmaster. "He opened one letter to see what was in it, and then the mailing just sat there until we went and got it. This is not uncommon," reported Perkins, "but it's irritating when your members get your mailings after the election."

If labor is king of the political education domain, it is partly because until recently business had never challenged the unions for the throne. This is not to say that there were no business activities in the field—far from it[167]—but most corporate officials tended to agree with one of their number who commented in 1978, "I question whether it is our business to educate [our] people on behalf of one candidate with stockholder money."[168] Gradually, however, business and trade groups are abandoning a tradition of noninvolvement, and in some cases they are taking up political education with fervor. There are signs of this trend in many individual corporate PACs. The LTV PAC gave each of its 80,000 employees a book compiling the 1980 presidential candidates' views on business, and organized get-out-the-vote rallies for employees.[169] Spring Industries PAC regularly holds meetings for its personnel with major candidates and elected officials as a way to interest staff in campaign duty. Loctite Corporation's PAC has set up town committees for each Connecticut locality in which employees reside; these committees hold "get to know your candidates" receptions and make formal recommendations on endorsements to the PAC.[170] The business-oriented trade associations have been particularly aggressive in political education. The political affairs division of the National Association of Realtors has established the Realtors Active in Politics (RAP) program. Each realtor enrolling in RAP pledges to commit at least 24 hours to some political activity, with those who devote greater time eligible for recognition awards. Several thousand realtors were signed up for RAP by 1984. Another trade group, the American Medical Association's AMPAC, planned to spend half or more of its budget on political education activities in 1984, according to its director, Peter Lauer. Thirty regional seminars were conducted in 1983 and 1984 for physicians and their spouses, stressing the nuts-and-bolts of voter registration, get-out-the-vote drives, the use of telephone banks, and the absentee-ballot process. AMPAC also launched the Participation '84 program, designed to encourage physicians and their families to run for delegate berths at the national party nominating conventions.

Business PACs have been joined by the ideological nonconnected PACs in exhibiting a growing interest in political education.[171] Paul Weyrich, founder of the conservative Committee for the Survival of a Free Congress, has made no secret of his intention to copy COPE's methods in his own organization. The Gun Owners of America Campaign Committee has been supplying voter registration and absentee ballot information to hunters. The antiabortion Life Amendment PAC trained over 500 volunteers to assist the campaigns of favored candidates in 1982, while the pro-choice National Abortion Rights Action League activated 10,000 individuals for campaign work at the state legislative level. Much as the PAC world itself diversified in the last decade, political education programs are proliferating on all sides. As Carter Wrenn of the conservative National Congressional Club explained, in politics as in physics, one action often begets an equal and opposite reaction:

> What we're seeing today is the liberals putting a lot of emphasis on registration. Jesse Jackson is cranked up all over the South, registering voters who will vote for liberal Democrats—which means we'll have to do the same thing as intensely with conservative groups. It's just political math.

The internal structures and operations of PACs exhibit once again the diversity which characterizes the PAC community—and also raise some disturbing questions about the PAC movement itself. As we have seen, some PACs have virtually no internal controls, while others are models of administrative efficiency. The fundamental concern can be stated succinctly: How democratic are PACs? Clearly, a few are autocratically run, but most are participatory, communicative, and in some respects democratic. The degree to which PACs diverge from the democratic model of organization and decision-making is crucial, however, and we will return to this central concern in the concluding chapter's evaluation of the PACs' role in the American system. For now, though, the focus will shift from the more private side of PAC activity to the role of PACs in the public eye, as we consider where PAC money goes.

CHAPTER 3

PACs in the Public Eye Their Candidates and Contributions

We have a friendly incumbent policy. We always stick with the incumbent if we agree with both candidates.

—Peter Lauer, executive director of the American Medical Association's AMPAC[1]

We are radicals who want to change the existing power structure. . . . It may not be with bullets, and it may not be with rockets and missiles, but it is a war nevertheless. It is a war of ideology, it's a war of ideas, it's a war about our way of life. And it has to be fought with the same intensity, I think, and dedication as you would fight a shooting war.

—Paul Weyrich, executive director of the Committee for the Survival of a Free Congress[2]

PACs differ dramatically in their approach to campaigns. Some are paragons of pragmatism, choosing only incumbents and likely winners as recipients for their largesse. Others prefer to do battle on an ideological field, backing challengers and insurgents who crusade for the causes they espouse. Some prefer to give money early, while others make most contributions late in the election cycle. Some favor fewer candidates with larger gifts, while others spread out smaller donations to many contenders. Some PACs use the special tools of independent spending and in-kind expenditure to supplement monetary gifts. Still other PACs have state and local affiliates carrying on their work at these electoral levels. The many forms of PAC organization and fundraising are matched by the variegated styles PACs have adopted in the political world they seek to master.

PAC CONTRIBUTIONS TO CANDIDATES

PACs show clear preferences in their choices of candidates to support, as Table 3–1 suggests. Incumbents are favored by a wide margin over challengers and open-seat candidates, most especially by trade PACs. Only nonconnected committees give challengers equal preference with incumbents, reflecting the significant number of ideological PACs included in that category. Labor, trade, and nonconnected PACs seem eager in varying degrees to support House candidates, while corporate PACs lean toward Senate contenders—but a large majority in all categories of PACs exhibit no strong inclinations in either direction. Similarly, in partisan terms, PACs in most categories claim to be even-handed, though labor is almost solidly Democratic while corporate and trade committees edge toward the Republicans. Ideologically, PACs are more forthcoming about their predilections. Labor is overwhelmingly liberal, corporate and trade PACs are solidly conservative, and few PACs identify with moderation. The nonconnected category is split both in party and philosophical identification, reflecting the bipolar nature of its ideological collection of PACs. Finally, PACs generally prefer to invest in close, marginal races where their money can have the greatest effect. This is particularly true for nonconnecteds, and least true for trade PACs, which have the strongest attraction for sure bets in safe races.

The actual contribution figures in Tables 3–2 and 3–3 bear out these stated PAC preferences. Overall, PACs have been decidedly incumbent oriented. Incumbents have never received less than half of all PAC money, and they achieved a near highwater mark in 1982 when 68 percent of the PAC largesse made its way to incumbent war chests. The PAC zenith for challengers came in 1980, when corporate PACs in particular backed a significant number of GOP insurgents. But even then, challengers received just 26 percent of total PAC contributions. There is substantial variation by PAC category, however. Corporate committees devoted as much as 31 percent of their resources to challengers in 1980, though the success of their 1980 efforts to elect Republican House challengers led the PACs to channel most of their 1982 money to these same candidates, now incumbents, in an attempt to hold those seats in a Democratic year. Labor has been consistently devoted to Democratic incumbents, though in 1974 and 1982, with the tide flowing to the Democrats, labor backed proportionately more challeng-

Table 3–1.
Kinds of Candidates PACs Prefer

PAC CANDIDATE PREFERENCES	CATEGORY OF MULTICANDIDATE PAC				
	ALL PACS	CORPORATE	LABOR	TRADE	NONCONNECTED
1. An incumbent	49%	39%	54%	62%	33%
A challenger	7	13	0	4	33
An open-seat candidate	4	0	8	8	0
No preference	40	48	39	27	33
2. A Senate candidate	13	20	8	15	11
A House candidate	18	3	31	19	33
No preference	69	76	62	65	56
3. A Republican	27	33	0	35	30
A Democrat	21	0	92	8	30
A third-party candidate	1	0	0	0	0
No preference	50	67	8	58	40
4. A liberal	21	0	92	0	44
A conservative	38	50	0	54	33
A moderate	18	28	0	15	0
No preference	23	22	8	31	22
5. A candidate in a marginal race	46	48	50	35	67
A candidate in a safe race	14	11	10	27	0
No preference	39	41	40	39	33

SOURCE: Responses to survey question "If all else were the same between two candidates, which one would you prefer to support?" from the questionnaire for the random-sample survey of multicandidate PACs conducted for this study; see Introduction, note 16.

ers to GOP incumbents. The trade PACs are truly committees that most congressional incumbents can love; they have lavished their monies upon officeholders without fail, never diverting even as much as a quarter to challengers. Nonconnected PACs are once more the odd man out. Incumbents have never received a majority of their funds—though they came close in 1982—while challengers have regularly gained a third to a half of the nonconnected booty.

Mainly because of incumbency addiction among PACs, the Democrats have maintained only a tenuous hold on the lion's share of PAC funding

Table 3-2.

PAC Contributions to Congressional Candidates by Candidate Status, 1972–1982[a]

PAC TYPE	YEAR	TOTAL CONTRI-BUTIONS (MILLION $)	INCUM-BENT (%)	CHAL-LENGER (%)	OPEN SEAT (%)
All PACs	1982	79.2	68	18	14
	1980	51.9	63	26	12
	1978	31.8	59	22	19
	1976	20.5	64	20	15
	1974	11.6	58	22	21
	1972	8.5	52	25	24
Corporate	1982	26.3	74	13	13
	1980	18.1	58	31	11
	1978	9.1	59	22	19
	1976	6.7	72	18	12
	1974	2.4	79	8	13
	1972	1.7	65	12	24
Labor	1982	19.3	58	28	14
	1980	12.3	74	16	11
	1978	8.9	63	21	16
	1976	7.4	64	22	16
	1974	5.7	49	30	23
	1972	3.6	53	28	19
Trade/ Membership/ Health	1982	20.6	76	13	12
	1980	15.0	66	23	11
	1978	10.6	60	20	21
	1976	2.6	65	19	15
	1974	1.8	78	6	17
	1972	1.0	50	20	30
Nonconnected	1982	10.0	49	35	16
	1980	4.5	33	51	16
	1978	2.3	30	44	22
	1976	1.2	33	42	25
	1974	0.7	14	43	43
	1972	—	—	—	—

SOURCE: For 1972–1980 data, Joseph E. Cantor, *Political Action Committees: Their Evolution and Growth and Their Implications for the Political System* (Washington, D.C.: Library of Congress Congressional Research Service Report No. 82–92 GOV, Nov. 6, 1981; updated May 7, 1982), pp. 116, 121–23. For 1982 data, Federal Election Commission.

[a]General elections only.

Table 3–3.
PAC Contributions to Congressional Candidates by Party, 1972–1982[a]

PAC TYPE	YEAR	TOTAL CONTRIBUTIONS (MILLION $)	DEMOCRAT[b] (%)	REPUBLICAN[b] (%)
All PACs	1982	79.2	54	46
	1980	51.9	52	48
	1978	31.8	54	46
	1976	20.5	66	34
	1974	11.6	68	32
	1972	8.5	68	32
Corporate	1982	26.3	33	67
	1980	18.1	35	65
	1978	9.1	34	66
	1976	6.7	43	57
	1974	2.4	38	58
	1972	1.7	29	71
Labor	1982	19.3	94	6
	1980	12.3	93	7
	1978	8.9	93	6
	1976	7.4	97	3
	1974	5.7	95	7
	1972	3.6	94	6
Trade/ Membership/ Health	1982	20.6	42	58
	1980	15.0	43	57
	1978	10.6	42	59
	1976	2.6	38	62
	1974	1.8	28	72
	1972	1.0	20	80
Nonconnected	1982	10.0	52	48
	1980	4.5	29	71
	1978	2.3	23	77
	1976	1.2	45	55
	1974	0.7	48	52
	1972	—	—	—

SOURCE: For 1972–1980 data, Joseph E. Cantor, *Political Action Committees: Their Evolution and Growth and Their Implications for the Political System* (Washington, D.C.: Library of Congress Congressional Research Service Report No. 82–92 GOV, Nov. 6, 1981; updated May 7, 1982), pp. 116, 121–23. For 1982 data, Federal Election Commission.
[a]General elections only.
[b]No third party is included because only about $22,000 was given by all PACs in 1981–1982 to candidates other than Democrats and Republicans.

(see Table 3–3). While Democrats no longer enjoy the two-to-one edge they had in the early 1970s—before the corporate and trade PAC movement began in earnest—they reversed a steady decline in 1982, increasing their share of PAC contributions from 52 percent to 54 percent. They recorded no gain among corporate PACs, however; Republicans secured a slightly larger proportion of PAC funds (67 percent) than they had two years earlier. Little change has been recorded in labor's pattern because it has been so reliably solid for the Democrats (94 percent in 1982). Since 1978 trade PACs have remained consistently bipartisan, but with about a 58 percent to 42 percent Republican edge. Once again those PACs recording the most noteworthy recent shift are the nonconnecteds. A major effort by ideologically liberal PACs after the 1980 Democratic election disasters transformed the nonconnected group from a 71 percent Republican majority (in 1980) to a 52 percent Democratic one in 1982. This comparison of direct contributions, however, does not take into account independent expenditures by the nonconnected PACs, which heavily favored GOP candidates.

Multicandidate PACs express little preference overall when offered a choice of a Senate or a House candidate (Table 3–1), yet PACs give most of their money to House candidates. The proportions have varied somewhat over the years, but House contenders have generally received about 70 percent of all PAC contributions, while 30 percent has gone to Senate candidates.[3] Of course it is not surprising that House candidates receive proportionately more PAC funds since there are so many more contenders for the 435 House seats each election year than there are for the 33 or 34 Senate posts up in each election cycle. But PAC contributions also comprise a larger percentage of all money raised for House than for Senate candidates; in 1982 PAC gifts accounted for 31 percent of all House contributions and only 18 percent of Senate campaign funds. This discrepancy exists in part because Senate candidates receive more publicity than their House counterparts and run in geographically bigger districts. Both conditions permit Senate aspirants to attract more donations from individuals, especially through broad-based direct-mail programs, and these proportionately reduce the weight of PAC money.[4]

These general patterns obscure some less obvious but perhaps more revealing trends in PAC contributions. First, while there is less money channeled to challengers, those resources given to nonincumbents are concentrated in close races where the funds can tip the electoral scales.[5] It would not substantially increase the competitiveness of politics if PACs gave a greater proportion of funds to challengers in districts they could not realistically hope to win,[6] so PACs' concentration on incumbents in many cases does not drastically decrease electoral competition. In fact some observers have marveled that so many PACs spend as much money on challengers as they do. In the 1980 election cycle, for instance, 17 percent of the

PACs spent over half their congressional budgets on challengers, and 40 percent spent no more than half of all their funds on incumbents.[7] Moreover, much of the money corporate and trade PACs give to incumbents goes to legislators who are safe—but when supposedly safe but unfriendly incumbents are seriously challenged, the business PAC "access" money contributed to those incumbents is withdrawn and sent instead to their challengers.[8] In this way, PAC money often seems to "go with the flow" of politics rather than generate tides of its own.

Overall, though, incumbents have an irresistible charm for PACs. Especially in the House of Representatives, incumbents win more than 90 percent of the time,[9] and so giving money to incumbents is a nearly foolproof strategy to ensure both access on Capitol Hill for the PAC's parent company, union, or association, and a favorable win/loss ratio for the PAC itself. The former helps interest groups to achieve their legislative goals and protect their economic interests,[10] while the latter helps to present a successful, positive face for fundraising and solicitation.[11] This incumbent strategy is often encouraged by the PACs' Washington offices, which tend toward pragmatism and acceptance of the legislative world as it exists on the Hill.[12] Smaller PACs are also more likely to favor incumbents disproportionately, since their kitty is usually exhausted after they make their gifts to incumbents who serve their home districts or who are on important committees; the well-endowed PACs have money for the challengers who are "left over" once key incumbents have been satisfied.[13]

Finally, PACs whose parent organizations are generally pleased with government and have a cooperative relationship with their regulatory agency and oversight congressional committees are more incumbent oriented than groups whose experiences have been adversarial.[14] The aerospace and defense industry PACs are examples of the former, and they typically support incumbents of both parties, especially those from districts where major plants are located.[15] The oil industry shows a dramatically different pattern. Buffeted by the energy crisis and enmeshed in the regulatory jungle that grew up as a result, the oil PACs have become some of the most fiercely ideological, least incumbent-inclined PACs. The oil PACs are clearly in the minority among corporate and trade PACs, however, where pragmatism dominates candidate selection: friendly incumbents receive priority attention, "open seats" where no incumbent is running are viewed as the next best opportunities, and disfavored incumbents are challenged only when they are considered to be in serious electoral trouble. CALPAC of the California Medical Association frankly summarized its policy for PAC members:

> CALPAC's first priority is to protect and assist incumbents who have proven their commitment to private health care. Beyond that, the PAC concentrates on "improv-

ing the breed" by supporting good candidates in open legislative districts, challenging unfriendly incumbents and opening lines of communication between local physicians and their elected representatives. Very few legislators can be defeated (only two were unseated in 1982), and CALPAC challenges uncooperative incumbents only when research shows they are vulnerable. The best opportunities for positive change occur when incumbents do not seek reelection.[16]

PACs do not offer money to just any incumbent or challenger, of course. Pragmatic PACs usually ask a series of questions much like the following in arriving at their candidate choices:[17]

—In whose districts do we have plants or local divisions?
—Which congressmen are on the House or Senate committees affecting us?
—Which congressmen have been particularly accessible to us and have attempted to understand our problems?
—Which congressmen have voted "right" on our issues and concerns?
—What is the political situation in the districts we want to target? Who especially needs help?
—For nonincumbents, where do they stand on our issues and how close to us have they been in the past? What are their electoral chances? What political consultants have they hired, what do their poll results say, and how much have they raised so far and from what groups? Which House or Senate committee assignments will they seek if elected?

Because of the PACs' emphasis on committee assignments, congressmen endeavor to get appointed to committees with well-financed constituencies and broad regulatory powers.[18] The House Energy and Commerce Committee and the Senate Committee on Commerce, Science, and Transportation, with jurisdiction over many important businesses, are particularly popular, as are the Banking Committees, the Appropriations Committees, and the House Ways and Means and Senate Finance Committees. Legislators in leadership positions and committee chairmen are also usually PAC priorities, whether unopposed or seriously challenged. For example, Democrat Jim Jones of Oklahoma, chairman of the House Budget Committee, received almost $165,000 just from corporate PACs in the 1982 election. His GOP opponent, who held him to 54 percent of the vote in a strong Democratic year, was given a grand total of $450 by corporate PACs.[19] But even freshman legislators are not ignored if they are on the committees vital to a particular union, company, or association. While the influence of freshmen is limited, they are attractive to PACs because, first, they often need the money most of all and gratefully remember those who help pay off their large first-election debts, and second, unlike veterans, they have not taken a position on many issues and are considered persuadable by the PACs and the parent organizations' lobbyists. "Every freshman represents a new chance for us," one lobbyist admitted. "They are not players now, but they will be some day, and we can be helpful as they learn the game."[20]

Like any decision-making process, PAC candidate selection is less rational in practice than it appears on paper. "It's really arbitrary," admits the National Rifle Association's Terri O'Grady. Loyalty to incumbents who are likely to lose but who have been faithful to a group's goals over the years is one reason for seemingly irrational contributions. For instance, despite South Carolina Democratic Rep. John W. Jenrette's conviction on Abscam corruption charges, the National Education Association PAC gave him $2,000 in his losing 1980 reelection campaign.[21] The fact that many PACs are decentralized makes it more difficult to describe a coherent PAC contribution scheme.[22] Union PACs are particularly tied to local endorsements. "I can't make contributions out of the D.C. office unless I check with the local affiliates first," explained the Teamsters' David Sweeney. "Most [locals] think the guys in Washington don't know shit from apple butter." A combination of loyalty and local control means that the United Auto Workers is almost compelled to make a contribution in virtually every Michigan congressional district, whether the money is needed by the favored candidate or not.[23] More centralized corporate PACs also have great difficulty on occasion in reconciling the views of competing plants and divisions. As BIPAC's Bernadette Budde suggested:

> In every major corporation you have a headquarters with a certain set of attitudes, and then facilities scattered all over the country with other attitudes. One facility's relationship with a member of Congress may be ideal, the headquarters' relationship with him may be nonexistent, and the Washington office might have mixed feelings. The more players you have the more complicated it becomes. . . . Suppose the company makes five products at different plants. All five compete against each other internally for attention and funding. So which candidate does this company support when products A, B, and C think incumbent X is great and products D and E think he's horrendous?

Contributions may sometimes flow from a PAC to a candidate simply because someone on the PAC's board of directors is a close friend and demands support. The Communication Workers of America was pressed for funds in 1980, and gave token gifts to some of its friends in close races, yet Sen. John Glenn of Ohio, coasting to reelection, received the maximum contribution of $5,000 for both the primary and the general election. A union official explained why: "Glenn is close to Marty Hughes, our vice president for Michigan and Ohio, who insisted Glenn get the full 10. There was not a heck of a lot we could do."[24] Occasionally a constituent of the PAC may run for office, expecting full backing even if his views are opposed to the PAC's stated philosophy or if his chances for victory are slim. Peter Lauer of AMPAC has answered his telephone a number of times to find a doctor on the other end who says, "O.K., I'm going to run. Where's my money?"[25] The PAC may have legitimate doubts about such a person, but it is difficult to refuse the request, especially if the physician has demonstrable support from local peers. And finally, PAC gifts do not always follow a committee's masterplan because from time to time money is used as a pawn in a political chess game. One union PAC manager reported that he had joined forces with others to attempt to persuade a certain candidate to run for the House rather than the Senate in a small northeastern state in 1984. Preferring another, reputedly stronger contender for the Senate seat, the PAC guaranteed the wavering candidate maximum support if he ran for the House race and no gift at all if he insisted on a Senate campaign. The candidate declared for the House.

Pragmatic PACs then tend to make their contributions after analyzing candidates through the prism of self-interest. Ideological PACs perhaps do the same thing, but they conceive of self-interest more broadly. Instead of asking whether the incumbent or challenger is accessible or helpful on specific economic concerns, they ask: Does the candidate share our philosophy and beliefs on issues of ideological or moral consequence? The political scientist Margaret Latus, using the journalist Edward Roeder's compilations, estimated that there were over 400 ideological PACs active in the 1982 election cycle.[26] About three-quarters were nonconnected PACs such as NCPAC and PROPAC, while the rest had parent organizations, and there were over twice as many conservative PACs as liberal ones. Few trade PACs are considered ideological, but a substantial minority of corporate PACs can be included in the classification. Stuart Rothenberg of the Free Congress Foundation found 44 corporate PACs that could be considered very ideological in the 1980 and 1982 elections.[27] Oil and natural gas firms as well as pharmaceutical and chemical companies headed Rothenberg's list, while others have found the construction, rubber, paper, and machinery industries also to be ideological and challenger oriented.[28] These corporate PACs are exceptional, however. The conservative ideological PACs regard most business groups as part of the problem. "Where we supported the tough conservative, the business PAC was always for the establishment, or for the moderate candidate," commented Paul Weyrich of the Committee for the Survival of a Free Congress. "Some of the most heated arguments I have had in the political process have not been with opposition groups, but with business groups. . . ."[29] In some of the larger trade PACs, committee managers will freely admit that their membership is often more conservative than the PAC endorsements indicate. Jerry Simpson, executive director of CALPAC, recalls, "Sometimes we have had liberal Democrats who vote with medicine 60 percent of the time, and the PAC will feel an obligation to support them. But that causes us all kinds of pain and suffering at the local level with our conservative constituency."

The ideological PACs on both right and left, as we noted earlier, are the

PAC group best characterized as pro-challenger. As one ideological PAC manager[30] put it, "If an incumbent can't get himself reelected with all the perks congressmen have, then there's something seriously wrong and our $5,000 wouldn't have made a difference. I mean, for an incumbent to lose, he's practically got to rape his sister on the Capitol steps." Ideological PACs are often willing to help even challengers who are opposing senior, entrenched legislators. NCPAC took on Senate Minority Leader Robert Byrd of West Virginia and House Majority Leader Jim Wright of Texas in 1982 because "we wanted to send a message to every member of the House and Senate that if we'll go after them, we'll go after anyone," according to chairman Terry Dolan. Ideological PACs will also look beyond a single election when deciding whether to support "risk capital ventures," as challengers are sometimes called. "We believe that many of our contributions to challengers are investments for the future; even when they lose, some will be candidates again one day, and better ones for the experience," explained NEA-PAC's Ken Melley.

Choosing which challengers and incumbents to support is no easier for the ideological PACs than for other groups. Given their bent for issues and philosophy, however, many ideological groups have systematic and precise means of evaluating candidates. Issuing "report cards" has become a cottage industry among PACs.[31] The Americans for Democratic Action, COPE, the Americans for Constitutional Action, and the Committee for the Survival of a Free Congress are just a few of the organizations that regularly rate incumbent legislators on a variety of issues important to their groups. These four scorecards tend to be broad based, covering a wide range of topics, while others—such as the National Christian Action Coalition's "Family Issues Voting Index"[32]—are more narrow. Some indexes are applied with mathematical precision to the candidate-selection process. The National Federation of Independent Business PAC uses a "70–40" rule, for instance; any incumbent who scores better than 70 percent on the group's report card is automatically eligible for a donation, and anyone scoring below 40 percent is likely to have a contribution made to his opponent.[33] Some indexes are not terribly popular even with allies. Russell Hemenway of the liberal National Committee for an Effective Congress wishes his compatriots at the Americans for Democratic Action would cease and desist: "ADA just kills our candidates. I wish they'd stop doing that goddamn index. It's great for the ADA, but our candidates out in the sticks are having to defend a 100 percent ADA record and it just helps their opponents. The NCEC has an index too, but we keep it to ourselves and nobody else sees it."

Voting indexes are not useful for evaluating challengers of course, unless they are House members running for the Senate, since challengers have no voting record to rate.[34] For this reason, and to nail down firm commitments from current and future legislators, many PACs require personal, recorded interviews, or dispatch detailed questionnaires to candidates. The National Education Association insisted that each 1984 presidential candidate desiring its endorsement prepare a videotape "show and tell" interview for its members and complete a lengthy questionnaire covering everything from collective bargaining and aid to education to civil rights and the nuclear freeze. Congressional candidates were quizzed in person and on paper about Social Security, tuition tax credits, and a host of other topics, some only tenuously related to education. The National Rifle Association and Handgun Control both restrict their candidate surveys to somewhat similar queries about firearms policy, though the expected answers are diametrically opposed. The Council for a Liveable World's Peace PAC not only sends out a questionnaire but makes a candidate sign a pledge to favor a nuclear freeze, support the termination of the MX missile and the B-1 bomber, and back other favored defense stands.[35] The Human Rights Campaign Fund asks pointed questions about candidates' hiring policy and their opinions on various forms of legal discrimination against gays.

The National Association of Realtors apparently holds the record for survey length: fifty-five questions on every major political issue on the national agenda even remotely connected to real estate. The "right" responses are not always obvious in some cleverly worded surveys, and a Realtor official notes that "Sometimes candidates call me and plead with me to give them the correct answers."[36] Candidates generally take the questionnaires seriously, and with good reason. When Wisconsin Democratic Sen. William Proxmire refused to fill out the NEA's survey in 1982, NEA-PAC gave Proxmire's little-known GOP challenger $2,500. Proxmire, as expected, won easily, but the NEA's Ken Melley reported that "After the election our people had a meeting with Proxmire and he was quite a different guy. He respected the fact that we stood behind our questionnaire, and there's a dialogue now with his office that hadn't gone on before."

Not all ideological PACs are as precise as the NEA in making their candidate selections. As we saw in Chapter 2, some nonconnected committees are chaotic "seat-of-the-pants" operations characterized by haphazard or autocratic decision-making. But few PACs in any category are really slaves to their report cards or questionnaire results when the final choice of candidates is made. Republican Rep. Lyle Williams of Ohio had a 68 percent favorable AFL-CIO rating in 1980 and had aided the United Steelworkers in a major court suit, yet the Steelworkers PAC, unfriendly to Republicans of any stripe, gave its money to Williams's 1980 Democratic opponent.[37] Two candidates in the same district may have identical positions on a group's issues, but most PACs will make a donation to the incumbent. And a PAC will often back a candidate unfavorable to it if his opponent is even worse. In 1982 the conservative-leaning Baltimore Gas and Electric PAC gave money to liberal Republican Milton Marks of California because he was running against the more liberal Democratic U.S. Rep. Phillip Burton. "In that particular district, you're not going to find Genghis Khan," observed a PAC spokesman.[38] Nor do two similar PACs necessarily agree on what a candidate's scorecard or voting record means. The antiabortion Life Amendment PAC gave Sen. Russell Long (D–La.) a 100 percent rating and $1,250 to his reelection campaign while the equally antiabortion National Pro-Life PAC, interpreting the senator's record differently, denounced Long as an infidel.[39]

Even if a PAC is certain that a candidate is completely in ideological tune with it, concerns outside the voting record may override an endorsement. One midwestern corporate PAC withdrew its previous backing for a philosophically agreeable congressman when unpublished reports reached it that the congressman had been having extramarital affairs in Washington. "Our PAC members believe personal characteristics and morality are important," explained the solemn PAC manager.[40] As in every other way, PACs differ markedly about such matters. The director of the Human Rights Campaign Fund bluntly ruled out any consideration of a candidate's personal life in his PAC's contribution process: "I don't care if they sleep with man, woman, or beast."

SIZE OF PAC GIFTS

Most PACs only rarely give the maximum donation of $5,000 per election, which they call a "max-out." Almost eight of ten of the multicandidate PACs[41] contributed not a single $5,000 chunk to any candidate in 1981–1982, and only 10 percent maxed out on a tenth or more of their beneficiaries. Only a few very large business and labor PACs regularly give the maximum to chosen candidates. In the 1982 election cycle, for instance, just forty-five PACs gave $5,000 or more[42] to the thirty-four Republican Senate candidates.[43] Among the labor PACs, some of the international labor organizations are inclined to max out: in 1982, for instance, the Machinists' MNPL gave nineteen of its twenty-five Senate primary candidates and twenty-five of its twenty-seven Senate general election candidates a $5,000 donation. The ideological and nonconnected PACs also tend to give larger contributions to smaller numbers of candidates.[44]

On the whole, though, PAC gifts are of relatively modest size. Since in 1982 only a few hundred PACs gave even as much as $25,000 to all federal races,[45] while each PAC contributed, on average, to about fifty candidates,[46] it is obvious that most PAC donations were well below $5,000. Nine of ten corporate PACs contribute an average per-candidate gift of $1,000 or less.[47] Of the 46,000 corporate PAC donations in 1981–1982, over 95 percent were for amounts of $2,500 or less, and the average corporate PAC gift to a congressional candidate was just $657.[48] For all categories of PACs in 1981–1982, the median contribution to a House candidate was about $500 and to a Senate candidate about double that.

Mainly, PACs max out in races that are both of high priority for them and considered to be close.[49] The National Education Association PAC, for example, has stated its "max out" policy this way:

> The Association commits the maximum possible and allowable resources to races involving a NEA-PAC endorsed candidate in which the race is considered marginal or special circumstances are involved. A race is considered marginal when a candidate won the previous election(s) with a margin of less than 56 percent and there exists a strong possibility that either candidate could win. . . . Special circumstances may include any number of factors. For example, the candidate may serve on or chair a key Congressional committee, may have played an important role in helping move legislation considered important by the Association, may have helped defeat legislation that would have been harmful to education, or may be challenging a candidate who is extremely hostile to NEA-supported pro-education legislation. . . .[50]

The NEA-PAC staff evaluates each endorsed candidate and rates him or her on a scale of one to seven:

1. A friendly incumbent in a marginal race deserving $5,000.
2. A challenger facing an unfriendly incumbent in a close race deserving $5,000.
3. An open seat, with a friendly candidate in a good position to win, deserving $5,000.
4. A friendly incumbent who is safe, deserving a contribution but less than the maximum.
5. An open seat with no friendly candidate, or a pro-NEA candidate who cannot win, deserving a token gift or none at all.
6. A friendly challenger facing an unfriendly incumbent, but with little chance to win. Token or no gift.
7. Uncertain political situation as yet; delayed contribution decision.

Until recently labor PACs frequently gave a maximum gift to friendly incumbents who were electorally safe, but the incidence of such "thank you" max-outs declined in 1982 when labor concentrated more of its resources on challengers.

The amount of money a PAC gives to a candidate at any time may simply reflect the state of the PAC's treasury. While Independent Action had hoped in 1982 to give $5,000 to each endorsed candidate as early seed money, its cash flow, coupled with a desire to help many candidates, made such a policy impossible to follow. Instead the PAC sometimes maxed out in installments, and this practice had an unforeseen advantage, as its director Ed Coyle explained: "We gave one Florida congressional candidate the maximum in five different checks stretched over the campaign. By doing this, the candidate and his staff stayed in touch with us. If we'd given the $5,000 all at once in January, I doubt they would have gotten to know us so well or kept calling. It also helped us make sure our money was being used properly."

While most PACs max out infrequently, there are a few PACs that evade even the $5,000-per-election limit in an attempt to give as much as possible. One technique is for a PAC to give a candidate the maximum gift, then donate $5,000 each to a number of friendly PACs, which may in turn give the favored candidate a contribution.[51] A PAC can also encourage its members, officers, or executives (and their friends and families) to give personal donations of $1,000 each to favored candidates. PACs such as the Council for a Livable World's Peace PAC collect and forward these individual contributions in a bundle to chosen candidates.[52] Finally, as we will soon see, the use of independent spending and in-kind gifts enables PACs to outmax a max-out.

D.C. FUNDRAISERS

If they want to say contributions are nothing but bribery, then receptions are nothing but blackmail.

—A trade PAC director

If there is one political institution the average PAC manager knows as well as his PAC, it is the Washington, D.C., fundraiser. This is usually a reception or dinner given by congressional candidates (mainly the incumbents) for a price per participant that varies between $100 and $1,000.[53] Most PACs receive 400 or more invitations a year to fundraisers held in the capital. "Lord Almighty, they're a pain," declared Donald Cogman of MAPCO. "Starting in August [over a year ahead of a congressional election] we'll get four or five invitations *every day.*" There are so many fundraisers that the national party committees try to prevent conflicts by mailing out lists of scheduled fundraisers well in advance, and the Democratic and Republican Clubs on Capitol Hill are often booked solid as incumbents scurry to fill their coffers early to scare (and often ward off) potential opposition. The price a congressman can command varies with rank, of course: a lowly freshman may only charge $100 a head, while a committee chairman rarely dips below $500 or $1,000 per person.

The PACs flock to the receptions in droves. About two-thirds of the multicandidate PACs regularly buy tickets, and those that do spend an average of 28 percent of their contribution total on fundraisers.[54] Corporate PACs are only slightly more likely than other PACs to attend, but those that do give an average of only 15 percent of their contribution budget. Trade PACs frequent the fundraisers to a much greater degree. Fully 82 percent of the trade PACs go to fundraisers, and as much as 40 percent of their money is spent on them. As we saw in Chapter 2, PACs with an office in Washington are more likely to attend fundraisers: 90 percent of them do so, compared to just 49 percent of PACs that lack a D.C. office. Similarly, PACs whose parent organizations have spawned a Washington lobby frequent fundraisers too: 78 percent of the lobbyist PACs go, while only 44 percent of those without a D.C. lobbying connection support the receptions.

PACs attend so many fundraisers for a combination of reasons. Perhaps most important is that their presence is expected by congressmen and staffers who have befriended them in their legislative pursuits,[55] and they are missed if they do not go. Many PAC officials also see in fundraisers the opportunity to talk to legislators personally (rather than just their staffs), the chance to make contacts of all sorts, and even the chance to massage their egos by being with the influential and those "in the know." "There's a certain aura of power, and someone who's been in Washington for a while likes rubbing elbows and wants to see and be seen," suggests Helena Hutton of the National Association of Manufacturers. (Her own perspective may come from being in Washington for a long while: "I find fundraisers to be deadly dull and boring—not my idea of a good time.") One additional reason why PAC managers frequently attend fundraisers is that they are increasingly asked to serve on the steering committees for the events. Gregg Ward of SMACPAC reported: "The steering committee thing has really gotten out of hand. . . . Last year I was asked [to serve] so many times I couldn't possibly have done a good job for all the sponsors."

Generally, the PACs assess fundraiser invitations with the same criteria they apply to regular requests for money. But about a quarter of the PACs, perhaps seeing fundraisers as "something more akin to social etiquette than to tough political decisions,"[56] seem to make special allowances and permit shortcuts. This is particularly true of trade and labor committees. The Realtors' R-PAC, for instance, has set up a permanent subcommittee of its trustees which can make decisions on the purchase of reception tickets costing up to $250 without prior approval of the entire group. Labor often gives its Washington offices full or partial discretion on fundraisers. Explains the Teamsters' David Sweeney: "If [GOP House Minority Leader] Bob Michel were having a reception, I would simply call the local guys [Teamsters in Michel's district] and say, 'Hey, we're going to buy a ticket.' It doesn't constitute an endorsement. If the local people objected, we wouldn't do it."

While only 34 percent of the multicandidate PACs refuse to contribute to fundraisers (and just 10 percent of this group cite a formal policy against fundraisers), many PACs are having second thoughts about this form of political giving. "They're an unproductive waste of your money because your contribution gets lost" in the "pack" of simultaneous givers, as one PAC official stated. Moreover, many home and district offices of both labor and business object to having their Washington representatives dispense so much of the PAC's largesse for reception tickets. "I know a lot of companies are getting tired of supporting the Waldorf-Astoria [Hotel], which along with the planning consultant takes 40–60 percent of the fundraiser's proceeds," says the Public Affairs Council's Richard Armstrong. John Perkins of COPE agrees: "Many of our unions hate to see their money spent this way. They want all of their funds to go into campaigns, not be squandered on overhead." Few PACs are likely to rule out fundraisers completely, but many more may place restrictions on their gifts similar to those of AMPAC. Having spent $83,000 on receptions in 1982, AMPAC has developed a firm set of "reception rules," according to Peter Lauer. "We've instituted a ceiling: a congressman can only get $250 per reception and a senator $1,000. We'll give at either a D.C. fundraiser or one back in the home state—not both. We only give to events of this type for incumbents. And that doesn't include a House member running for the Senate." And if Congress should pass any sort of overall limitation on the total amount candidates can receive from PACs, "fundraisers will be out," insists Lauer.

GIVING TO BOTH SIDES

Like gamblers at a racetrack, PACs sometimes hedge their bets by giving money to both sides of a single contest. Sometimes such split giving (often termed "double dipping") occurs when a PAC contributes simultaneously to both the Democratic and Republican nominees in a general election. Other times the PAC gives to one party contender in the primary election, perhaps to prevent a more objectionable candidate from becoming the party's nominee, then switches to the other party's standard-bearer (presumably the PAC's first choice all along) in the general election. Third, some PACs make a contribution to one candidate before the election, and if he should lose, to his successful opponent after the election.

Instances of split giving usually receive a great deal of publicity, partly because the practice tends to confirm the critics' view of PACs as vote buying influence-seekers. There is little doubt that split giving is cynical and distasteful, with the possible exception of the primary/general election splits mentioned above. Yet it is also true that split giving is rare. For almost all the major PACs I interviewed, there were no more than half a dozen cases of split giving (out of dozens or hundreds of contributions) over several election cycles.[57] Many PACs' policies or by-laws discourage or prohibit it, or allow it (as does the Honeywell Employees' PAC) only "in rare cases in primary elections where encouraging more than one qualified candidate may be advisable."[58] For some PACs, of course, split giving is far more common. In 1980 and 1982, for instance, the auto dealers' PAC contributed to two or more candidates in eighteen of the sixty-six U.S. Senate races.[59] But instances such as this one are exceptional.[60]

When split giving occurs it is normally in a close race pitting two candidates with similar records on a PAC's area of interest. Both candidates may also have vociferous supporters on the PAC's decision-making board. Many PACs resolve these cross-pressures by staying out of a race entirely and giving to neither side, but split giving is an alternative. Occasionally the PAC will give each of the two candidates a different amount, perhaps indicating whose side a slim majority of the PAC board favored.

Redistricting also seems to produce many cases of split giving. As one trade PAC manager explained, "In some cases we weren't certain where the state legislatures were going to draw the lines, but we contributed early and ended up giving to two candidates who found themselves running against each other in the same district." Earmarking[61] is another PAC practice that can easily result in split giving; if a large group of employees is allowed free rein to choose the recipients of their PAC donations, inevitably some will choose opposing candidates. (Few PACs allow this wide-open form of earmarking, though.) Additionally, some PACs that do not often give to opposing candidates do so regularly to the opposing parties; this is especially common among those PACs that wish to demonstrate their bipartisanship. In the 1982 election cycle BANKPAC gave $10,000 each to the Republican and Democratic National Committees, and additional gifts to all four of the parties' congressional campaign committees and several other party-affiliated groups. Finally, split giving is used on the odd occasion to remedy an error. Terri O'Grady of the National Rifle Association's PAC cited the case of a South Dakota congressional race in which the PAC gave a donation to the GOP candidate, only to discover later that the Democratic nominee had precisely the same positions on gun issues. The problem was resolved with the dispatch of a similar grant to the Democrat.

While there are credible and legitimate explanations for some examples of split giving, many cases are simply naked attempts to buy access and influence whoever wins the election. Most PACs have recognized this and shun the practice. Those that do not bring disrepute to the PAC system, and may themselves be too clever by half. Don Cogman of MAPCO PAC, who previously served as a senator's aide, saw it this way: "I sure as hell think [split giving] is a bad policy. On the Hill the attitude is, if they're going to give to the other side they should not give to us. What they're doing is so obvious and it doesn't do them any good. They might as well save their money."

THE TIMING OF PAC GIFTS

The timing of PAC contributions springs from vital choices of strategy. In 1978 and 1980 many business PACs set aside a substantial portion of their budgets to give to congressional candidates (mostly Republicans) in the final weeks before the election. This is when extra money can give a campaign the added boost necessary for victory.[62] At the same time more and more PACs appear willing to consider early contributions for spring or summer primary contests,[63] and some are contributing even as much as a year or two prior to the November general election. Very early giving almost always goes to incumbents. Fully fifteen months ahead of November 1984, incumbent U.S. senators seeking another term had amassed a collective war chest of almost $10 million, and $2.5 million of that total came from PACs.[64] A dozen incumbents had by that time already raised more than $100,000 each in PAC gifts.

Overall, PACs active in the 1981–1982 election cycle gave about a fifth of their contribution total in 1981, a quarter in the first half of 1982, a third from July to September 1982, and another quarter from October 1 to election day.[65] About half of all the PACs also participate in primaries to some degree, though on average only about 10 percent of their funds go to primary candidates. Corporate PACs are slightly more likely to contribute prior to October 1 than are other categories of PACs: under a fifth of their gifts are made from October 1 to election day, compared to a quarter for all PACs. But corporate PACs spend only about half as much of their resources as the average PAC does in the primaries, so their giving seems more concentrated in the pre–Labor Day period for candidates (mainly incumbents) without primary opposition. By contrast, ideological PACs are often eager to take an active role in primaries when they see a chance to nominate candidates closer to their viewpoint in low-turnout elections.[66]

There are certain advantages to both early and late giving.[67] "It's worth three times the money to give early compared to late," flatly declares FEC member Lee Ann Elliott. Early substantial contributions permit a committee such as BIPAC to send a signal to other PACs that a candidate is of a certain ideological bent and has a good chance to win. Preprimary giving also enables a PAC to double its maximum contribution to a favored contender, since it can contribute the limit of $5,000 in each election. Of course, in some parts of the country, particularly the South, and in heavily one-party districts across the nation, a primary victory is tantamount to election; if a PAC wants to influence the congressional choice in such a district, it must give early. Even in hotly contested districts, early contributions can be very influential because, first, they draw the attention of the candidate since fewer PACs give at that time, and second, they provide the "seed money" so crucial to getting a campaign—especially for nonincumbents—off the ground organizationally. A direct-mail campaign, for example, demands the early investment of much capital for prospecting. Moreover, as Ken Melley of NEA-PAC suggests, "If you want to have some input on the issues you care about, you'd better give early. . . . It gives you access when the candidate's positions are being formulated." (Melley's remark brings to mind an observation attributed to Louisiana Gov. Earl Long: "Those who give early get whatever extra there is to be had; those who give late get good government.") Finally, incumbents appreciate early contributions because the size of their reelection accounts can deter strong challengers from running against them.

But early giving can cause misgivings. "You make more mistakes," admits Gregg Ward of SMACPAC, and therefore "I don't necessarily hold to the premise that early money is the best money." The National Federation of Independent Business PAC agrees. As one of the officers reported it, after the PAC broke with its no-primary policy and backed a losing candidate, "NFIB succumbed to [the early money] pitch once, and we will not again."[68] The many PACs that are strongly incumbent oriented and winner biased are unlikely to give early: they do not have the gambling instinct that early giving demands, and they want to be reasonably sure of a candidate's electoral fortunes before committing the PAC's name and resources. There is another reason for late giving as well: to evade preelection disclosure of a controversial gift.[69] The gay Human Rights Campaign Fund withheld their contributions until late in the 1982 election season partly to spare its recipients some bad publicity. As HRCF's Stephen Endean explained it: "A lot of our candidates wanted money late, and a lot of our friends even had the perception that a contribution from us was political doom. I think some of them have gotten over that. They better have —it's on their record now!"

The timing of contributions is not always determined solely by the PACs. Some primaries are held so late (in September or October for a number of states) that PACs that give only to general election candidates are forced to contribute just a few weeks prior to the November election day. PAC contributions also depend for their timing on cash flow. As Charles Orasin of Handgun Control PAC recalled, "*When* we gave was really a function of when we had the money." Since many members contribute to their PACs during election seasons, when the races are headline news, there is often simply more money to dispense in the autumn months, which encourages later giving. Occasionally a PAC that intends to give money early but anticipates a late flow of receipts will take out a loan a year before the election and secure it with projected revenues.[70] (Raising funds through payroll deduction is particularly useful in making these arrangements.) Pressure from candidates may also affect a PAC's contributions schedule; campaigns need money by specific dates for media advertising "buys," for instance. Last, some PACs allow legislative priorities to determine the timing of their contributions. When the auto dealers were lining up cosponsors for a 1981 congressional resolution to veto a Federal Trade Commission rule requiring used-car dealers to disclose defects in their merchandise, they made contributions to sixteen House members within ten days of the date the congressmen signed on as cosponsors.[71] (We will take a closer look at this episode in the next chapter.)

POST-ELECTION CONTRIBUTIONS

If you're trying to buy access, giving after the election is like buying tickets on a horse race once the race is over.

—Richard Armstrong, president of the Public Affairs Council

For those PACs that are challenger shy and winner oriented, nothing beats a contribution once the election is over. Many candidates, especially successful challengers, run up large budget deficits during a campaign, and a gift to help the officeholder-to-be retire his debt is welcomed by both the winner and the PAC, which probably supported the incumbent. "Basically, what you're doing is buying off a mistake," as SMACPAC's Gregg Ward explains it. In 1976, for instance, the American Trial Lawyers Association's PAC gave substantial contributions to five new U.S. senators-elect after their November victories; before the election, each of their incumbent opponents had received the PAC's maximum $5,000 donation.[72] With very few exceptions, only winners are assisted in debt retirement; losers, though burdened with even more massive debts, are without influence and must fend for themselves. Some PACs are selective in the mistakes they correct. Rather than giving to just any winner, the American Bankers Association's BANKPAC and the National Association of Broadcasters' TARPAC, among others, wait until the winners' committee assignments are announced, so they know which congressmen-elect will have the most influence or effect on their groups.

While the amount of PAC money devoted to campaign debt retirement may be significant in individual cases—BANKPAC, for instance, gave about $75,000 in the 1982 election cycle—overall only about 3 percent of the average multicandidate PAC's funds go to post-election contributions.[73] A few PACs have by-law restrictions against debt retirement, while some others have adopted policies which discourage it. Because in many cases post-election gifts represent obvious influence peddling, the occasional PAC manager has decided the practice should cease. "I'm recommending we get out of it," says SMACPAC's Ward. Most PAC managers apparently disagree though, with the result that congressional incumbents are resting easier financially. In just their first six months in office in 1983, the eighty House freshmen collected nearly $1.6 million from PACs to help them retire their election debts, a sum representing 43 percent of their total receipts during this period.[74]

IN-KIND CONTRIBUTIONS

One of the first "in-kind" contributions in American political history was made in 1757 when George Washington ran for the Virginia House of Burgesses and local merchants donated liquor for Washington to ply the voters with. An in-kind contribution to a campaign, then, is basically a gift of goods or services instead of money,[75] and it is a practice that a growing number of PACs are adopting. Close to a fifth (18 percent) of all multicandidate PACs reported making in-kind contributions in 1981 or 1982, and another 13 percent of those that did not do so in the last election cycle foresee making in-kind gifts "in the next few years."[76] Trade and labor PACs are especially inclined to use the in-kind option, and 22 percent of the trade committees and 17 percent of the labor PACs are planning to add in-kind services in the future. PACs with a Washington, D.C., office are also more likely to be found among the in-kind contributors: 21 percent of D.C.-office PACs, and only 11 percent of PACs without Washington representation, make in-kind gifts. Corporate PACs are clearly the most reluctant to adopt the practice. Just 9 percent of the corporate PACs report any in-kind spending in 1981–1982, and only 7 percent foresee its use in the next few years. The corporate PAC managers I interviewed were frequently not even familiar with the in-kind concept, or if they were, claimed that it was too burdensome for their PAC, too cumbersome for their accountants, and too unappealing to their favored candidates. This corporate resistance to in-kind expenditures has proven frustrating to key officials of the business PAC movement who believe the in-kind option could greatly expand PAC influence. One of these individuals explained corporate reluctance about in-kind contributions this way:

> In-kind just does not fit their mentality. Most of them don't understand what they could do and they don't appreciate the intricacies of in-kind giving. They're in the

business of making tires or whatever the hell they make, and they don't want to be confused with all these details about buying stamps for a brochure for John Smith.[77]

Those PACs that do use in-kind giving are generally pleased with the results. They believe that a donation of money is often invisible and quickly absorbed by the campaign organization, while in-kind expenditures are usually prominent and draw attention to the PAC, making its gift a memorable one for the candidate and his staff. The candidate frequently benefits substantially since the PAC can often provide services at a lower cost than an individual campaign can secure. Since 1974 the liberal National Committee for an Effective Congress, for instance, has entered long-term contracts with a number of political consultants; this "package deal" has meant that consultants who would charge a single campaign a large sum have been provided to campaigns by the NCEC under much lower "group rates."

Besides garnering increased attention, PACs themselves benefit from the in-kind option in important ways. First, in-kind giving allows the PAC to retain some control over how its money is spent. Many PAC officials expressed anger that their money was so often wasted by campaigns that were floundering without proper direction or expertise. This observation has led to increased in-kind expenditures in a few cases. One trade PAC manager declared, "We now like to go to a campaign and say 'We know what you need based on our own experience and solid data. If you don't believe it then we've got a real problem and we're not sure we're going to take the money that our members have donated to us and put it down a rat hole." A second way the PAC benefits from in-kind giving is through staff interaction. In-kind gifts bring the PAC staff and the candidate's staff together. The personal relationships thus established become very useful if the campaign is victorious and, as usually happens, campaign staffers become office staffers. PACs are then in a better position to influence the officeholder's legislative aims.

One form of in-kind expenditure which has proven particularly successful for groups such as NEA-PAC and AMPAC is "survey sharing."[78] During the 1982 campaign, for example, AMPAC funded surveys for thirty-six congressional candidates, all but one of whom was an incumbent. While the total cost of the surveys exceeded $380,000, only about $89,000 was reported as AMPAC contributions because of a special Federal Election Commission in-kind regulation known as the "sixty-one-day rule." This regulation recognizes that poll data become less valuable as time passes,[79] and therefore permits a PAC to depreciate the cost of a poll by 50 percent if it waits sixteen days after the poll's completion to deliver it to a candidate, and by a massive 95 percent if delivery is postponed more than sixty days after completion. AMPAC's polling was a financial bonanza for candidates, but AMPAC was also a clear beneficiary. One condition AMPAC placed on its survey assistance was that it required the candidate to involve himself directly in designing the poll and receiving the results, in order to acquaint the AMPAC staff personally with the potential congressman. The candidate was first given a choice among the prominent party pollsters who had contracted with AMPAC. (In 1984 Republicans could select Robert Teeter, Lance Tarrance, or Richard Wirthlin, while Democrats had a choice of William Hamilton, Hugh Schwartz, or Hugh Parmer.) Then the candidate and his staff joined with AMPAC personnel and the pollster to design a questionnaire, which included standard trend and demographic questions plus another dozen or so queries specified by the candidate and tailored to his needs. AMPAC also added five "American Medical Association questions" on health care issues whose results were not transmitted to the candidate; rather, AMPAC retained them for its own data files, and used those strictly in-house questions as a basis for assigning to itself some of the poll's cost, reducing the charge to candidates still further.[80]

Other trade PACs besides AMPAC, especially large well-staffed association committees centered in Washington, have been leaders in the in-kind contribution field. The Realtors' R-PAC lends members of its national staff to candidates for organizational and fundraising chores; their salaries are charged as an in-kind gift. SMACPAC has assisted campaigns in putting on fundraising dinners and soliciting support from other PACs. The Chamber of Commerce's PAC counts each candidate listing in its important weekly "Opportunity Race" report as an in-kind donation. Besides trade committees, the PACs formed by prospective presidential candidates (which we will discuss later in this chapter) also make frequent in-kind contributions. These usually include production of television advertisements featuring an endorsement by the presidential hopeful, or payment for a White House aspirant's travel to a local candidate's district.

Ideological and nonconnected PACs are particularly likely to choose in-kind gifts as well. Handgun Control PAC has lent its direct-mail donor list to favored candidates, and the Committee for the Survival of a Free Congress has trained candidates and staff at seminars, paid salaries for campaign assistants, provided strategic and technical advice through CSFC field representatives, and supervised get-out-the-vote operations. Several environmental "Green PACs," including those of the League of Conservation Voters, the Sierra Club, and Environmental Action, marshalled hundreds of volunteers for canvassing and phone bank efforts in key 1982 states and districts.[81] And the National Committee for an Effective Congress capitalized on "star power"—the political influence of entertainers in the age of television—by recruiting Hollywood's most visible liberals to give benefit performances for candidates with views similar to the stars' own. More than twenty stars and candidates were matched up by NCEC in 1982.

INDEPENDENT SPENDING

One thing we've done is wreck the federal election laws, and thank God for that.[82]

We could elect Mickey Mouse to the House or Senate.[83]

I'm not after respectability. The only thing I care about is if we're effective.[84]

The only difference between Republicans and Democrats on a Presidential level is the Democrats tell you they're going to screw you and the Republicans tell you they're not going to screw you—and do it anyhow.[85]

All these statements, and many more like them, have been made over the years by the eminently quotable John T. "Terry" Dolan, a founder and longtime chairman of the National Conservative Political Action Committee (NCPAC). NCPAC has been a primary focus of election-year publicity for four successive election cycles mainly because of its use of "independent expenditures." Under federal election law an independent expenditure is money spent by an individual or a group to support or defeat a candidate *which is made without consultation with, or the cooperation of, any candidate or campaign.*[86] In other words, the expenditure truly must be independent, and if it is, there are *no limits* on the amount of money that can be spent.[87]

Despite the attention that independent expenditures have drawn, relatively few PACs engage in them. Only 4 percent of all the multicandidate PACs reported making any independent outlays in 1981 or 1982.[88] Only a minority of nonconnected PACs and a few trade PACs have so far shown a real affinity for independent spending, and just a handful of corporate and labor PACs have used independent expenditures to any significant extent. But another 6 percent of the PAC community has also indicated a desire to expand into the independent arena in the near future,[89] and that proportion might well grow if Congress should pass major limitations on PAC giving. (This possibility will be discussed in the concluding chapter.)

Despite the limited number of PACs so far participating, independent spending has increased dramatically in recent years. In the 1976 congressional elections just $386,000 was expended independently, and in 1978 a bit less than that, $317,000. In the 1980 elections for the House and Senate, though, $2.3 million in independent expenditures were recorded, and by 1982 that amount had increased by 146 percent to $5.75 million. In the presidential sphere the $1.6 million in independent spending during the 1976 contest had grown to $13.7 million by the 1980 election. Ronald Reagan was the primary beneficiary: $10.6 million of the total was devoted to advocating his election, while Jimmy Carter received only about $28,000 in independent support.[90] Reagan received unsolicited but very helpful aid not merely in the general election but also in the primaries.[91] As Reagan approached New Hampshire's spending limit before that state's critical primary, the Fund for a Conservative Majority (FCM) bought $60,000 worth of pro-

Reagan media time and campaign literature, and the antiabortion Life Amendment PAC operated phone banks and conducted canvassing for Reagan in targeted wards. The FCM again came to the rescue in the Texas primary. When Reagan approached that state's spending limit, FCM pumped in $80,000 in pro-Reagan advertising and activities.

These positive expenditures for Reagan are the exception, since most independent spending is negative: it pays for attacks on the opposition. In the 1980 election cycle almost three-fifths of all congressional independent expenditures were negative; and in 1982 fully 80 percent of the independent money expressly advocated the defeat of some ninety House and Senate candidates. Ideological nonconnected PACs accounted for 93 percent of all 1980 independent expenditures and 84 percent of the 1982 total.[92] Even by 1982, after the formation of a number of liberal PACs, conservative groups outspent liberal committees independently by better than three to one. Consequently, most of the independent targets were Democratic incumbents, particularly those in the Senate (see Table 3–4). The seventy PACs making independent expenditures in 1982 comprised 91 percent of all independent spending recorded in that year[93]—and yet the total spent by PACs independently accounted for only 3 percent of all PAC outlays and less than 2 percent of all money devoted to the 1982 congressional elections. Indepen-

Table 3–4.
Independent Expenditures in 1981–1982

PACS REPORTING SPENDING THE MOST MONEY INDEPENDENTLY	INDEPENDENT EXPENDITURES		
	FOR	AGAINST	TOTAL
1. National Conservative Political Action Committee (NCPAC)	137,724	3,039,490	3,177,214
2. Citizens Organized to Replace Kennedy (of LAPAC)[a]	0	416,678	416,678
3. Fund for a Conservative Majority (FCM)	0	388,399	388,399
4. Life Amendment Political Action Committee (LAPAC)	36,455	219,055	255,510
5. NRA Political Victory Fund (National Rifle Association)	232,250	477	232,797
6. American Medical Association PAC (AMPAC)	211,624	0	211,624
7. Realtors PAC (R-PAC)	188,060	0	188,060
8. Progressive PAC (PROPAC)	8,090	134,795	142,885
9. Independent Action, Inc.	0	132,920	132,920
10. League of Conservation Voters (LCV)	129,163	0	129,163

Table 3–4. *(Continued)*

CANDIDATES FOR/AGAINST WHOM MOST MONEY WAS SPENT	ELECTION RESULT	INDEPENDENT EXPENDITURES		
		FOR	AGAINST	TOTAL
Senate				
1. Edward Kennedy (D–Mass.)	Won	500	1,146,135	1,146,635
2. Paul Sarbanes (D–Md.)	Won	29,501	697,763	727,264
3. Robert Byrd (D–W.Va.)	Won	9,184	270,749	279,933
4. John Melcher (D–Mont.)	Won	40,118	228,011	268,129
5. Lloyd Bentsen (D–Tex.)	Won	0	226,662	226,662
6. Lowell Weicker (R–Conn.)	Won	21,248	200,508	221,756
7. Howard Cannon (D–Nev.)	Lost	0	192,801	192,801
8. Edmund Brown, Jr. (D–Calif.)	Lost	7,632	146,346	153,978
9. Orrin Hatch (R–Utah)	Won	22,081	82,772	104,853
10. Harrison Schmitt (R–N.M.)	Lost	5,682	76,575	82,287
House				
1. Thomas P. O'Neill (D–Mass.)	Won	0	318,114	318,114
2. Jim Wright (D–Tex.)	Won	0	217,115	217,115
3. Jim Jones (D–Okla.)	Won	13,266	127,029	140,295
4. Dan Rostenkowski (D–Ill.)	Won	0	57,507	57,507
5. Bob Edgar (D–Pa.)	Won	24,762	8,943	33,705
6. Bill Chappell (D–Fla.)	Won	30,332	0	30,332
7. Jim Dunn (R–Mich.)	Lost	24,013	5,500	29,513
8. John Kasich (R–Ohio)	Won	27,294	0	27,294

Table 3–4. *(Continued)*

CANDIDATES FOR/AGAINST WHOM MOST MONEY WAS SPENT	ELECTION RESULT	INDEPENDENT EXPENDITURES FOR	AGAINST	TOTAL
9. Jim Coyne (R–Pa.)	Lost	25,019	1,681	26,700
10. Edward Weber (R–Ohio)	Lost	17,442	5,500	22,942
TOTALS				
All Democrats		369,461	4,047,034	4,416,495
All Republicans		882,579	550,046	1,432,625
All Incumbents		815,300	4,425,222	5,240,522
All Challengers		290,226	24,669	314,895
All Open-Seat Candidates		146,514	147,189	293,703
Grand Total		1,252,040	4,597,080	5,849,120

SOURCE: Federal Election Commission.
[a]Citizens Organized to Replace Kennedy was a special project of the Life Amendment Political Action Committee (LAPAC).

dent expenditure then is a growing but still relatively minor part of campaign finance in the United States. It assumes disproportionate importance because it draws the attention of the press and politicians with its often negative, hard-hitting character.

The notoriety of independent spending is due more to NCPAC than to all other PACs combined. Founded in 1975 by the conservative activists Charles Black, Terry Dolan, and Roger Stone, with the financial assistance of the direct-mail specialist Richard Viguerie, the survey prowess of pollster Arthur Finkelstein, and the imprimatur of Sen. Jesse Helms (R–N.C.), NCPAC has grown into a PAC conglomerate with a staff of several dozen and interests stretching across the conservative spectrum.[94] NCPAC is perhaps best known for its 1980 efforts to oust liberal Democratic Sens. Birch Bayh of Indiana, Frank Church of Idaho, Alan Cranston of California, John Culver of Iowa, Thomas Eagleton of Missouri, and George McGovern of South Dakota. NCPAC spent over $1 million attacking the six, and four (Bayh, Church, Culver, and McGovern) were indeed defeated —though how much NCPAC had to do with their downfalls in the midst of the Reagan landslide is an open question. NCPAC has relied heavily on media advertising, which has ranged from slickly produced, sophisticated spots to rough-cut pieces such as one aired against Democratic Sen. Robert

Byrd of West Virginia in 1982. This spot featured Elmer Fike, an unphotogenic member of the NCPAC policy board from Nitro, W.Va., belting out a personally composed song, "Bye-Bye, Bob Byrd." Far more effective was a 1980 NCPAC anti-Carter advertisement which utilized footage from the 1976 Ford-Carter debates.[95] After Carter's glowing 1976 promises on inflation and unemployment were contrasted with the disappointing reality of Carter's performance in office, the spot concluded with a jarring, rhythmic recording of Carter saying "I keep my promises, I keep my promises, promises, promises" and the announcer intoning, "We trusted Jimmy Carter once. Can we afford to trust him again?"

NCPAC's newsmaking is not limited to election seasons. For example, NCPAC led a protest march in Washington after the Russians downed a Korean Air Lines passenger jet in 1983. (Dolan, speaking at the rally, attributed the Soviet action "directly to [congressmen] who believe in appeasing the Soviet empire.")[96] Jane Fonda has been another NCPAC foil; Dolan urged a nationwide boycott of her health spas and "workout" books since some of their profits were devoted to the political activities of Fonda's husband, left-wing California Assemblyman Tom Hayden.[97] NCPAC underwrote a $50,000 radio advertising campaign on Washington, D.C., stations "to expose the regular and consistent leftist bias of the *Washington Post.*"[98] The Panama Canal treaties and the SALT II arms accords were also targets of NCPAC organizers in cooperation with other New Right groups.[99] NCPAC has even had its own television show, a weekly program in interview format called "American Forum," hosted by Dolan and aired intermittently in major media markets since 1981.

Such anti-incumbent, negative advertising has guaranteed NCPAC front-page headlines. The publicity has not always been to NCPAC's liking, however, because the committee has gotten its facts wrong with some frequency. As NCPAC cofounder Charles Black has admitted, "There have been a few mistakes made in terms of research."[100] In fundraising letters and other communications, NCPAC has made at least fifteen major blunders, accusing its targets of votes they did not cast or actions they did not take.[101] Sens. John Melcher (D–Mont.) and Quentin Burdick (D–N.D.) were charged with voting for the Panama Canal "giveaway," but Melcher and Burdick had voted against the treaties. Sen. Henry Jackson (D–Wash.), one of the staunchest proponents of a strong military defense during his years in Congress, was accused of being against "increased defense spending." Sen. Thomas Eagleton (D–Mo.), NCPAC said, had voted for giving $75 million in aid to Nicaragua and against funding for the neutron bomb; he had in fact voted against the Nicaragua aid and for continued neutron bomb outlays. Sen. Birch Bayh (D–Ind.) was supposed to have voted to slash the 1979 defense budget by $1.4 billion, according to NCPAC, but Bayh in fact had not even been present for the vote. Sen. Frank Church (D–Idaho), it was charged, voted for a congressional pay raise and also to empty Titan

I missile silos in his home state; Church had opposed the pay raise and gotten the U.S. Air Force to replace outdated Titan missiles with more advanced Minuteman missiles. Virginia Democratic gubernatorial candidate Henry Howell was accused of "urging that Virginia school children be bused into D.C.," a complete misrepresentation of his views. Antiabortion Sens. Melcher and Dennis DeConcini (D–Ariz.) were called pro-abortion, and so on. Some, though not all, of these errors were corrected by NCPAC, but only after the false charges had received wide publicity.

Other NCPAC tactics have also been roundly criticized. Democratic Rep. Stephen L. Neal of North Carolina filed a complaint with the U.S. Justice Department charging NCPAC with attempted bribery after he and other congressmen received "carrot and stick" letters containing a two-part NCPAC offer: (1) a pledge to run $40,000 in radio and newspaper ads praising each legislator if he would vote in favor of President Reagan's 1981 tax cut package, and (2) a threat to air the same amount of advertising attacking him if he didn't.[102] Another blunt instrument employed by NCPAC was a deceptive 1983 fundraising letter which used the death by cancer of congressman-elect Jack Swigert as the basis for an emotional appeal. Claiming a good bit of credit for Swigert's victory—when in fact NCPAC had given him only $500 in the general election—Dolan, who had never met Swigert personally, delivered the bad news of the death of his "good friend" to recipients of the letter. Dolan combined a moving plea for more cash with encouragement to send an enclosed sympathy card to Swigert's mother, who was never notified of NCPAC's efforts and was reportedly bewildered and upset when the notes started arriving.[103]

Aside from near-universal condemnation of many of NCPAC's tactics, political observers differ about the effectiveness of NCPAC's work. On the one hand Victor Kamber, who has adopted NCPAC's negative strategy for his own PROPAC, concluded, "If you plant the seeds of doubt about a senator, and back it up with facts and figures, then someone else can capitalize on it. I don't like it, but it's effective."[104] The advantage of this approach for groups like NCPAC is the ability to come into a state a year or more ahead of the general election and set the agenda for the nascent campaign with saturation advertising that attacks an incumbent on his perceived weaknesses, and almost inevitably raises the incumbent's "negative" in poll ratings.[105] Frequently, the challenger—the candidate NCPAC is indirectly favoring—is able to have the best of both worlds by benefiting from the incumbent's decline while keeping NCPAC and the fallout from the group's negativism at arm's length. As Dolan himself has explained it, "A group like ours could lie through its teeth, and the candidate it helps stays clean."[106] Or as NCPAC critic Lloyd Bentsen of Texas asserted, "These so-called independent groups . . . reap the advantage of lies and distortions and then force a candidate to spend funds to set the record straight."[107] Survey evidence suggests that NCPAC's advertising has had at least limited effectiveness in some Senate races;[108] even in cases where NCPAC failed and the incumbent won, says Dolan, "the incumbent's negatives were much higher when we finished."

These same surveys also reported significant voter backlash against NCPAC's negativism, however, and some of that backlash tarred the challenger as well as NCPAC.[109] Generally, the longer NCPAC stayed in a state, the higher visibility it achieved and the more controversial and harmful to its candidate it became. As a consequence, to the legion of NCPAC's critics such as Russell Hemenway of the liberal National Committee for an Effective Congress, independent expenditure is "totally inefficient. . . . Everything Dolan did was counterproductive."

Incumbents, moreover, have gradually learned how to respond to NCPAC's attacks.[110] Rather than ignoring NCPAC, as many made the mistake of doing several years ago, candidates have taken on NCPAC frontally and full force, decrying its negativism and directly tying it to their opponents.[111] Sen. John Melcher of Montana aired a television spot in 1982 showing suspicious-looking actors descending from a plane carrying NCPAC briefcases full of money. ("Have you heard what they're saying about 'Doc' Melcher?" one talking cow asks another about the veterinarian Melcher later in the commercial. "Looks like they've been stepping in what they've been trying to sell.") Sen. Robert Byrd's 1982 campaign in West Virginia featured an advertisement with his opponent's face sinking into a sea of mud. Sens. Paul Sarbanes of Maryland and Daniel Moynihan of New York used NCPAC's involvement in their races to generate enthusiasm for their candidacies among Democrats and liberal activists. Sen. Quentin Burdick attacked the "outsiders" who were trying to tell North Dakotans how to vote in 1982. And while these candidates' statements and commercials made it on the air, many of NCPAC's spots were not even broadcast by television and radio stations wary of NCPAC's reputation for inaccuracy.[112] In some states leading Democrats urged media outlets to reject the NCPAC ads, warning the stations that they might not be immune from libel suits if misrepresentations were aired.[113] (NCPAC filed suit against the stations that refused its advertising, but the complaint was later dismissed.)[114]

Some challengers were just as happy when NCPAC was sent packing. As one PAC manager surmised in explaining why his committee will not use independent expenditures:

> The candidate we would want to help already has a strategy. If we go out and put up billboards for him it might be the reverse of what's needed to get the message across. Then we've done him more harm than good. Basically, with independent expenditures you're substituting your own judgment for the judgment of the candidate and his campaign managers, and I don't think that's appropriate.[115]

Another PAC officer, a former campaign manager himself,[116] put it more forcefully: "Independent expenditure scares the daylights out of me. A third party comes in that doesn't know my strategy or my budget and interjects itself. This could terribly jeopardize a campaign." There have been cases of precisely this kind of well-intentioned but inept independent expenditure.[117]

Despite these doubts and all the criticism directed at it, and a less than successful 1982 electoral track record,[118] NCPAC shows no signs of fading away.[119] Its fundraising has remained strong (after a brief dip following NCPAC's 1982 defeats), and ambitious plans for future independent expenditures abound. The focus and tone of many of these expenditures will be different, however. First, the aura of invincibility that had surrounded NCPAC—whether justified or not—since its 1980 triumphs has dissipated. Dolan himself acknowledged in a letter to supporters after November 1982 that "Our experience in Maryland [with Sen. Paul Sarbanes] and West Virginia [with Sen. Robert Byrd] simply demonstrates that NCPAC cannot defeat Democratic Senators without the help of other factors."[120] Second, the approach taken in much future NCPAC advertising will be positive as well as negative. "It's a change recognizing the changed political atmosphere," says Dolan. "We want to keep the negatives off as much as possible." So NCPAC has instituted a "Constituent Congratulations Program" which will air television and radio commercials in selected media markets to highlight certain favored congressional incumbents' records and to salute voters in those areas for exercising their franchise wisely.[121] (The ads in each case conclude: "Congratulations . . . you've elected a winner.") For the 1984 presidential contest NCPAC formed a "Blacks for Reagan" committee and, more practically, produced a $60,000, twenty-five-minute film, *Ronald Reagan's America,* to air on television stations at crucial points during the election.

NCPAC's fundraising is also geared to positive, pro-Reagan themes. It commissioned a 200-page book on Reagan as a gift for direct-mail contributors, and held "American Heroes for Reagan" rallies (featuring Dale Evans, among others) to sign up grassroots volunteers and donors around the country. Dolan called the efforts NCPAC's new face: a "shameless appeal to patriotism that Ronald Reagan, the modern-day FDR, so well embodies." But then in a return to NCPAC's old negative face, Dolan added, "Of course we also want to focus on the fact that whoever the Democratic nominee is will be a committed leftist." As early as the New Hampshire primary in February 1984, NCPAC launched a $2-million negative advertising campaign aimed at Democratic presidential candidate Walter Mondale.

On the congressional level NCPAC retains plans for some purely negative independent expenditures, but their timing may well be altered. The NCPAC pollster Arthur Finkelstein has suggested that NCPAC should use early negatives to set the campaign agenda and to introduce doubts about the incumbents, then cease and desist for the rest of the campaign, perhaps with a final volley in the closing hours of the election so that backlash does not have time to build.[122]

NCPAC has shared the independent spotlight with the Congressional Club, the highest spending PAC in the nation, which was founded in 1973 by Sen. Jesse Helms and the Raleigh, N.C., lawyer Thomas Ellis to pay off a $150,000 debt from Helms's first Senate race.[123] As with NCPAC, Richard Viguerie provided direct-mail services, which helped the Club accumulate more than 300,000 donors and an election year staff of nearly fifty by 1982. In 1980 the Club spent $4.5 million in independent expenditures on Ronald Reagan's behalf, although the PAC's main job, according to Terry Dolan, "is to create a political constituency for Jesse Helms." The Club's relationship with Helms, who remains honorary chairman, is close but still detached. "Helms is a sort of philosophical cover," explains the Club's manager Carter Wrenn. "He does not get involved in the day-to-day operations of the Club . . . [but] if we see something we think will impact him personally, then we'll call him. . . ." Nevertheless, the Club seems keenly attuned to Helms's needs and activities. In 1983 when Helms strenuously opposed establishing a national holiday to mark Dr. Martin Luther King, Jr.'s birthday, the Club quickly capitalized on the senator's stand among conservative direct-mail recipients.[124] And while the Club could not pretend to spend money independently of Helms for his 1984 reelection campaign, it did undertake nonpartisan but selective registration drives to benefit Helms. The Club also spent $300,000 to attack the tax plans of Helms's projected Democratic opponent, Gov. Jim Hunt, in 1982.

Another conservative PAC that has invested heavily in independent expenditures is the Fund for a Conservative Majority (FCM), which planned a $3.5-million series of television commercials and a major volunteer recruitment drive for Ronald Reagan's 1984 reelection campaign. Most of the FCM's independent spending has been devoted to presidential contests,[125] but FCM aired some spots in the 1982 congressional election, including one of GOP New Right Rep. John LeBoutillier urging the electorate to "repeal [House Speaker Tip] O'Neill" and sweep in a Republican Congress. (Voters had other ideas; LeBoutillier himself was ousted.) Antiabortion groups have also favored independent spending. The Life Amendment PAC, for instance, during Sen. Edward Kennedy's 1982 reelection effort in Massachusetts, distributed over a million copies of a vicious comic book entitled "Every Family Has One," which dwelt in lurid detail on the Chappaquiddick accident.[126]

Gun PACs, led by the National Rifle Association's Political Victory Fund (NRA-PVF), have been inclined to independent spending too.[127] The NRA-PVF spent about $675,000 independently in 1980 and 1982, sending postcards or letters of endorsement to NRA members and hunters, producing brochures endorsing certain candidates, and airing radio commercials and printing newspaper advertisements.[128] Unlike the practices of many PACs, most of NRA-PVF's independent spending has been of a positive nature, though the PAC made a $166,000 exception to attack Sen. Edward Kennedy during his 1980 presidential campaign. The Committee for the Survival of a Free Congress, which concentrates on organizing campaigns and training political workers, supplements its in-kind contributions with one independent spending effort: it has bought newspaper advertisements in congressional districts throughout the country trumpeting incumbents' liberal voting records and asking for potential conservative candidates to step forward and write a CSFC "Candidate Search Committee." (This device may seem a bit outlandish, but Richard Nixon was recruited for his first congressional race by similar newspaper ads run in California in 1946.)[129] Finally, the Christian Right PACs have also used independent spending methods despite the doubts of some in the movement about the spiritual morality of negative campaigns.[130]

Independent spending is less frequent on the liberal side of the PAC spectrum for several reasons.[131] First, most of the liberal groups were begun later, and have far smaller budgets than many conservative PACs. Second, progressive PAC leaders remain skeptical that independent expenditures are effective, or at least as effective as other campaign techniques to which their money can be devoted. And third, there reportedly remains considerable resistance among grassroots liberal donors to the idea of negative independent expenditures, making it difficult for a number of liberal PACs to raise money for independent purposes. The oldest liberal PAC, the National Committee for an Effective Congress (NCEC), founded in 1948 by Maurice Rosenblatt with the backing of Eleanor Roosevelt, takes a stand on this issue. NCEC refuses to undertake any independent expenditures both because it regards its other programs as more important and because it actively recruits candidates, which makes uncoordinated expenditures legally dubious in many cases. Other liberal PACs that prefer to make only positive, nonindependent outlays include the Americans for Democratic Action PAC and the Council for a Liveable World's Peace PAC.[132]

The Progressive Political Action Committee (PROPAC) took the opposite view when it was formed by Victor Kamber in 1981. As "an outgrowth of the frustrations of the 1980 elections," PROPAC adopted negative independent spending as a legitimate tool to fight similar conservative tactics, even while viewing the strategy as distasteful. "The theory was that as long as there was an independent expenditure committee on the right that was successful, the only way you could do away with independent expenditures was if you balanced the system and caused enough frustration with the political forces to make them throw out the whole system," Kamber explained.[133] Kamber also found the press receptive: "It was easy to get press coverage and attention just because we were perceived as the alternative to NCPAC."[134] PROPAC launched newspaper advertising campaigns attacking NCPAC and defending one of the conservatives' prime targets, Maryland Sen. Paul Sarbanes. It placed a series of North Carolina newspaper ads lampooning Sen. Jesse Helms as a "circus ringmaster" and a Rube Goldberg–like "congressional obstacle." It aimed hard-hitting negative ads against Republican Sen. Orrin Hatch of Utah, S. I. Hayakawa of California, and Harrison Schmitt of New Mexico. The anti-Schmitt pieces, portraying the incumbent as a do-nothing pretty boy, were later cited by GOP officials in the state as having helped prepare the way for Schmitt's defeat by Democrat Jeff Bingaman in 1982.[135]

Even more so than NCPAC, PROPAC is controversial within its own ideological tent. While some Democrats like Rep. Barbara Mikulski of Maryland call PROPAC "one of our front line S.W.A.T. teams,"[136] the Democratic chairman of Utah demanded that PROPAC stay out of his state in 1982, lest its negativism backfire.[137] PACs like NCEC that do not use independent expenditures are not terribly tolerant of PROPAC either. Says NCEC's Russell Hemenway: "PROPAC has not been that successful, they don't do much. . . . As for Kamber, I once fired him. He's incompetent. . . . He's very good at his own public relations." Kamber has a similar view of NCEC and Hemenway: "I think NCEC is ineffective. They don't do anything. They live on a reputation thirty years old. I deal with too many candidates who are . . . tired of getting second-rate services [from NCEC]. . . . It's an elitist group that hasn't opened its ranks to the younger community." These sorts of quarrels among ideological soulmates are standard across the spectrum, of course; Terry Dolan warned Kamber that PROPAC would receive more criticism from its allies than from its enemies. The criticism (along with mounting debts) exacted a toll in 1984, when PROPAC became at least temporarily moribund.[138]

A few other liberal groups have engaged in independent spending. Rep. Morris Udall's Independent Action PAC aimed negative mail and newspaper advertising at many of the same 1982 targets as PROPAC. (Like PROPAC, though, Independent Action essentially abandoned independent spending in the 1984 election cycle.) Democrats for the '80s, a PAC founded by Mrs. Averell Harriman in 1981,[139] paid for $20,000 in radio advertisements defending Sen. Paul Sarbanes from the 1981 NCPAC onslaught.[140] The League of Conservation Voters (LCV) has mounted extensive door-to-door canvasses and literature drops independent of the campaign organizations of favored candidates; some contenders have credited the LCV efforts with providing their margins of victory.[141] These substantial independent efforts on the left are clearly exceptional, however. Most liberal activity on the independent front is far outdistanced by conservative groups. In the 1980 election, for example, twenty-one antiabortion groups independently spent over $250,000 on congressional races; just a single pro-choice organization, the National Abortion Rights Action League, recorded any independent expenditure (a total of less than $3,000).[142] And while the NRA-PVF was expending $442,000 and the Gun Owners of America another $114,000 independently in 1980, Handgun Control's PAC spent just $43,000 on independent activities.

Corporate PACs have been even slower than liberal ideological groups to add independent spending to their political repertoire. As early as 1977 the U.S. Chamber of Commerce was encouraging corporate PACs to adopt the tactic,[143] but for the most part the plea fell on deaf ears. "Since we don't use it," says BIPAC's Bernadette Budde, "I can't imagine the average corporate PAC undertaking it." In both 1980 and 1982 all corporate PACs together spent about $20,000 on independent expenditures, and barring major legislative limitations on PACs, it is doubtful that more than a handful will seriously launch independent ventures in the near future. In general the corporate committees are too small, too politically inexperienced, and too reluctant to devote the significant staff time and planning resources necessary to undertake independent activities successfully. This is not true of large trade association PACs, however, which often have the staff and technical expertise required. Both the American Medical Association's PAC (AMPAC) and the Realtors' PAC (R-PAC) have already demonstrated a readiness to conduct independent efforts. AMPAC has been making independent expenditures since 1978; in 1982 it spent $212,000 on television and radio spots and targeted direct mail for thirteen House candidates. In previous elections AMPAC paid for buttons and magazine advertising independently.[144] All of AMPAC's spending, like R-PAC's, has been of a positive nature, supporting rather than opposing candidates. In 1982 the Realtors allocated $188,000 to independent efforts, most of which went to direct mail but some also to telephone voter-identification and get-out-the-vote activity.[145] R-PAC's direct mail made sure that their independent expenditure, though separate from a campaign, did not go unnoticed. Each voter receiving an R-PAC letter was urged to mail an enclosed postcard to the candidate which read in part: "I have just received a letter from the REALTORS® Political Action Committee in support of your reelection . . . and I wanted you to know that I will cast my vote for you. . . ."

PACS AS A CAMPAIGN ISSUE

ANNOUNCER: Who owns Charlie Dougherty? Well, when Dougherty needs money for his reelection he turns to every special-interest group imaginable.

VISUAL: PAC money totals flash on screen.

ANNOUNCER: Corporate PACs own Charlie Dougherty.
Republican groups own Charlie Dougherty.
National conservative groups own Dougherty.

Oil PACs own Dougherty.
The National Rifle Association has a piece of Charlie Dougherty.
Everybody but the people who count—the people of the Northeast [Philadelphia].
We need Bob Borski, the Democrat, for *us.*[146]

This anti-PAC television advertisement helped Philadelphia Democrat Bob Borski to oust Republican U.S. Rep. Charles Dougherty in the 1982 election. Borski was not alone in his use of the PAC issue; the subject was a focus of debate in at least four dozen other congressional races that year. Because of the growth of PAC campaign contributions and the attention paid by the press to them, PACs are fast becoming a consistently important issue in House and Senate elections.

The PAC issue is raised in a number of different ways at election time. Sometimes the stress is on the sheer amount of PAC money a candidate has accepted. The successful 1982 Democratic challenger Robert Torricelli of New Jersey capitalized on Republican incumbent Harold Hollenbeck's PAC receipts by pledging to limit his PAC gifts to one-third of his expenditures; Hollenbeck had secured 58 percent of his 1980 reelection treasury from PACs. Other candidates are criticized for taking "out-of-state" PAC funds. Incumbent Democrat James R. Jones of Oklahoma managed to turn back spirited 1982 opposition from the GOP's Richard Freeman, who claimed that a majority of Jones's war chest was filled by out-of-state PACs.

In still other races the emphasis is placed on the alleged connection between a congressman's floor votes and his acceptance of PAC gifts at campaign time. Democratic incumbent Thomas A. Luken of Ohio successfully weathered allegations in 1982 that he had fought for the positions of the American Medical Association and the auto industry in exchange for their reelection cash. In addition some candidates, assisted by interest groups, have sought to use PAC contributions as evidence of an opponent's ideology, relying on the old refrain that "birds of a feather. . . ." Politicians who accepted PAC money from Environmental Action's "Filthy Five" corporations (Weyerhauser, Dow Chemical, Occidental Petroleum, Amoco Oil, and Republic Steel) were tagged antienvironmentalist and tolerant of industrial pollution.[147] In a few cases PACs have become an issue because PAC officials decided to run for Congress themselves.[148] Their access to money can be a powerful asset, as Republican William Moshofsky of Oregon proved in 1982. A former board member of BIPAC and a government relations executive for Georgia-Pacific Company, Moshofsky raised almost $450,000 and held entrenched incumbent House Democrat Les AuCoin to 54 percent of the vote.

Occasionally a PAC itself is so controversial that its involvement in a race may steal the spotlight from the candidates. On the conservative side of the spectrum, NCPAC is certainly one of these, while on the left there is no better example than the Human Rights Campaign Fund (HRCF). In 1982 the HRCF, the gay rights political action committee, gave about $150,000 to 119 congressional candidates (69 of whom were incumbents and 95 of whom were elected.)[149] At least sixteen House incumbents, about equally split between Democrats and Republicans, refused the HRCF gifts, and according to the PAC's treasurer Stephen Endean, "We purposely did not always ask people [in advance] if they wanted our money because it was my perception that another thirty or forty candidates would have declined." There were some surprises for HRCF. A few on-the-record gay rights supporters refused the contributions anyway, possibly to avoid drawing more attention to their stand. Others, such as David Sellers of Georgia, who challenged incumbent Democrat Larry McDonald, a sponsor of antigay legislation, kept the donation. "I would have bet money he would have sent it back," said Endean. "I'm sure he won't be running again." In fact Sellers did run to succeed McDonald after the incumbent's death in the 1983 Soviet shooting of a Korean airliner; the HRCF gift was not a prominent issue, but Sellers lost again.

Other than Sellers and a few regional compatriots, HRCF avoided the South generally and the Bible Belt in particular in choosing the recipients of its funds, realizing that a Bible Belt candidate who accepted its money "would have to sweat blood," as Endean put it. Despite its careful selectivity, the HRCF donations became an issue in a number of races. In some cases the candidates simply declared ignorance of the gift or of HRCF's mission, despite a very explicit letter that accompanied the transmission of the PAC's contribution.[150] Other candidates reacted to the criticism by turning to the HRCF for even more help. Pennsylvania Democratic Rep. Robert Edgar's acceptance of an HRCF donation resulted in signs reading "Homos for Edgar" along a local freeway. HRCF responded to an Edgar campaign request by getting local gays to set up telephone banks on Edgar's behalf. The HRCF is yet another PAC whose political effort generates more PAC activity by those who disagree. Some of the evangelical Christian and New Right PACs are gearing up to make gay rights—and the HRCF—a major focus of future elections.[151]

The PAC issue has not been entirely restricted to congressional elections. In 1984 it became a major topic in the race for the Democratic presidential nomination. At the outset of his campaign Walter Mondale vigorously denounced PACs, despite operating a large political action committee himself (to be discussed later in this chapter). Pledging to accept no PAC money in his presidential bid, Mondale declared: "No citizens with genuine and legitimate interests in the conduct of government will have to pay me to listen to them, either on the campaign trail or in the White House."[152] As it happened, however, Mondale's "no-PAC money" pledge did not apply to committees formed by supporters who were seeking to win election as Mondale delegates to the Democratic National Convention. Provided they were independent of direction from the official Mondale campaign, these committees were permitted under Federal Election Commission guidelines to raise and spend unlimited amounts of money on such election-related activities as campaign literature and telephone bank canvassing. Moreover, these committees' expenditures did not count toward the overall $24.2 million campaign-spending ceiling in effect for the preconvention period—a substantial advantage for Mondale since his organization was much closer to the spending limit than was the late-blooming campaign of Sen. Gary Hart.

Approximately $300,000 in PAC gifts (mainly from labor unions) were accepted by the 129 Mondale delegate committees operating in nineteen states, and the infusion of funds was particularly helpful to Mondale in the crucial New York primary. Hart wasted no time decrying the Mondale delegates' violation of their candidate's PAC pledge, though. A complaint was filed with the FEC questioning the legality of the separate delegate committees, some of which had been formed with direction from the national Mondale campaign, and a thirty-second Hart television advertisement saturated the airwaves in April, declaring that Mondale's "manipulation of money through the backroom is politics as usual and it's wrong." In the face of Hart's continuing assaults Mondale retreated, finally agreeing to shut down all his delegate committees and even to return all their PAC contributions. While admitting no wrongdoing, the Mondale campaign paid an $18,500 civil penalty and refunded almost $380,000 in public matching funds to the U.S. Treasury in December 1984 in order to end the FEC investigation of the matter.

Hart's purity on the PAC issue, like Mondale's, withers a bit upon closer examination. While neither Hart's presidential campaign nor his delegates took PAC money in 1984, the senator solicited and accepted $255,770 in PAC gifts during his close reelection campaign in Colorado in 1980. And significantly, while Hart may have made some political capital by banning PAC money from his campaign, his financial sacrifice was probably not great. No presidential candidate has ever received more than about 3 percent of his war chest from PACs. (Even Mondale's delegate committees did not exceed this proportion.) Public funds and individual donations comprise the bulk of preconvention presidential financing,[153] and PACs choose to concentrate their efforts on congressional races.

A number of congressional candidates and incumbents of both parties have made a more substantial sacrifice than Messrs. Mondale and Hart by refusing all PAC money. They have succeeded in defusing the PAC issue for themselves and at the same time have positioned their campaigns to attack opponents who do accept the gifts. Sens. David Boren (D–Okla.), William Proxmire (D–Wis.), and Warren Rudman (R–N.H.), and Reps.

Barber Conable (R–N.Y.), Andrew Jacobs (D–Ind.), Jim Leach (R–Iowa), and Bud Schuster (R–Pa.) are among the roughly two dozen congressmen with an announced policy of refusing all or most PAC gifts. (Some go further: Proxmire refuses all contributions of any kind, while Conable accepts no more than $50 from any group or individual.) Most of these legislators are motivated by a sincere belief that campaign contributions are, or appear to be, corrupting. But a few, like ex-Rep. Eugene Atkinson of Pennsylvania, may be motivated more by expedience. As a Kennedy Democrat, Atkinson refused on principle to accept PAC money, but after his conversion to Reagan Republicanism in 1981 he raised more than $40,000 from business and trade PACs when faced with a difficult (and ultimately losing) reelection campaign.

The PACs themselves have treated these nay-sayers in interesting ways. One PAC director said, completely seriously, "I wish I had a list of all the congressmen who won't take PAC contributions. I'd give to all of them: I'd get noticed and get my money back too!" Many PACs treat any incumbent respectfully, even one who is critical of them. When anti-PAC Rep. Jim Leach of Iowa was opposed in the 1984 GOP primary by an outspoken conservative who was closely associated with two PACs, the challenger had a difficult time raising business PAC money. As one business PAC official put it, "The PAC people are too much practical politicians to [oppose Leach]. They won't throw their money away just for spite."[154] Another congressman who had sought legislative limits on PAC contributions, Republican Thomas Railsback of Illinois, received more than 30 percent of his early 1982 campaign funds from PACs, especially those connected to the pharmaceutical and entertainment industries which had bills pending in a House committee on which Railsback sat.[155] And in a wry twist, incumbent Republican Rep. Cooper Evans of Iowa, who had refused PAC money in 1980 and won only narrowly, decided to accept it in 1982, but met some resistance from PAC managers resentful over his earlier stance. Evans agreed to let PAC manager Peter Lauer of AMPAC intervene to smooth ruffled feathers. As an in-kind contribution, Lauer sent "a letter of explanation" about Evans's transgression and conversion to 800 of the major PACs. A nonincumbent challenger who alienates PACs is less likely to be given such consideration. In fact a challenger's refusal to take PAC funds can cause political prognosticators virtually to write off the candidate's chances of victory, since they assume his campaign will be inadequately financed.[156]

SOLICITATION OF PACS BY CANDIDATES

Some of those [anti-PAC] officeholders call me a whore so I'll call them hypocrites. The best example is [Sen.] Bob Dole [of Kansas] who says, "When the PACs give, they want something in return besides good government." Then I get a letter from him asking for money for his PAC. I also get a telegram from him two weeks out from the election saying, "I see you have not supported [a Dole-backed candidate in Kansas]. Deeply disappointed. Signed, Bob Dole, Chairman, Senate Finance Committee." What kind of sledgehammer is that? I find those things deeply disturbing.

—Peter Lauer of AMPAC

As Lauer suggests, Sen. Robert Dole has received a good deal of publicity, most of it favorable, for his critical one-liners about PACs. What Dole does not add is that he accepted over $420,000 from PACs in his 1980 Senate reelection campaign.[157] Dole has plenty of company on both sides of the congressional aisle: many legislators are becoming familiar with the two-way street of campaign finance. They careen up one side with the voters, piously decrying special interest politics and calling for reform, and then quietly slip down the other side soliciting the PACs. Congressmen like Democrat John Bryant of Texas understand the contradiction, even hypocrisy, contained in the divergence of their rhetoric and electoral habits, but say the system forces them into it: "I'm a realist and I play by the rules of the day. Right now, I am pursuing campaign contributions in any way I can, and I'll continue to play by those rules until they are changed."[158]

The rules by which candidates solicit PACs are dramatically different for incumbents and challengers. Incumbents are known quantities who usually have contacts galore from previous elections. They know whom to call and how to apply pressure. "The amount given is directly proportional to the amount of pressure [the congressman] puts on you," observed Ben Albert of COPE. "You know, they always say they're in trouble."[159] The incumbents often do not have to make a special effort to initiate contact; they are asked to speak before many groups that have PACs and they attend hearings and receptions by the hundreds which are populated with PAC representatives. (Of course, other congressmen compete for PAC attention at these receptions. In June 1982 the National Association for Association PACs held a modest wine-and-cheese party and eighty congressmen showed up, outnumbering the PAC managers present by better than two to one.)[160]

Often incumbents protect themselves from charges of influence peddling by completely delegating campaign fundraising to staff members, who nonetheless solicit PACs in their boss's name. "If the congressman is smart, he just stays the hell out and lets his staff handle PACs," says Steven Stockmeyer of TARPAC. Both the staffs and their employers can play rough, though. Richard Armstrong of the Public Affairs Council calls some of their tactics "bordering on extortion. . . . I get calls from their office or a senator calls and says he's surprised my name is not on the [contributor's] list. . . . It's brutal." Almost all the PAC managers I interviewed decried the increasing pressure incumbents put on the PACs to make earlier and earlier gifts to their reelection kitties. One PAC official mentioned that a request for a maximum contribution of $5,000 had been received in 1983 from GOP Sen. Pete Wilson of California. Wilson had just taken office in January 1983, but the money was not needed to retire a debt; it was to be deposited in his 1988 reelection account. Incumbents hope that a bulging bank balance will deter challengers, and "tactically, it's a very smart move," agreed the PAC manager. "But it puts a lot of pressure on us in the PAC community."

Incumbents may solicit PACs, but challengers must truly seduce them. As we discussed earlier, most PACs are not inclined to support challengers, so the competition among nonincumbents is much stiffer for the fewer dollars available. The National Republican Congressional Committee tries to disabuse its challengers of their preconceived PAC notions early on:

Don't expect to understand why a PAC acts as it does. Each PAC is different from all others and is as unpredictable as most human behavior.

Don't expect a PAC to give to you simply because you're a Republican and support the free enterprise system.

Don't think you're going to get a lot of PAC money early in your campaign.[161]

PAC-hungry challengers are also urged to send "PAC kits," a kind of investment portfolio, to the appropriate officials. The kits usually contain a profile of the candidate and district, past voting results, a sketch of the candidate's orientation, budget, issue stands, endorsements, and perhaps derogatory information about the opponent. While some candidates send out a "Dear PAC" form letter, the wiser ones personalize the kit's cover letter, perhaps including specific comments on each group's legislative agenda. The cover letters also frequently emulate the emotional appeals of direct mail; the candidates passionately explain why their election is essential to the PAC's goals as well as to the survival of Western civilization. To round out the packet, excerpts are included from the latest poll of their district, assuming it is favorable or can be construed that way; one good survey is worth a thousand other enclosures to political businessmen seeking hard data to guide their investment decisions. Sophisticated campaigns do not stop with a PAC kit mailing. They follow up with frequent "newsnotes," telephone calls from the staff, and personal visits from the candidate. Repeated solicitation is often the key to a PAC contribution for a challenger. A PAC chairman, when asked why one particular nonincumbent was funded, spoke admiringly of the candidate's campaign manager: "He's a persistent sonofabitch."[162] Moreover, a number of political consultants and firms now offer PAC solicitation services which include targeted direct-mail or telephone fundraising. These specialists work for a commission fee on the PAC gifts they secure.[163]

Most challengers schedule one or more forays to Washington, D.C., to visit PACs, though their time spent campaigning at home is precious. "Challengers have an illusion that there is this vast rainbow over the country that comes to an end over the Beltway [that rings the District of Columbia]. So there's this pot of gold in Washington and all they have to do is go there and come out clutching $50,000," notes Marty Franks, executive director of the Democratic Congressional Campaign Committee. His counterpart at the National Republican Congressional Committee, Joe Gaylord, agrees: "Considering all the hoops that challengers have to jump through to get $250 contributions from PACs, if they spent that time raising money back in their home districts they'd be better off. . . . But they have this strange logic that to be legitimate back in the home district they have to get Washington PAC money." The irony is that most of the large corporate and trade PACs with Washington offices simply tell visitors that before any consideration can be given them, they must secure the support of the local PAC officials. Still, the myth persists, and the hopefuls come in droves. BANKPAC, for instance, meets in Washington with about eighty candidates each election cycle. "When a candidate come to town," says TARPAC's Steve Stockmeyer, "he feels he's got to make the rounds. He thinks it's like going through fraternity rush."

CANDIDATE PACS

Some candidates not only solicit political action committees, they are forming their own. This has been especially prevalent at the presidential level, and in recent years most major White House hopefuls have created PACs as the vehicles to take them to 1600 Pennsylvania Avenue. Creation of a PAC has some important political and financial advantages beyond signaling that a presidential candidate is serious. First, it enables a contender to travel widely, make speeches, and establish contacts before formally announcing his candidacy. This can be done without charge to the eventual presidential campaign committee or against the overall or state spending limits imposed by FECA.[164] Second, a candidate PAC can afford a head start on organizing and funding the campaign by training potential staffers and developing a file of contributors through direct mailings to prospects. The money raised by the PAC can be used as a fund not only for the candidate, his staff, and his headquarters, but also for contributions to state and local candidates which create debts of gratitude that can be repaid at the presidential nominating convention. The PAC allows greater financial latitude as well; as an individual the presidential hopeful can give each favored candidate only $1,000, but his PAC can donate $5,000. Similarly, his supporters can give him only $1,000 apiece but can quintuple that amount for his PAC.

The first presidential PAC belonged to Ronald Reagan. Formed in January 1977 and called Citizens for the Republic (CFTR), the Reagan PAC replaced his 1976 nomination committee and inherited its balance of over $1 million.[165] In the 1977–1978 election cycle CFTR spent $4.5 million, including almost $600,000 on contributions to 400 candidates and many local parties. With a staff of almost thirty (including even a cartoonist), CFTR expanded the Reagan direct-mail contributor list from 100,000 to 300,000, held political workshops, sponsored Reagan's speaking tours, and published a bimonthly newsletter that was a showcase for Reagan's views. Even after Reagan announced for president, and indeed after he took office, CFTR continued operating separately from the campaign committee and the White House and raised nearly $2 million for the 1980 elections and almost $2.4 million for the 1982 midterm contests. Over that period GOP candidates' coffers were enriched by about $575,000 of CFTR's money. Reagan's PAC was not alone on the GOP side. The John Connally Citizens Forum, George Bush's Fund for Limited Government, Sen. Robert Dole's Campaign America, and Sen. Howard Baker's Republican Majority Fund were all active in the pre-1980 maneuvering. Baker's and Dole's PACs continued to function after their 1980 defeats in anticipation of future presidential bids. The Dole PAC raised over $270,000 during 1981–1982, while Baker's garnered almost $2 million and contributed $578,000 to GOP candidates. Baker and Dole were joined by another congressman who occasionally hums "Hail to the Chief," U.S. Rep. Jack Kemp of New York. His PAC, Campaign for Prosperity, raised almost $250,000 and gave $106,000 to 111 GOP House and Senate candidates in 1982.

The Democrats have been almost as active on the PAC front. Walter Mondale's Committee for the Future of America, established shortly after Mondale left the vice-presidency in 1981, raised and spent $2.5 million before Mondale launched his presidential campaign. It gave about $700,000 to 200 Democratic candidates.[166] It spent almost $1 million to develop a direct-mail list of 23,000 Mondale donors, a bonanza which it rented to the Mondale presidential campaign committee for less than $1,200.[167] Some of its contributions to other candidates benefited Mondale as much as the recipients. The PAC produced two one-minute television advertisements which showed Mondale discussing Social Security and unemployment; at the end of each spot Mondale would add a personal endorsement of any 1982 congressional candidate who wanted to use it. The Mondale PAC absorbed the production costs, but the congressional candidates paid to air the spots —which advertised Mondale as much as the candidate sponsors.

Mondale's frequent attacks on PACs did not extend to his own, of course. Despite his pledge not to accept any PAC money for his presidential campaign, Mondale's PAC took in $200,000 in PAC gifts—including more than $50,000 after the Mondale "no-PAC funds" declaration.[168] Mondale's early chief opponent for the 1984 Democratic presidential nomination, Sen. John

Glenn, also formed a PAC, but like his entire campaign Glenn's PAC was slow in starting and just a pale shadow of Mondale's. Called the National Council on Public Policy, it began in the autumn of 1982 and raised only about $120,000 to finance Glenn's midterm election travels.[169] Far more impressive was noncandidate Sen. Edward M. Kennedy's Fund for a Democratic Majority, which slightly exceeded the Mondale PAC's fundraising total in 1981–1982. Another ex-presidential contender, California's former governor Jerry Brown, formed a small PAC, the Committee for California, after leaving office in 1983.

Candidate PACs are hardly reserved for presidential candidates alone. A growing number of individual congressmen and state officeholders are acquiring PACs as well. North Carolina Sen. Jesse Helms's Congressional Club is second on the list of PAC fundraisers, trailing only NCPAC. Supporters of Helms's 1984 Democratic opponent, Gov. James Hunt, formed a competing PAC, the North Carolina Campaign Fund, to prepare the way for Hunt's senatorial challenge.[170] House Speaker Thomas P. O'Neill has his Democratic Speaker's Club to support the party's House candidates, and Senate Minority Leader Robert Byrd has a similar PAC for Democratic Senate contenders. U.S. Rep. Andy Ireland of Florida, at the time a Democrat, founded America's Small Business PAC, which gave half of its ten $2,500 gifts in 1982 to Republicans[171]—presaging Ireland's personal switch to the Republican party in 1984. Another congressman, Democrat Henry Waxman of California, used his PAC to distribute almost $73,000 to twenty-five liberal House and Senate contenders in 1982. (One Democratic political consultant called Waxman's PAC "the closest thing to a Democratic political organization we've got right now.")[172]

It is not uncommon today for several officeholders in a single state to operate competing PACs. In Virginia, for example, Republican Sen. Paul Trible, Democratic Gov. Charles Robb, and GOP Rep. Stanford E. Parris have used PACs to extend their influence within the state; all three made large outlays to state legislative candidates in 1983. Robb's committee, called Virginians for Good Government (or "ChuckPAC," after the governor's nickname), also demonstrates the hazards of PAC operation for an officeholder.[173] Robb was first embarrassed when it was publicly revealed that the PAC's formation had never been announced, and that half the committee's original funding had come from undisclosed gifts made after Robb's election as governor. Robb then directed that all donors be publicly named, and the General Assembly passed a law (with Robb's backing) making such disclosure mandatory. But soon after, ChuckPAC had to return contributions totaling $3,000 to two individuals who had been linked to financial scandal (one of them a convicted highway bid-rigger). And some of Robb's contributors griped publicly and privately about the use of $36,000 of ChuckPAC's funds to renovate office space for his wife, the former Lynda Bird Johnson, and to support a pet project of hers. Robb gave up and did what few of his political fellows have done: he closed up shop, decommissioning his political action committee in late 1983.

STATE AND LOCAL PACS: "NEW FEDERALISM" IN CAMPAIGN FINANCE

American politics, perhaps even more than American government, is decentralized, and the PAC community has begun to reflect fully this federated arrangement. The growth of PACs at the national level has been matched, and in some cases exceeded, by the increase in PAC number and size recorded in states and localities across the country. Almost a third (32 percent) of all multicandidate PACs had associated state-level committees by 1982; most PACs have one or two, but the large trade associations usually have PACs in most or all of the fifty states.[174] Labor PACs have traditionally been the most active in the state arena, and 42 percent have at least one separately registered PAC at the state level. Nonconnected committees, by contrast, have been the least ambitious state organizers: just a fourth have formed any state affiliates.

There is little question that PACs contribute a growing proportion of campaign money in states and localities, particularly in races for the state legislature.[175] In Washington state there were 114 PACs with receipts of $2 million in 1978; just two years later, 200 PACs raising a total of $4.3 million were on the scene.[176] In Illinois the number of PACs registered with the state board of elections has grown from 54 in 1974 to 372 in 1982, with a record number of new entrants in the latter year.[177] In Michigan the number of active state PACs rose from 325 in 1978 to 478 in 1982; six local Chamber of Commerce PACs were in existence in 1980, and fifty-four two years later.[178] In California, state PACs accounted for 45 percent of all $100+ contributions to 1980 candidates for the state legislature, and by 1982 eight different PACs were pouring more than $200,000 apiece into races for the state House and Senate.[179]

The growth of state-level committees is only part the "new federalism" of PACs. More than four in ten of the *federal* multicandidate PACs also contributed to state and local candidates in 1981–1982.[180] During that period an average of 12 percent of all PAC funds was devoted to state candidates, and another 6 percent went to local candidates. Once again labor PACs were especially likely to contribute to state and local candidates, while nonconnected PACs were the least inclined. Moreover, in those states where it is legal to do so, 63 percent of the parent unions of labor PACs and 31 percent of the parent companies of corporate PACs make contributions to state and local candidates and parties directly from union or corporate treasuries. (Twenty-eight states permit direct corporate contributions and forty-one states allow union treasury gifts.)[181]

State PACs, like the national variety, are not a completely new phenomenon. Labor unions have had active state PACs for decades,[182] and a number of trade associations operated state PACs before their national PAC was formed. Organizations like the California Public Health League (predecessor of the California Medical Association's CALPAC) along with an activist group of physicians in Oregon "were what really got the American Medical Association going" at the federal level, according to AMPAC's Peter Lauer. Much PAC development has moved from the national to the state level, however. The major political decision for most companies and trade associations seems to have been the one to form a national PAC. Once that threshold was crossed, it was relatively easy to expand the terrain; additional costs were not great, the legal research had been done, and the accounting mechanisms were in place. Many groups recognized that state legislatures were playing an increasingly important regulatory role, particularly in the late 1970s and 1980s when the federal government was attempting to trim its sails. Even if the U.S. Congress were still the center of a group's attention, it had good reason to look to the state capitals: most recent congressmen first served as state legislators, and a contribution made early in their careers was likely to be well remembered. In addition, Watergate caused many states to pass laws similar to the Federal Election Campaign Act, and just as FECA stimulated the growth of PACs at the national level, so too did the state statutes encourage PAC formation at the state level.

Many state PACs are not connected in any way to a national PAC or group, and are completely based in a single state or even a single locality. Unless they contribute to federal candidates or transfer funds to a federal PAC,[183] they are not required to register with the Federal Election Commission.[184] Other state PACs are tied in some fashion to a national PAC, but the strength of the affiliation varies. In some cases the PACs fit a "parent/-child model," and the state PACs are mere creatures of the national PAC, subjugated to it with little independent decision-making authority on candidate selection (though they can recommend endorsements to the national committee). The parent PAC files all reports for its affiliated children. In other cases state PACs are more like "independent adults." They may share fundraising and solicitations with the national, but they retain much authority to contribute to candidates of their own choice without prior approval from above.[185]

There are seemingly endless variations on these two models. COPE has a "three-legged partnership," as its director John Perkins terms it, which calls for frequent negotiation among national, state, and local union PACs on how funds should be raised and spent, and which candidates should be selected. Each of the fifty state Realtors' PACs has its own board of trustees which determines which state and local candidates to support; the national R-PAC restricts itself primarily to congressional races. BANKPAC has thirty-five state affiliates, thirty-three of which are registered as both state and federal PACs. The Honeywell Employees' PAC contributes to federal candidates everywhere but California, where a state PAC is empowered to make all federal endorsements. Standard Oil of Indiana's federal Amoco PAC handles all administrative and fundraising chores for twenty-two state PACs, but the state committees receive about half of all PAC funds to donate as they see fit.[186] The Machinists' PAC, as do many labor PACs, takes the opposite approach; the national PAC is funded by the state branches, which retain a portion of monies raised to be given to state-level candidates.[187] The most elaborate national-state PAC arrangements belong to AMPAC. Several of AMPAC's forty-eight state associates (including those in California, Texas, and Illinois) are among the largest state PACs in the country, and just CALPAC alone raised $1.7 million and gave $800,000 of it to state legislative candidates in 1981–1982.[188] AMPAC and the state PACs jointly solicit for funds, but they strictly[189] separate their contributions: AMPAC gives to federal candidates and the state PACs give to state politicians. Yet AMPAC also relies heavily on research and information provided by its state PACs in making decisions on congressional races.

While nonconnected PACs generally are less likely to have state affiliates, many of the Washington-based ideological PACs do. Since 1981 the Committee for the Survival of a Free Congress has had a "Committee for Effective State Government," which offers many of the same services as CSFC to conservative candidates for state legislative seats. NCPAC also has a State Election Fund (NCPAC-SEF) for much the same purpose, and frequently sets up individual state committees to target a disfavored politician and act as a conduit for NCPAC's money. In recent years, for example, NCPAC has created "Republicans to Replace [Sen.] Lowell Weicker" in Connecticut and "Independent Virginians for Responsible Government," aimed at Virginia's 1977 Democratic gubernatorial nominee Henry Howell.[190] Progressive ideological PACs, slower to develop at the national level, have also lagged in establishing state divisions. A few, like Handgun Control PAC, have them on the drawing board, while other state-based groups, such as the liberal Illinois Public Action Council, have set up PACs on their own.[191]

Despite the confusing array of state-federal relationships, most state PACs have a number of basic characteristics in common with the national PAC community.[192] State as well as national PACs have grown disproportionately in the corporate and trade categories, and have given business interests the localized political network available before just to labor.[193]

State PACs, like their national counterparts, have focused their activity primarily on legislative rather than executive offices, and they most often favor incumbents and legislative leaders, not challengers or freshmen. New directions among state PACs parallel those at the federal level: participation in primary elections, extensive involvement in ballot referenda campaigns, more expansive and innovative fundraising techniques, and the use of in-kind expenditures (though so far not to the same extent as the more sophisticated federal PACs). Business and trade PACs in many states are also developing coordinating and informational umbrella groups similar to those in Washington. Examples of this kind of state PAC include United for California, United for Washington, Maryland Business for Responsive Government, Montanans for Effective Government (MEGPAC), Pennsylvanians for Effective Government, Texas Businessmen Are Concerned (BACPAC), and the Louisiana Business PAC.

The dangers of overgeneralization are great on the subject of state PACs. Each state's political action committees are somewhat distinct because election laws—which determine the character of a state's PACs—vary dramatically from Maine to Iowa to California.[194] Unlike other states, for example, Montana prohibits any state House candidate from receiving more than $600 from PACs and any state Senate contender from accepting more than $1,000 during an election cycle; as a result, Montana PACs are spending less on contributions and are concentrating more on in-kind expenditures and political education efforts (registration, get-out-the-vote, and the like) among their own members.[195] The states also differ greatly about who can be solicited for PAC funds, how much PACs can give individual candidates, to what extent and how often PACs must disclose their spending and list their contributors, and whether corporate, union, and association treasuries can pay the administrative expenses of their PACs.[196] States even disagree about what groups can form PACs; West Virginia, for example, prohibits public utilities and railroad companies from having political action committees.

PAC growth at the state and local level will almost certainly be sustained in the near future, and it may even outstrip the expansion rate of national PACs, which has begun to level off. At the same time there are limitations that will keep state and local expansion somewhat in check. The complicated variations in law and regulation from state to state undoubtedly will deter some national groups. Others will be reluctant because of the single contribution limit of $5,000 per election for each group of formally affiliated organizations. Already a number of business and union PACs have been cited by the FEC for violations of this unitary limit.[197] (The AFL-CIO now bars its state and local PACs from giving to federal candidates in order to prevent a violation.) In some states, too, PACs are not a necessity for politically active groups, since corporations and unions can donate money to candidates directly from their treasuries.[198] And finally, state PACs may simply not be feasible for certain kinds of national committees. Several national nonconnected PAC managers who find the idea of state PACs appealing nevertheless wondered whether there is enough public interest to maintain them, especially through the medium of direct mail. "It's hard for people to get excited about state politics," claimed Russell Hemenway of the liberal National Committee for an Effective Congress. His conservative counterpart at the Committee for the Survival of a Free Congress, Paul Weyrich, agreed:

> It's really difficult to interest people in state legislatures other than their own. It's hard to explain to the guy in Illinois why he should contribute to someone in Virginia to defeat the Equal Rights Amendment. I was hoping that with Reagan's "New Federalism," things would change . . . but not so far.

Still, the PAC "new federalism" appears much healthier on the whole than President Reagan's intergovernmental affairs program of the same name, and the likelihood is that the state PAC movement will continue to prosper.

We have now seen how political action committees are organized, how they operate, and how they use their contributions to influence the conduct and outcome of elections. But if PACs clearly have an impact on elections, what is their effect on government after the ballot boxes have been stored? We now move to the most controversial aspect of PAC politics: the relationship between PAC contributions and the actions of elected representatives in Washington. Simply put, does PAC money buy votes in the halls of Congress?

CHAPTER 4

After the Election
PACs and Lobbying

Why do you think the biggest, brightest business people in America are raising millions of dollars to give to members of Congress? They're trying to buy votes. There's no other purpose to it. Labor unions, trade associations are all doing the same thing.

—Former Rep. William Brodhead, D–Mich.[1]

Saying "PAC money buys votes" is the equivalent of looking at the obituary page and concluding that people die in alphabetical order. There is *not* a *quid pro quo*. . . . The presumption is that congressmen are dishonest and on the take, that PAC givers are sleazeballs, in the business of bribery—and neither is the case.

—Lee Ann Elliott, Federal Election Commissioner[2]

We're just looking to cultivate personal relationships so down the line when we need a congressman's vote, that base of a relationship will be there. The PAC approach is the pursuit of the future. It's part of the goodwill process.

—Steven Stockmeyer, director of the National Association of Broadcasters' Television and Radio PAC[3]

It was Justin Dart, longtime friend of President Reagan and head of Dart Industries, who once observed that talking to politicians "is a fine thing but with a little money they hear you better."[4] Popular wisdom has long held that politicians are corrupt and greedy, and the correlations between donations of PAC money and congressional action seem to confirm the axiomatic view:[5]

PACs representing the banking industry, which waged an intense lobbying effort to win repeal of a provision requiring withholding of taxes on interest and dividends, contributed $3 million [to congressional candidates] in 1980 but gave $5.3 million in 1982—a 79 percent increase.

Aerospace industry PACs, successfully fighting for increased defense spending and for specific weapons systems (such as the MX missile and the B-1 bomber), gave $1.1 million in 1980 but contributed $2.3 million in 1982—a 104 percent increase.

Teachers determined to defeat a proposed tuition tax credit for private schools gave $0.6 million in 1980 but contributed $1.6 million in 1982—a 152 percent increase.[6]

We saw in the previous chapter that PACs contribute primarily to incumbents, sometimes right after the election to help with debt retirement or early in the legislator's term to provide "intimidation money" which helps the congressman frighten away potential opposition. PACs usually prefer to help members of those committees that affect their profession or trade. Members on committees without PAC constituencies can be nearly ignored; a *New York Times* survey of PAC gifts to members of twenty-two House committees found the panel with the leanest per-member PAC contribution to be, appropriately, Standards and Conduct, commonly known as the ethics committee.[7]

These contribution patterns are suggestive, especially when coupled with the fact that most PACs are connected to organizations that lobby Congress for legislative favors on a regular basis. PACs of course do not give money for the sheer fun of it, and most PACs make little attempt to hide the connection between their contributions and congressional activity. As one PAC sternly warns its own potential donors in its solicitation brochure, "Unless *your* presence is felt in Congressional campaigns, *your* voice may not be heard in the legislative deliberations that follow."[8] The California Medical Association PAC goes even further: "Medicine's involvement in campaign politics is intended to *influence public policy.* The 'bottom line' is the support CMA receives in Sacramento and Washington, D.C."[9] To entice contributors, many PACs proudly list in their fundraising letters and pamphlets not just their election winners but also the legislative successes achieved since the PAC was formed.

Yet conceding all this, the relationship between PAC contributors and the votes cast by congressmen is far more complex and less easily classified than it appears at first blush. We must take a closer look at what is probably the most severe charge made against PACs—"buying votes."

PACS AND LOBBIES

My theory is that in modern-day Washington you have to have three elements to be influential and effective: (1) a PAC, (2) a lobbying division, and (3) a strong grassroots organization. The lobbying is central and you back it up with the other two.

—Steven Stockmeyer of Television and Radio PAC

The recent focus on PACs obscures the other elements of most groups' legislative relations. The PAC is often just a part—sometimes a minor part—of an organization's lobbying strategy. Fully 68 percent of the corporations, associations, and unions that have formed multicandidate PACs also have a lobbying office or representative in Washington, D.C. And 57 percent of all multicandidate PACs (72 percent of the trade PACs) are merely one division of a larger "governmental affairs" department in the parent organization.[10] Nearly a third of the nonconnected PACs (31 percent) are also related to a lobby, either as its direct offspring or in association with a lobbying body.[11] The relationship between the PAC and the lobby in any organization is crucial, and it has real consequences for the way the PAC makes decisions.[12]

In the first place, PACs are usually not even formed by groups that have not seen fit to establish a governmental affairs or legislative lobbying department.[13] By contrast, it is not unusual for large corporations and trade associations to judge a legislative division more vital than a political action committee; many have a bustling lobbying division, but no PAC at all.[14] The business-oriented Public Affairs Council, for instance, gives many more seminars on lobbying techniques than on PAC formation each year. For those groups with both operations, though, there is a good deal of evidence that the lobbying division has a greater impact on the PAC than the reverse. For instance, those PACs with a Washington lobbying division are much more predisposed toward congressional incumbents (and Democrats) than PACs without such a connection.[15]

The main reason for the predominance of the lobby may simply be that it is much bigger, better staffed, and more generously funded than the PAC in most groups. The American Dental Association's ADPAC has two staff positions, while its lobby has six. At BANKPAC the ratio of staff is doubly worse for the PAC: twelve to two. (BANKPAC, in its basic brochure, flatly pledges not to "engage in lobbying, exact pledges in return for its support, nor seek legislative favors from candidates after they are elected"[16]—activities that are obviously unnecessary in light of the lobby's strength.) At SMACPAC about two dollars is spent on lobbying for every one dollar devoted to the PAC. The SMACPAC proportions may actually understate by a wide margin the overall comparison between lobby and PAC expenditures. In 1982 alone approximately 6,500 registered lobbyists reported spending an estimated $35 million to support, oppose, and otherwise influence congressional legislation.[17] But because of loophole-ridden disclosure rules, most observers believe the real lobbying expenditure to be at least ten times that amount, or $350 million. By contrast, when *both* 1981 and 1982 are taken together, all PACs in every category spent about $190 million, and contributed $83 million of that to congressional candidates.

Specific examples of the enormous size of lobbying expenses abound. Business groups supported a Senate filibuster of a labor-law revision during the Carter administration with estimated lobbying outlays totaling $5 million. This expenditure on one bill compared to $9 million in congressional contributions from all corporate PACs combined in the same year.[18] In 1981 the Savings and Loan Foundation spent $4.5 million mainly on their successful drive to secure passage of the All-Savers Certificate,[19] and the American Council of Life Insurance budgeted nearly $2 million in 1983 and 1984 for its print and television campaign against pending legislation to ban insurance rate and benefit schedules based on sex.[20]

Even if the lobby is the dominant partner, PAC managers usually develop an informal relationship—though not necessarily a close one—with the lobbyists, if only because they are normally housed together in the home office or in Washington. In the biggest organizations the lobby and PAC staffs are kept nearly or completely separate, but in more modest groups the PAC chairman often serves as the lobbyist too. Even when the leadership of PAC and lobby are not joined, the staffs frequently are, shuttling back and forth as need dictates. "If there's a crucial issue coming up on the Hill, we'll bring our political people in from the field to lobby," according to the Teamsters' David Sweeney. In the National Rifle Association, the lobbyists are the ones who trade roles, sometimes doubling as political field representatives. Money raised by a PAC is occasionally used for lobbying purposes, a practice sanctioned by the Federal Election Commission,[21] and lobbying funds can also be transferred to a group's PAC if the contributors agree.[22]

Despite such cooperative ventures, relations can be strained between a group's PAC and its lobby, especially in larger organizations where the two divisions often operate at cross-purposes. "I'm not going to tell you that some of our legislative issues managers [lobbyists] like our political program," reveals John Kochevar of the U.S. Chamber of Commerce's PAC. "It hinders them when they have to deal with an incumbent targeted for defeat." Peter Lauer of AMPAC elaborates:

> We're 180 degrees apart. The PAC is here not to keep the status quo. The lobbyists say, "We may disagree with this congressman but I can talk to him. I don't want

somebody new I'm not sure of." . . . At least since [the PAC and lobby] are separate, the lobbyist can say, "Congressman, those SOBs up at AMPAC—I told them not to do this. I'm really with you but I have no control over them."

Of course if AMPAC actually contributes to a congressman, the AMA lobbyists can say something different: "Hey, listen, I got you a thousand bucks."

Generally PAC managers insist that lobbyists have very little power to determine which incumbents receive campaign donations. And without exception they are appalled at the intimation that lobbyists ask for contributions to be distributed before a key legislative vote. One PAC director huffed: "We're not that crass. We would do our cause an injustice by making that kind of blatant overture."[23] Most PAC officials, however, will admit to having lengthy discussions or sharing information with their organization's lobbyists when it comes time to endorse candidates, and this is hardly suggestive of pure independence. Some will also acknowledge that many Washington reception tickets are purchased by the PAC "so that our lobbyists can have access," as Ken Melley of the NEA-PAC commented. Access—the ability to meet with legislators and state one's case—may be the most important common interest linking a group's PAC and its lobby. Don Cogman of MAPCO was referring to corporate PACs, but his remark applies as well to many PACs in other categories: "Some companies use their PAC for nothing but to buy access. . . . the PAC *is* their lobbying, period."

BUYING ACCESS OR BUYING VOTES

Anytime someone, whether a person or a PAC, gives you a large sum of money, you can't help but feel the need to give them extra attention, whether it is access to your time or, subconsciously, the obligation to vote with them.

—Rep. John Bryant of Texas[24]

I take money from labor, and I have to think twice in voting against their interests. I shouldn't have to do that.

—Rep. Richard Ottinger of New York[25]

We are the only human beings in the world who are expected to take thousands of dollars from perfect strangers on important matters and not be affected by it.

—Rep. Barney Frank of Massachusetts[26]

I fear we could become a coin-operated Congress. Instead of two bits, you put in $2,500 and pull out a vote.

—Rep. Barbara Mikulski of Maryland[27]

The only reason it isn't considered bribery is that Congress gets to define bribery.
—Rep. Andrew Jacobs of Indiana[28]

If you give a dog a bone, he'll be loyal forever. And if you give a congressman some money, he may not fetch your slippers for you, but he'll always be there when you need him.
—Rep. Dan Glickman of Kansas[29]

Members of Congress have themselves frequently offered the harshest interpretations of the effect of PAC money on their voting proclivities. While some legislators confess that PAC dollars affect their judgment of the issues before them, PAC officials are adamant that all they get for their investment is access to congressmen—a chance to "tell their story." Political analysts have long agreed that access is the principal goal of most interest groups,[30] and lobbyists have always recognized that access is the key to persuasion. As one of their number commented:

I know what it means to put in a call to a legislator and get a call back and not to get a call back. And if that $500 is going to increase my chances of getting a call back, that is a heck of a lot, because frequently all it takes is the opportunity to talk to a legislator 10 or 15 minutes to make your case. He may not have 10 or 15 minutes to hear the other side.[31]

A congressman's time is often as valuable as his vote because, as the Public Affairs Council's Richard Armstrong declares, "except maybe for some guy from Idaho . . . they haven't got time to see everybody. Some congressmen *say* they see everyone, but that's bullshit." Both of the major political parties have merchandized the time of their top legislative leaders, providing numerous opportunities for PAC officials to meet with senior senators and representatives if the PACs give money to the party committees. Some congressmen are also not shy about personally making the connection between their "open door" and PAC money. A trade PAC manager told of his success in arranging a private session with a powerful House committee chairman shortly after the PAC bought high-priced tickets in advance of a Democratic fundraising dinner held in the chairman's honor: "At that meeting [the congressman] was quick to point out his appreciation for our support—and he knew about this two full weeks before the dinner."[32]

Most PAC managers will agree that their money buys some degree of access. "Maybe we do get more access than Mr. Constituent," admits AMPAC's Peter Lauer, "but I don't think this country is going to fall apart if my phone call is returned before a congressman's constituent." It is certainly true that access and vote buying are not the same, and probably true that most parent organizations of the large PACs are weighty enough to get access without PAC gifts.[33] Moreover, at least one class of PACs—

the ideological groups—are demonstrably uninterested in access to the incumbents they are avidly trying to replace. But no one seriously disputes that access, for those organizations which desire it, is sometimes secured by means of campaign cash.

MOTIVES AND MONEY

PACs give money in a variety of ways, and these depend on what motivates the gift. Most PACs have chosen a distinctive style. One of these methods, most common among labor and some trade PACs, is to offer "reward money," or PAC gifts awarded to candidates on the basis of their favorable voting records.[34] PACs cannot afford to forget their friends in a constantly shifting political world, and few do. For example, according to the *Wall Street Journal,* the National Education Association PAC closely pegged its 1980 gifts to congressmen's support of the bill creating the Department of Education in 1979.[35] Another *Wall Street Journal* report tied the Realtor's PAC donations to the voting records of congressmen on certain housing legislation.[36] Others have claimed that AMPAC gave "thank you" money to the sponsors of Medicredit, the AMA's alternative to national health insurance.[37] Most PAC managers deny that they use their contributions as rewards, but at the same time they point out that rewarding legislators for votes cast independently prior to a donation is more wholesome than attempting to buy future votes. As Wayne LaPierre of the National Rifle Association's Political Victory Fund (NRA-PVF) testified before a congressional committee:

> Contributions are given to those candidates already supportive of NRA positions on the preservation of the Second Amendment and hunting rights. The NRA-PVF does not support a candidate hoping that our support will change his/her mind on our issues or that somehow a contribution from the PVF will change a vote in the future. Candidates, both incumbents and challengers, are supported by the NRA-PVF because of their issue positions *prior* to the decision to support them.[38]

LaPierre's PAC adversary, Charles Orasin of Handgun Control PAC, concurred: "We don't contribute until we're certain the guy's with us. It solidifies the bond. . . . You have to be able to show these people who stand up for you that you'll help them get reelected. That's what it all boils down to."

While PACs as a group reward more than they punish, the use of "punish money" is far from uncommon. Congressmen can be punished in several ways. A PAC might simply choose not to make the usual contribution to a previously favored candidate. George Meade of the American Trucking Association reported: "We did nothing for [Arizona GOP Sen.] Barry

Goldwater [in 1980] because we had problems with him in committee."[39] Or a PAC can threaten to support a rival candidate in the primary or general election. One congressman complained: "The AMA [American Medical Association] is especially aggressive that way. Although I'm generally sympathetic to their views, if I seem to be straying from their line in their view, they will let me know that they can always support another candidate in the primary."[40] The next level of "punish money" signifies excommunication. AMPAC gave the maximum contribution to defeat New Jersey Democratic Rep. Andrew Maguire in 1980 after some quarrelsome health care sessions in the House Commerce Committee. "Our lobbying shop found him not easy to work with," said an AMA official. "We died a thousand deaths with Andy Maguire."[41] Similarly, Amoco's PAC donated $5,000 to Jack Fields, the GOP candidate who defeated Rep. Bob Eckhardt (D-Tex.), with the PAC chairman noting, "We would've given to any name on the ballot against [Eckhardt]. He had a very bad oil record."[42]

Occasionally PACs threaten punishment in order to defeat a particular piece of legislation they find noxious. BIPAC and other committees have repeatedly spread the word that candidates supporting certain campaign finance reforms (such as public funding and limitations on the amount of PAC money a candidate can receive) would find the business PAC pipeline shut off.[43] When a Democratic congressman from Pennsylvania sought a contribution from the Holiday Inn's INN-PAC, for instance, he received a letter from the PAC chairman noting that his support of a PAC limitation bill made a gift impossible at this time—but if the congressman were to reconsider his position, the PAC might reconsider its.[44]

Punish money is, of course, the stock-in-trade of many ideological PACs. Sometimes ideological groups use the threat of an independent expenditure campaign to steer legislators in their philosophical direction. For example, Terry Dolan of NCPAC announced "potential targets" for 1982 but noted that "if these individuals would move noticeably to the right, they would improve their chances substantially" of a reprieve.[45] On other occasions ideological PACs follow through with the sledgehammer approach in the hope that punish money, even if unsuccessful in defeating congressmen, will cause them to modify their offending positions in order to avoid another negative blitz in the future. Charles Orasin of Handgun Control PAC recalled airing a powerful negative television spot in the districts of certain pro–National Rifle Association congressmen in 1982. A woman whose grandson had been killed with a handgun movingly explained the connection between her tragic loss and the congressman's pro-gun voting record. "When you vote, think what happened to my grandson," she concluded. Orasin claims that his PAC's "punish" campaign caused two of the target legislators (both reelected) to cease active support of an NRA-backed bill to weaken current gun restrictions.

Except perhaps for ideological groups, the PAC bark is usually worse than the bite. Of the thirty-eight congressmen who received campaign money from the car dealers in 1980 but voted against their most important legislative priority in the following session, eighteen received additional donations at reelection time in 1982 (though the average gift fell by about $400).[46] And like parental sanctions, PAC punishments are often lifted once the anger of the moment passes. When Pennsylvania Democratic Rep. Doug Walgren refused to support industry amendments to the Clean Air Act in 1982, the enraged chairman of U.S. Steel sent a memorandum to hundreds of company executives only three weeks before the general election that read, in part:

> Since he was elected in 1976, we have tried very hard to work with Mr. Walgren. These efforts were made with the hope that he would be understanding and helpful concerning issues which bear heavily on our industry. Further, to demonstrate our confidence, he has received contributions in the past from the Good Government Fund [U.S. Steel's PAC].
>
> To no avail. For instance, in almost every vote on the Clean Air Act amendments, he has voted contrary to our interests. In recent months, he voted for a very unwise and damaging amendment which resulted in killing any chance for significant changes in the Clean Air Act this year. He was advised before he cast his vote of its importance to us, but we were unable to persuade him to support us on this issue of vital importance. . . . Congressman Walgren should be replaced.[47]

But after Walgren won reelection, he held a debt-retirement fundraiser; among the participants was a PAC representative from U.S. Steel carrying a check for $300.

Cases like Walgren's do little to assuage congressmen's fears about PAC retribution, however. Whatever the reality may be, the perception on Capitol Hill is that one wrong move on a vote of major importance to a large PAC could trigger a "max-out" to one's political rival. "We're forced to always look over our shoulders and figure out whether this vote will cost us $10,000 from a PAC, or worse yet, whether it will provoke a PAC into giving $10,000 to an opponent," claims Democratic Rep. David Obey of Wisconsin.[48] Some PAC leaders assert that the threat is enough to make hostile legislators more friendly. "The people who we targeted for defeat in 1982 have improved their voting record with us by 16 percent compared to the last session of Congress," boasted John Kochevar of the U.S. Chamber of Congress.

In addition to "reward" and "punish" gifts, PACs dispense "present needs" and "future needs" money. "Present needs" PAC cash is timed to arrive at such critical moments in the *legislative,* not the electoral cycle, as when the recipient legislator is preparing to vote on a group's pet bill. In the spring of 1981 twelve major oil companies each gave $1,000 or more to a U.S. senator's 1982 campaign fund; two weeks later the senator introduced a bill to repeal certain aspects of the windfall profits tax.[49] June 1981 was a busy month for PAC gifts from investment houses to members of tax-writing committees, which were then considering new tax breaks for investors.[50] When the auto dealers were attempting to line up cosponsors for a bill to veto a restrictive Federal Trade Commission ruling concerning them, they made contributions to sixteen congressmen within ten days of the date the legislators signed on as bill patrons.[51]

"Present needs" money is also visible on the state level. In Georgia, for example, five state legislators received "belated" contributions from a bank PAC three months after the 1980 election—on the very day of a critical, close vote on a banking bill.[52] PAC managers usually insist that such timing is coincidental; in the Georgia case, bank PAC officials insisted that the gifts had not been made earlier merely because of an oversight. In California the state medical association's CALPAC made what its director called "the boo-boo of the century" after a PAC representative presented a key legislator with a check forty-eight hours before a vote on a medical bill.[53] The legislator in this case promptly returned the check, and some congressmen in similar situations have done the same.[54] The not-infrequent rejections of "present needs" money as too crass is one reason why this particular method of contribution is not widely used.

This is not the case with "future needs" money, also known as "goodwill" cash. As a Florida legislator once explained it while attending an "appreciation dinner" held for Florida state legislators in midsession, "You've got to appreciate someone for their past service—or their future service."[55] "Future needs" money is given to maintain goodwill and in anticipation of legislative favors that will be required in the months and years to come. Sometimes a group has a specific bill or subject in mind, and money is distributed with the expectation that the bill or subject will be brought up in the next legislative session. The House Merchant Marine Committee, which in previous years ranked twelfth among House committees in total PAC gifts received by members, rose to first place in 1983 as shipbuilders, construction companies, and unions scrambled to prepare for deliberations on the shipping act of 1983, a watershed bill concerning regulation of the maritime industry.[56] When the Iowa Beef PAC wrote Rep. Dan Glickman (D–Kans.) asking support of another measure, it began the letter by saying, "As we trust you will recall, the Political Action Committee of Iowa Beef Processors, Inc., has heretofore supported your candidacy. . . ."[57] Congressional observers were shocked when U.S. Rep. Henry Waxman (D–Calif.) upset more senior Rep. Richardson Preyer (D–N.C.) in 1979 to become chairman of a prominent subcommittee of the House Energy and Commerce Committee. Although Waxman claims his election was owing purely to his beliefs and stands on the issues, his personal PAC had contributed about $24,000 to Democratic committee colleagues in the months preceding the vote.[58]

Much of the "goodwill" cash is donated without such specific goals in mind, however. The large labor and trade PACs, as well as certain corporate PACs, disperse contributions widely, and the cumulative impact can be impressive. Every single U.S. senator seeking reelection in 1980, and all but 54 of 401 incumbent representatives who sought another term, got some financial assistance from chemical manufacturers.[59] During the 1978, 1980, and 1982 elections taken together, AMPAC and state medical association PACs gave money at least once to more than 90 percent of the 287 House members who served continuously from 1976 to 1982, and 61 percent of them received gifts in each of the three election cycles.[60]

PAC MONEY AND CONGRESSIONAL VOTING: A CLOSER LOOK

"As long as I've been with AMPAC—more than nine years—we've never given money because of a legislative issue," flatly declared Peter Lauer. Yet the liberal-leaning citizen's lobby Common Cause regularly issues "correlational studies" purporting to show a relationship between the cash AMPAC and other groups have contributed and vote tallies on bills in the Senate and the House. Common Cause has cited the defeat of President Carter's Hospital Cost Containment Act of 1977 as an example of AMPAC's influence.[61] Of the 234 House members who voted for a crippling amendment to the act, 202 had been given $1.65 million in contributions during their 1976 and 1978 campaigns, with an average receipt of over $8,100 per member. While 122 of the members voting against the crippling amendment had also been given contributions, their average gift was a much lower $2,300 each. Yet as conclusive as these statistics seem on the surface, there is no "smoking gun"; a correlation does not prove causation.[62]

There can be many explanations for a congressman's vote for or against any given bill. His party might strongly favor or oppose a measure. The bill might positively or negatively affect his constituents in some way. The legislator's long-held beliefs might predispose him one way or the other. Or as Common Cause and others claim, he might be thinking of PAC support for him, or his opponent, at election time. Even if the last explanation suffices—and most decisions human beings make are hardly so simplistic and unidimensional—there is still the "chicken and egg" question: Does money follow votes or do votes follow money? Do PACs give congressmen campaign contributions as a reward for their previous voting records or as an inducement to vote for their bills in the future? We have already heard from the PAC managers and congressmen on this question. We can now go further.

A number of political scientists have been able to shed some light on this subject through the use of more sophisticated statistical techniques than simple correlations.[63] They have been able to "control" (i.e., account for or hold steady) such variables as party, ideology, and past voting record to determine what independent effects on congressmen's votes gifts actually have.[64] W. P. Welch, for example, analyzed the effect of 1974 dairy PAC contributions on the following year's congressional vote for milk price supports.[65] He found that the PAC gifts had a relatively small effect on the vote. Rather, congressmen's positions were determined more by how important dairy production was in each legislator's home district, as well as by their ideology and party affiliation. Nevertheless Welch established that legislators' votes on dairy price supports were clearly related to the contributions dairy PACs made in the next election; the PACs offered "reward" money on this issue.

Henry Chappell studied the effects of PAC contributions on seven different bills, and found a significant positive relationship between PAC money given in the previous election and voting results in only one case, which involved Rockwell International and the vote on the B-1 bomber.[66] Diana Yiannakis examined two bills—the windfall profits oil tax (part of President Carter's energy package) and the Chrysler loan guarantee—both passed by Congress in 1979.[67] Like Welch and Chappell, Yiannakis concluded that the influence of 1978 PAC gifts on roll-call voting in the House the following year was very limited. Congressmen who voted for either of the two bills followed their party and ideological leanings far more than the trail of PAC money.

Yiannakis was careful to note, however, that the oil tax and Chrysler bailout bills were high-visibility ones in the press and, presumably, in the home districts of congressmen. Taking a position against "big oil" by voting to tax their windfall profits could well have been worth far more toward victory at the next election than the campaign contributions that might have flowed from oil companies had a congressman voted against the tax. But what of lower visibility and more technical issues on which a congressman's vote might not draw the attention of his constituency yet might garner the financial backing of a wealthy PAC? John Frendreis and Richard Waterman investigated just such a situation in the U.S. Senate vote on deregulation of the trucking industry in 1980.[68] The issue was not of headline quality, nor did it necessarily pit Democrats against Republicans or liberals against conservatives. Yet the issue was of critical importance to the American Trucking Association, whose PAC made contributions to 54 senators and 319 representatives in 1979 and 1980. The results of the study showed a strong linkage between congressional votes and PAC money; in fact this relationship was stronger than those between votes and party, ideology, and constituency, and it was firmest for those senators nearest to an election (those whose seats were up in 1980).[69]

Similarly, Kirk Brown looked at bills passed by the House of Representatives in 1982 directly affecting two powerful organizations with large PACs, the National Automobile Dealers Association (NADA) and the American Medical Association (AMA).[70] First, the House approved a veto of the Federal Trade Commission's so-called lemon rule, which required that used-car dealers list all known defects in their automobiles for prospective buyers to see. Of 286 House members who supported the veto resolution, 242 had previously received donations from NADA's PAC. This simple correlation was merely suggestive; but when other variables such as party and ideology were statistically controlled, an independent relationship between the House vote and the PAC money still existed. For those congressmen whose ideology matched the PAC's leanings, PAC gifts only marginally increased the probability that they would vote the NADA line. But for congressmen who were decidedly more liberal or conservative than NADA, PAC money substantially raised the probability that they would cast their vote with NADA.

Furthermore, a vote favorable to NADA resulted in more generous gifts for congressmen's 1982 reelection campaigns. Of the 251 legislators who supported the veto resolution and ran again in 1982, 89 percent received contributions from NADA, which averaged over $2,300. This total included 66 legislators who had not been backed by NADA at all in 1980, before the veto resolution vote. Just 22 percent of the 125 congressmen who voted against NADA received 1982 money, and they averaged only about $1,000 apiece. Assuming two congressmen held the same ideological views, served on the same committees, and faced equally close and costly reelection campaigns, the one who voted with NADA could expect to receive $1,050 more than the one who voted against. NADA also rewarded the *intensity* of effort displayed by congressmen on its behalf. Those House members who had been cosponsors of the veto resolution were given an extra increment of nearly $400 each in 1982.

Six months after the NADA issue, the House voted in favor of exempting professionals (including doctors, dentists, and lawyers) from regulation by the Federal Trade Commission. The AMA and the American Dental Association (ADA) were the chief organizational backers of the bill, and the "reward" money for congressmen siding with them was generous. A favorable vote was worth, on average, nearly $1,000 additional for a legislator's campaign kitty, and any cosponsor of the bill was in line for $1,800 more than went to House members who did not cosponsor the bill but had similar voting records and reelection prospects. As the study concludes, "Since only seven votes would have had to be changed for the professionals' exemption to have been defeated in the House, it is not difficult to conclude that the AMA's and ADA's campaign contributions of over $1.5 million to House members during the 1982 election provided the margin of victory."[71]

PACS AND THE VOTE-BUYING CONTROVERSY: A SUMMARY JUDGMENT

What conclusion, then, can we draw about the charge that PAC money buys votes in the halls of Congress?[72] The best answer based on the available evidence seems to be that PAC contributions do make a difference, at least on some occasions, in securing access and influencing the course of events on the House and Senate floors. But those occasions are not nearly as frequent as anti-PAC spokesmen, even congressmen themselves, often suggest.

PACs affect legislative proceedings to a decisive degree only when certain conditions prevail. First, the more invisible the issue, the more likely that PAC funds can change or produce congressional votes on it. After the Federal Trade Commission exemption for professionals passed the House and went over to the Senate, for example, it became something of a cause célèbre in the press. When the media turned the spotlight on the bill and its alleged unfairness to consumers, generous doctors' and dentists' PAC gifts could no longer save the measure, and the Senate decisively rejected it by a fifty-nine to thirty seven margin.[73] A corollary of this invisibility rule might be that PAC money has more effect on the early stages of the legislative process, such as agenda setting and votes in subcommittee meetings, than on later and more public floor deliberations. Press, public, and even "watchdog" groups are not nearly as attentive to initial legislative proceedings.[74]

PAC contributions are also more likely to influence the legislature when the matter at hand is specialized and narrow, or unopposed by other organized interests. PAC gifts are less likely to be decisive on broad national issues such as American policy in El Salvador, or the adoption of a nerve-gas program or an MX missile system.[75] But the more technical measures, such as those discussed in the last section, seem tailor-made for the special interests. Additionally, PAC influence in Congress is greater when large PACs or groups of PACs (such as business and labor PACs) are allied. In recent years, despite their natural enmity, business and labor have lobbied together on a wide range of issues including defense spending, trade policy, environmental regulation, maritime legislation, trucking legislation, and nuclear power.[76] The combination is a weighty one, checked in many instances only by a tendency for business and labor in one industry (say, the railroads) to combine and oppose their cooperating counterparts in another industry (perhaps the truckers and Teamsters).[77] More frequently, the dozens or even hundreds of PACs in a single field (such as banking, oil, transportation, and so forth) will join forces to back legislation.[78] Each of these PACs, of course, can contribute up to $5,000 per election; even though max-outs are uncommon, modest gifts from most or all of an industry's PACs amount to a considerable sum. A congressman may be able to dismiss $5,000 with ease, but $20,000 or more from one group of PACs is a sizable chunk of any reelection campaign's needs. When PACs travel in packs, says Rep. David Obey (D–Wis.), "The pressure generated from those aggregate contributions is enormous and warps the process. It is as if they had made a single, extremely large contribution."[79]

Finally, certain PACs enhance their leverage on Capitol Hill by cleverly adapting the techniques of the lobbying trade to their contribution strategy. Pragmatism and single-mindedness in both endeavors help enormously. George Meade of the American Trucking Association reported that his membership occasionally objected to his PAC's candidate selections: "We'll want to support a guy and they'll say, 'Don't do it. He's so far left he meets himself coming around.' We keep telling them that we can't afford a political philosophy. We'll buy a ticket to anyone's event as long as he didn't vote the wrong way on trucking issues."[80] The successful PACs also combine grassroots lobbying with campaign contributions. In the example cited earlier of AMPAC's effort to secure a regulatory exemption for professionals, the AMA had doctors swarming over the Capitol. Commented Sen. Warren Rudman (R–N.H.): "I noticed something very interesting in the last week. For the first time in 20 years doctors are making house calls. They made house calls in the Dirksen Building, they made house calls in the Russell Building. They are so concerned with our health that the reception room is packed with them."[81] And as skillful lobbyists know, PAC money can also ensure that congressional allies are used to the group's best advantage. As Rep. Les Aspin (D–Wis.) explained, "There are various degrees of being for a bill—co-sponsoring it, or fighting for it in committee, in debate, on the floor, or in a leadership role on the floor. PAC funds can determine a member's intensity as well as position."[82]

In short, PACs have legislative influence, and that influence is occasionally decisive because, as Michael Malbin has stated, "PAC money is and will remain the easiest money for most incumbents to raise."[83] Candidates these days need a great deal of cash to run for office, and PACs, especially those in Washington, are convenient, economical, and usually willing sources of contributions for congressmen whom they favor—and who favor them.

It is worth stressing, however, that most congressmen are *not* unduly influenced by PAC money on most votes. The special conditions I have outlined simply do not apply to most legislative issues. Other considerations —foremost among them a congressman's party affiliation, his ideology, and his constituents' needs and desires—are the overriding factors in determining a legislator's votes. Much has been made of the passage of large tax cuts for oil and business interests in the 1981 omnibus tax package. The journalist Elizabeth Drew said there was a "bidding war" to trade campaign contributions for tax breaks benefiting independent oil producers.[84] Ralph Nader's Public Citizen group charged that the $280,000 in corporate PAC money accepted by members of the House Ways and Means Committee had helped to produce a bill that "contained everything business ever dared to ask for, and more."[85] Yet as Robert Samuelson has convincingly argued, the "bidding war" between Democrats and Republicans was waged not for PAC money but for control of a House of Representatives sharply divided between Reaganite Republicans and liberal Democrats, with conservative "boll weevil" Democrats from the southern oil states as the crucial swing votes.[86] The Ways and Means Committee actions cited by Nader were also more correctly explained in partisan terms.[87]

If party loyalty can have a stronger pull than PAC contributions, then surely the views of a congressman's constituents usually take precedence over those of political action committees. PAC gifts are merely a means to an end: reelection. If accepting money will cause a candidate embarrassment, then even a maximum donation will likely be rejected. If an incumbent is faced with a choice of either voting for a PAC-backed bill that is very unpopular in his district or foregoing the PAC's or even a whole industry's money, the odds are that any politician who depends on a majority of votes to remain in office is going to side with his constituency and vote against the PAC's interest. The flip side of this proposition makes sense as well: if a PAC's parent organization has many members or a major financial stake in the congressman's home district, he is much more likely to vote the PAC's way—not so much because he receives PAC money but because the group accounts for an important part of his electorate. Does Sen. David Durenberger of Minnesota vote for dairy price supports because he received 11 percent of his PAC contributions from agriculture, or because the farm population of his state is relatively large and politically active?[88] Do congressmen generally vote the National Rifle Association's preferences because of the money the NRA-PVF distributes, or because the NRA, unlike gun-control advocates, has repeatedly demonstrated the ability to produce a sizable number of votes in many legislative districts? Even a severe PAC critic like Rep. Dan Glickman (D–Kans.) admits that district votes are more persuasive:

> My city produces half the [small] airplanes in the world. Maybe one of their PACs will give me a campaign contribution. I'm not going to vote for them because they

gave me a contribution from their PAC, but as a general proposition I'm going to help them because they employ 15, 20, or 25,000 people in my district.[89]

Nor should the number of fundraising alternatives available to congressmen be underestimated. Not only do individuals, parties, and direct mail provide ready sources of campaign cash for most incumbents, but PACs (except for labor) are hardly monolithic.[90] While there are exceptions (such as those occasions when business and labor join forces), by and large the alienation of one PAC can open up a path to a competing group. Among business PACs, for instance, divergence is a way of life. Observes Don Cogman of MAPCO PAC:

> We don't agree with Mobil Oil which is in our same business, much less International Paper, which ain't. We see issues differently, we often take opposite sides, and we basically have a different agenda. Too much coordination among business? That's hogwash. Most of the time half of us are fighting with each other on candidates or issues or whatever.

For all their vaunted power, business PACs have repeatedly lost out in coordinated attempts to alter established legislation or secure new statutes. The roster of their failures is at least as impressive as their successes. Assaults on the Clean Air Act, Clean Water Act, the Federal Insecticide, Fungicide, and Rodenticide Act, the Consumer Product Safety Commission, and the Freedom of Information Act, among others, have fallen short in recent years.[91] Similarly, labor has suffered humiliating congressional defeats on issues such as labor law reform and common situs picketing even when Democrats retained large majorities in both houses. Labor and business PACs have each discovered the enormous difficulty of passing legislation in a system honeycombed with checks and balances—mechanisms that check the power of PACs as much or more than that of presidents.

If PACs have appeared more influential than the American system should permit them to be, perhaps it is partly because many people's views of congressmen have been tainted by scandals such as Abscam, as though all legislators were looking for opportunities to exclaim (as one on Abscam's candid camera did), "I've got larceny in my blood!" It is certainly disturbing, and maybe amusing as well, to find that the National Republican Congressional Committee felt it necessary to warn its PAC-soliciting candidates: "Don't *ever* suggest to the PAC that it is 'buying' your vote should you get elected."[92] Yet all knowledgeable Capitol Hill observers agree that there are few truly corrupt congressmen. Simple correlations notwithstanding, when many legislators vote for a PAC-supported bill, it is because the *merits* of the case (or their party leaders, peers, or constituents), not the money from the PAC, convinced them. In the case of the auto dealers and the used-car "lemon rule" cited earlier, there were sound reasons to support the dealers' efforts to veto the rule, which some claimed was vague, too punitive, unfair in that it applied only to some sellers of used cars, and inflationary.[93] Furthermore, a purely political calculation may have called for a vote in *favor* of the "lemon rule," even if the auto dealers' money was lost by doing so. As Rep. Tom Tauke (R–Iowa) explained:

> I voted against the rule because I thought it would do more harm than good. I thought it would just make it harder for low-income people to buy cars. But from a political point of view, I got $3,000 from the car dealers, and the best thing I could have done would have been to vote for the rule, against them. That would have helped me politically. For one thing it would have stopped my opponent from going around carrying this little lemon on wheels as a campaign gimmick.[94]

The image of the "congressman on the take" has been promoted, ironically, by a number of congressmen who seek limitations on PACs and dramatize their opinions by citing anonymous colleagues who have confessed to them that their votes have been bought. Rep. Millicent Fenwick (R–N.J.), for instance, recited one incident to the *Washington Post:* " 'I took $58,000. They want it,' was the explanation one colleague gave me for his vote."[95] PAC managers insist that these examples are more imagined than real. Claims Peter Lauer of AMPAC:

> You never hear any of those guys say who that individual was. Because it never happened. I can understand congressional license and their stretching of the truth to make their case, but I don't have that privilege. I would love to have the opportunity to say, "Okay—put up or shut up." Several years ago Common Cause was challenged by [Rep.] Newt Gingrich [R–Ga.] to give him the names of congressmen on the take so he could prosecute. The AMA and other groups agreed to provide financial backing for the prosecution. They never came up with a name.[96]

Whatever the degree of contemporary corruption caused by PAC money, it pales by comparison to conditions prevailing before the Federal Election Campaign Act and the amendments of the 1970s.[97] If contributions of $5,000 are thought to buy congressional votes, then the Capitol must have been a covered market in the days when groups could make contributions as large as the National Committee for an Effective Congress did. Before the limits on contributions were passed, reported the NCEC's Russell Hemenway, "Dick Clark [Democratic candidate for U.S. Senate from Iowa in 1972] walked into my office one day and he walked out with $50,000. We got his winning campaign started. I can't do that anymore, but it was fun. You really had a lot of influence." It is also the new campaign finance system's stringent requirements for reporting and disclosure that make it possible to correlate PAC money and congressional votes so easily; before FECA, the flow of cash was substantially hidden from public view. Rep. Al Swift (D–Wash.) recognized the effect FECA has had:

> When we went to the PAC system, it made it easy to identify the special interests and their money. It became easy to tie votes to money. Members of Congress spend

half their time doing it to each other. Any vote you make in our committee, someone can make a case that you did it on something other than the merits of the case. This is not to say money has no effect, but in so many ways you find it compensated for. Ultimately, you get back to the basis of merit.[98]

When the PAC phenomenon is viewed in the broad perspective, and when the complex nature of the congressional and electoral process is fully considered, Swift's belief that *merit* matters in the votes most congressmen cast—merit as defined by ideological beliefs, party loyalty, and the interests of district constituents—seems sound. It is ludicrously naïve to contend that PAC money never influences congressmen's decisions, but is it irredeemably cynical to believe that PACs always, or even usually, push the voting buttons in Congress.

The general view is that in recent years the rising influence of PACs has been accompanied by the declining influence of the two major parties. But the truth is that the national arms of the political parties have grown and expanded their capacities to elect candidates as dramatically as have political action committees. PACs and parties are rivals in many ways, but of necessity they have cooperated and forged ties, some tenuous and others tenacious. We will focus on these in the next chapter.

CHAPTER 5

PACs and the Political Parties

> When you look at it on paper, it would seem that PACs and the parties should be rivals. But in practice, we've come to very important accommodations. . . . Our party has become a broker, a facilitator, and a sometime matchmaker for the PACs.
>
> —Ann Lewis, political director of the Democratic National Committee

> If we ever were rivals, we're not anymore. . . . We see ourselves as the people in the middle. To PACs we try to offer ourselves as a service organization to provide information about Republicans who are running for Congress. For our candidates we try to help match them to PACs.
>
> —Joe Gaylord, executive director of the National Republican Congressional Committee

As Ann Lewis of the Democratic National Committee suggests, on paper one can make a strong case that PACs and the political parties are bound to be competitors. They both raise money from the same limited universe of political givers, large and small. They both try to elect candidates, but in doing so they adopt very different perspectives: most PACs act on the basis of relatively narrow or even single-interest viewpoints, while the parties operate from a fisheye, broad-based, overarching vantage point. And they both vie for the attention, affection, and loyalty of candidates and officeholders.

While there is in fact evidence of considerable competition between PACs and parties, what is more surprising is that despite their natural tensions the two have learned to coexist symbiotically: they use one another quite well. PACs need the information about candidates, intelligence about congressional contests, and access to political leaders that parties can provide. The parties seek PAC money for their candidates and their own organizations, which of late have modernized and expanded at a rate that matches the growth of PACs.

The still-developing relationship between PACs and the political parties is a fascinating one which illustrates the new realities of campaign finance as well as some eternal verities of the adaptable American political system.

PAC "BIPARTISANSHIP"

"We will never be partisan," declares Brian Meyer of BANKPAC, a committee that regularly gives maximum contributions to both parties and occasionally donates to both candidates in the same race. "I'm strictly between the two parties ideologically; you could call me a whore if you wanted to," jokes Gregg Ward of SMACPAC. Meyer and Ward are typical of a large majority of business PAC managers who eschew partisanship and fervently embrace—for the record at least—a policy of nonalignment. As Table 3–1 showed, an overwhelming proportion of corporate and trade PACs expressed no preference between a Republican and a Democratic congressional nominee in a race in which party label was the main distinction.[1] (Among those who did name a choice, the GOP standard-bearer was the clear favorite.) Even when a business PAC's track record is highly partisan, the claim of even-handedness is often made. "We're definitely bipartisan," insisted John Kochevar of the U.S. Chamber of Commerce, which endorsed ninety-one candidates, every one a Republican, in the 1982 election. "It's just that there simply wasn't a business-oriented Democrat running against a more liberal non-business-oriented Republican in a close race in 1982." Kochevar's distinction is supported by Bernadette Budde of BIPAC:

> It was not our goal to get [the Republican U.S. Senate] elected. We deal more with the ideological outcome. . . . 1984 is definitely critical for the Republicans and yet when you look at the [Senate] Democrats who are up, the business community cannot afford to abandon most of those Democrats with good records. And at least half of them have good records.[2]

Budde's and Kochevar's philosophy has generally prevailed. Since 1978 about a third of the corporate PAC contributions and 42 percent of the trade PAC gifts in congressional races have gone to Democratic candidates.

(They are almost always incumbents, however; business challenger money is mainly reserved for Republicans.) Business PACs actually supplied more money to Democrats in 1980 than did labor PACs, and in 1982 the business groups supplied almost as much.[3] Thanks to the growth of business PACs, the relative importance of labor money for Democrats has declined sharply since 1974.[4] If business PACs gradually become more involved in primary elections, as many expect they will,[5] then the amount of corporate and trade cash flowing to Democrats will certainly increase, if only because of the remaining number of one-party Democratic districts in the South and Border states.

Labor PACs have much less a claim to bipartisanship than business committees. Not only do almost all labor committees express a clear Democratic preference in an otherwise "equal" race (see Table 3–1), but an average of nearly 94 percent of all labor PAC money has flowed to the Democrats since 1978. John Perkins of COPE offers reasoning similar to his counterpart in the U.S. Chamber of Commerce: "Now that we've lost Republicans like [ex-Sens.] Ed Brooke [of Massachusetts] and Jacob Javits [of New York], there are only a handful of GOP moderates left and so we don't have many opportunities to give to Republicans. We'd like to show bipartisanship but we're not going to slit our own throats." Yet many labor PACs, like the Machinists Non-Partisan League, take pains in their solicitation materials to deny a party bias. "The MNPL is non-partisan," reads their fundraising pamphlet. "Endorsed Republicans are treated just the same as endorsed Democrats."[6] An occasional labor PAC, such as the Teamsters' DRIVE, does take a more bipartisan approach, if only for the sake of practicality. "If there's a Republican who's been up there [in Congress] for years, our membership will say, 'You know, we ought to endorse that son-of-a-bitch instead of having him mad at us for the next two years,' " explains DRIVE's Dave Sweeney.

Like the labor PACs, a solid majority of nonconnected committees are willing to express a clear partisan preference. (We will see later in this chapter that many nonconnected PACs express contempt for the American political party system despite their affinity for one or the other party.) The formation of a number of liberal committees has shifted the partisan affiliation of nonconnected PACs more toward the Democrats when only direct gifts are considered (see Table 3–3). But their independent expenditures remain tilted heavily toward the Republicans. In 1982, for example, ideological PACs of all stripes spent $4 million independently to defeat Democratic congressional candidates, and just $550,000 to defeat their Republican counterparts. In the same year just $369,000 in independent expenditures supported Democratic candidacies, while $883,000 was spent to support GOP contenders.[7]

THE MATING DANCE OF PAC AND PARTY

PACs and parties court one another, but the parties are more assiduous in their attentions. This is because parties are rarely called on to contribute to PACs, while PACs almost always donate to at least one party's candidates and frequently to the party itself. A multicandidate PAC is permitted to give $15,000 each year to all national-party political committees combined, and while few contribute that large an amount, about a third of all multicandidate PACs donated some amount to the parties in 1981–1982.[8] PACs swelled the parties' treasuries by a total of about $6 million in those two years. While this sum comprised a modest 3 percent of all PAC funds raised, the money was not insubstantial, and was welcomed especially by the financially hard-pressed Democrats. The Democrats received $4.1 million to the Republicans' $1.9 million, an edge attributable in part to the GOP's desire to steer all available PAC money to its candidates.[9] The Republican committees are generally well funded from other sources as well, and less in need of infusions of PAC cash.

Most PACs secure some of their information about candidates and elections at regular party briefings and through party newsletters. As Table 2–3 showed, 44 percent of the multicandidate PACs receive information from the Democrats, and 47 percent from the Republicans. This nearly equal overall division averages in (and thereby conceals) the tilt of corporate PACs to GOP briefings and labor PACs to Democratic sources. Trade and nonconnected PACs give balanced attention to the two parties, though trade is more likely than any other category of PAC to rely on the parties' information, while the nonconnecteds are the least likely to do so. The PACs that attend the briefings given by each party are somewhat more inclined to contribute to that party's candidates.[10] It may simply be that those who are predisposed to one party's philosophy usually assemble at its table, but the briefings may also nudge undecided PACs in the direction of the party's marginal candidates.

The PACs are somewhat wary of the slant they receive at party briefings. "The parties always have a built-in bias," notes Don Cogman of MAPCO PAC. "Everybody in the PAC community realizes that and takes some of the parties' information with a grain of salt." Many PAC managers have held the parties accountable for "bum steers" that have caused the PACs to back losers. One corporate PAC official complained, "We invested heavily in Dave Emery [Maine's 1982 GOP nominee for the Senate] because the Republican Senatorial Committee told us his was the top-priority race and he had a good chance to win. In fact, Emery's campaign was a shambles, he lost in a landslide, and we wasted our money."

Yet one can only sympathize with the parties, which are caught in the crossfire between PACs and candidates. "The PACs won't listen to us if we're not honest with them, yet the pressure from candidates to present them in the best possible light is unmerciful," reports Joe Gaylord of the National Republican Congressional Committee (NRCC). He continued, "We're a convenient excuse for campaigns that aren't successful in raising money from the PACs; on the other hand PACs make it tough on us because they have no hesitancy using us as the excuse for not giving when a Republican candidate calls them, telling [the candidate] that we said he can't win." Gaylord's counterpart at the Democratic Congressional Campaign Committee (DCCC), Marty Franks, has had similar experiences. "By the end of each PAC briefing we always had four or five candidates mad, calling on the phone about what we'd said about them. One candidate threatened to come over to my house and spit in my eye."

Both parties' officials choose to brave the slings and arrows of outraged candidates rather than to mislead the PACs seriously, however. "We have to be relatively honest because PAC resources are finite and tough judgments have to be made about which of our candidates can be helped to victory," says Gaylord. "We don't want to waste [PACs'] money any more than they do." Still, *caveat emptor* is not an inappropriate slogan for PACs at party briefings. As Mike Mulligan, PAC liaison for the National Republican Senatorial Committee (NRSC) admitted, "Our job is to elect Republicans, and we're going to try to sell Republicans in the most effective manner possible, just like Proctor and Gamble sells their product in the best way they can."

As PACs have become more sophisticated, they have begun to demand more precise and accurate information from the parties, and as in virtually every category of modern-day political organization, the Republicans are in a much better position to provide it. "Our job is to develop a dialogue and a close relationship with the PACs," declares the Republican National Committee (RNC) chairman Frank Fahrenkopf. The RNC and associated committees have established numerous programs and channels of communication with the PACs in order to meet Fahrenkopf's objective. Just as PACs have special donor clubs, the RNC has the PAC 40 Club and the Eagles' President's Club. Any PAC contributing $5,000 or more to the RNC each year gains a PAC 40 membership, entitling it to meet with Republican congressional leaders for off-the-record breakfasts once a month at the Capitol Hill Club in Washington. The admission price for a PAC to the Eagles' President's Club is $10,000 a year. More important than the limited-edition paintings signed by Presidents Reagan and Ford and the Steuben glassware club members receive, they gain more access to officeholders in special meetings held throughout the year, and secure reserved seats at the GOP National Convention. Along similar lines, the National Republican Senatorial Committee (NRSC) has a $10,000-per-PAC-member Senatorial Trust Club, and the National Republican Congressional Committee (NRCC) has a $2,500-per-PAC-member Republican Congressional Leadership Council.[11]

Any PAC, not just members of expensive clubs, enjoys access to certain Republican services. The Senatorial Committee maintains a toll-free telephone number for PACs' use, and the Republicans dispense not only updates on their own candidates but suggestions to improve PAC fundraising. Briefings for the PACs are provided by both the Congressional and Senatorial Committees on a quarterly basis in Washington and in major cities around the country. The NRCC also periodically publishes an "Opportunity Race" report, sent to 2,200 GOP-leaning PACs, that provides data on key congressional races. Large PACs, such as the Realtors, AMPAC, and the Homebuilders, do not have to attend formal GOP briefings because they are given personal attention at their convenience. "It's all personal contacts," says Tim Crawford of the RNC's PAC division. "One-on-one relationships are very important," agrees the NRSC's Jackie Lowe. And the GOP certainly pays attention to the needs of its candidates, particularly unknown challengers. When a challenger comes to Washington, the appropriate Republican committee will help to set up appointments with PAC managers in the capital and to design a PAC solicitation program tailor-made to the candidate's strengths. Along with the frequent workshops and training sessions for candidates held by the GOP, the party also throws in a cocktail reception with the PACs.

Republican appeals to corporate and trade PACs are enhanced by the presence of a number of former party staffers in key positions in the PAC community. BIPAC, the U.S. Chamber of Commerce, the Realtors, the National Association of Broadcasters, the National Association of Business PACs, and many other organizations have hired Republican party operatives in PAC leadership posts in recent years. The GOP's path to business PACs is also smoothed by their leaders' firm advocacy of the PAC movement and stern opposition to any attempt to limit the PACs' influence. For instance, Sen. Richard Lugar (R–Ind.), chairman of the NRSC, wrote PAC managers in 1983 assuring them of his determination to defend them legislatively.[12]

But relations between business PACs and the GOP are not always completely friendly. The NRCC's Joe Gaylord insists, "Despite what people think, business PAC money does not flow from the heavens just because you are a conservative Republican nominee." Ronald Reagan complained directly to business leaders before the 1978 election about the proportion of PAC funds being given to Democrats: "I don't think the Republican party has received the kind of financial support from corporate PACs that its record deserves. . . . The best thing you can hope for by following [a split-giving] policy is that the alligator will eat you last."[13] Even though business PACs have increased the GOP's share of their contributions since then, dissatisfaction remains among Republicans. In 1983 the executive director of the NRSC sent a letter to all Republican U.S. senators which listed the business and trade PACs giving significant amounts to Democratic committees and candidates, and described those PACs as "hostile to the interests of our majority" and as contributing "to the cause of turning you back into a ranking minority member."[14]

Republicans are uneasy in part because the Democrats have recently devoted greater efforts to securing corporate and trade PAC money. Since 1981 Rep. Tony Coelho (D–Calif.), chairman of the Democratic Congressional Campaign Committee (DCCC), has made a concerted appeal to business to "not let your ideology get in the way of your business judgment."[15] Coelho and the DCCC executive director Marty Franks systematically visited many of the larger corporate and trade PACs. As Franks reports:

> It got us some money, but more important, it put them on notice. We told them that the party might not have done a very good job at marketing itself or its candidates to you, but we're putting you on notice that we're going to do better, and a year or two down the road if we're still not successful, we'll know it's not our marketing skills but your ideology. . . . [Take] the Chamber of Commerce, for instance. When we went there, we heard a great deal of professed bipartisanship. It doesn't really bother me if the Chamber [backs all Republicans] so long as they don't claim to be bipartisan. I'm a big boy, I like the game, don't kid a kidder. Now I've got no gripe with the Realtors. They're conservative people . . . but I feel it's a more honest process and generally we get a fair shake.

Democratic leaders consider this "self-interest" argument the most persuasive to business PACs. The Democrats frankly admit that they are selling access to a currently Democratic House of Representatives, and to a Democratic Senate and White House sometime in the future. "The point I make to business PACs is that Democrats are clearly going to control the House for many years, and regain the Senate shortly and, we hope, the White House too," relates the DNC political director Ann Lewis. "It's in your interest to make sure you have access to these institutions. It's not in your interest to shut yourselves off."

Democratic officials concede that they have not increased their party candidates' share of corporate and trade PAC funds, but they have kept the situation from worsening (as Table 3–3 shows). Franks also notes, "We're getting more calls from PAC directors who need to balance out their contributions." In addition to their visits to business PACs, Democratic leaders have enlisted the aid of influential House and Senate leaders to approach PACs that may be friendly to the legislators individually but not to the party as a whole. Conservative Texas Democratic Reps. Charles Wilson and Kent Hance, for instance, were delegated the task of contacting the independent oil PACs, among the most ideological and Republican of all corporate PACs. In meetings and by letter, the congressmen told the oilmen, as Wilson put it, "You've got to stop trying to change the world or you are going to get hurt."[16]

Democrats have also followed the Republican lead in using exclusive clubs and offering special access to attract the PACs. The DNC has a Business Council which PACs can join with a $15,000 annual contribution, and a $2,500-per-year PAC Council which is the rough equivalent of the RNC's PAC 40 Club. Like its GOP counterpart, the PAC Council gathers together legislators and PAC officials for monthly breakfasts. Reflecting labor's prominent role in the Democratic party, there is a separate DNC Labor Council whose price is $15,000 per year for a PAC and a whopping $50,000 for a labor union proper. The Democratic senatorial committee has a $15,000 Leadership Circle, and a cut-rate $5,000 Senate Roundtable which is aimed particularly at business PACs. The Congressional Committee also has two groups, a $15,000 Speaker's Club and a $2,500 Chairmen's Council. The activities of the Chairmen's Council have drawn the admiration of even former rivals. TARPAC's Steve Stockmeyer, former executive director of the NRCC, calls the Council "irresistible to most of the PACs in this town. You get an invitation to have dinner with John Dingell [chairman of the business-regulating House Energy and Commerce Committee] and all his key subcommittee chairmen are there too."[17]

Moreover, Democratic officials like Coelho have made peace gestures to the business PAC community. For example, despite the fact that the vast majority of PAC-limitation measures in Congress are sponsored by Democrats, Coelho appears in the Public Affairs Council's pro-PAC film *PACs under Fire* saying: "The press has not really researched what is going on with business PACs. . . . If they did that, they would not be as prejudiced against business PACs. . . ."[18] Democratic party staffers have begun to appear regularly at business PAC briefings "as part of the monitoring process to make sure we get a fair shake," explains Marty Franks. The previously uninvolved Democrats were not at first familiar to all the participants at these briefings. Early on, Franks joined a briefing session held by the U.S. Chamber of Commerce for its regional political directors. As the speaker finished, a prominent member of the GOP's PAC staff interjected, "Look, let's cut through this stuff. We're all Republicans here. What can we do to help you?"

For its candidates as well as the PACs, the Democratic party has been slow to match superior Republican services. "Until 1981 we didn't work terribly effectively with PACs," admits the DSCC's executive director Brian Atwood. Charles Orasin of Handgun Control PAC compared the two parties this way:

The Republicans have a phenomenal amount of information available on their candidates. I receive reams of stuff from them. The Democrats have a hard time even telling you the name of a campaign's treasurer so you can send them a check. . . . I went to one Democratic party gathering for PACs to meet candidates, and only four or five other people were there. You know why? The Democrats were sending out invitations to the meeting bulk rate, so people never even got the mailing in time. Republicans are just light-years ahead of the Democrats in data collection and candidate presentation.

Democratic services to PACs and party candidates are gradually improving, however. The party committees have expanded the size of their PAC liaison staffs, conduct regular briefing sessions for PACs, and distribute informational newsletters about key races. While Democratic congressional candidates receive much less direct party aid in lining up PAC gifts, the DCCC has been holding a series of large PAC-candidate forums, each involving about two dozen candidates and 50–100 PACs. The candidates are stationed at various locations in the meeting room, and PAC officials are free to roam from booth to booth. "It's just intended to break the ice," says Marty Franks. "Few candidates walk out with checks."

In essence, the role of ice breaker is the fundamental one played by both parties with the PACs. The parties' uneasy alliance with PACs is formed and maintained of necessity—the necessity to elect party candidates. Republican and Democratic leaders alike may understand the competing nature of PACs and parties, but they also realize that under the current system of campaign finance, PAC money gives congressional contenders an often crucial competitive edge. So PACs and parties are learning to support each other.

PRO-PARTY AND ANTIPARTY PACS

So far the only certain "generalization" we have been able to make about PACs is that it is very difficult to make broad generalizations about the diverse cluster of groups that huddles under the PAC umbrella. This holds true when we consider PACs' relations with the major parties, which can be cozy on the one hand or rocky on the other. First of all, there are a number of strongly pro-party PACs. Labor PACs are so closely allied with the Democratic party that they are sometimes seen as a dual or shadow Democratic structure performing many of the same tasks for Democratic candidates that the Republican party organization accomplishes for its nominees.[19] Fifteen seats on the DNC Executive Committee are reserved for labor officials, and labor returns the favor. In 1981, for example, labor alone raised almost $1 million for the national party.[20] Democrats have also worked hand-in-hand with most of the liberal nonconnected PACs we have looked at (see Chapter 3). Pamela Harriman's Democrats for the '80s has even engaged in joint fundraising with the party. Her PAC cosponsored a $1,000-a-plate black-tie dinner with the DNC at the February 1983 National Governors Association meeting, and split the $350,000 proceeds with the party. (Harriman promised her half to Senate candidates, and the DNC share was targeted to House and gubernatorial contenders.) Similar cooperative efforts have occurred at the state level as well.[21] When the North Carolina Campaign Fund disbanded in July 1983, the PAC donated its golden direct-mail list of 35,000 donors to the state Democratic party.[22]

While there is no set of PACs as closely tied to the GOP as labor is to the Democrats, the Republicans have had very smooth working relationships with many of the corporate, trade, and coordinating business PACs over the years. The independent oil PACs in particular have been enormously supportive of GOP candidates and party needs since the mid-1970s.[23] Occasionally, GOP activists and allies have themselves taken the PAC route to shore up party efforts in various ways. In 1983 a PAC called American Women Supporting the President was formed to help Ronald Reagan close his "gender gap."[24] Sen. John Heinz (R–Pa.), a recent former chairman of the National Republican Senatorial Committee, served as advisory chairman of a PAC called the Republican National Independent Expenditure Committee, which made $185,000 in direct-mail independent expenditures to assist appointed Washington GOP Sen. Daniel J. Evans's successful bid for an elected term in 1983.[25] (The PAC drew loud protests from Democrats, and aroused fears among Republican party officials that Heinz's connections to the NRSC could jeopardize the "independent" status of the PAC's spending.[26] Heinz resigned from membership in the NRSC to help defuse the controversy.)[27]

But the parties' relationships with some other PACs are far rockier. The conservative ideological PACs lead the list of party antagonists and, surprisingly, there is concern about them in both parties. Democrats, of course, expect little but hostility from groups such as NCPAC, and are not surprised when Terry Dolan attacks them as socialists:

> The process of the Democratic party is frankly a bidding war between fairly committed leftist forces, fanatics who are socialist. . . . Jesse Jackson isn't a leader for blacks; he's a leader for socialism, statism, and he hides behind the fact that he's a black.

But Republican leaders are often taken aback when they read of Dolan's assessment of their party: "The Republican party is a fraud. It's a social club where rich people go to pick their noses."[28] Similarly, Dolan's New Right ally, Paul Weyrich of the Committee for the Survival of a Free Congress, takes a dim view of the GOP: "The problem with Republicans is that most of them in leadership positions never had to work for a living. Those people in the White House who have clout are from the upper crust. If you wear a certain kind of mink fur, if you are a Hollywood star, or David Rockefeller, or one of the biggies from California, you're welcome."[29]

It is not just their rhetoric but their actions that characterize many New Right PACs as antiparty. In some cases the conservative PACs are clearly attempting to usurp the functions of the two parties and establish themselves as substitutes by recruiting and training candidates and creating pseudo-party organizations of their own.[30] Sen. Jesse Helms's Congressional Club has in many ways supplanted the regular Republican party organization in North Carolina, to the consternation of some GOP officials in the state.[31] Weyrich, among other New Right leaders, has called for the disbanding of the GOP and the establishment of a separate "conservative party."[32] NCPAC, which has been accused of stealing contributors' names from Republican party finance report lists,[33] seriously considered declaring itself to be a political party in 1982.[34]

Even though the New Right groups usually end up supporting Republican candidates (or opposing Democratic ones), their antagonism has caused some GOP leaders to take a critical view of their activities. Richard Richards, during his tenure as RNC chairman in 1981, said publicly that the New Right PAC efforts "hurt us more than help us."[35] Before the Senate Rules Committee, Richards remarked that "I find them obnoxious to the whole scheme of things. . . . They have been the biggest sources of antagonism for me as chairman of the national party."[36] Richards's successors at the GOP helm have been somewhat more amenable to the conservative PACs. Paul Weyrich indicates that he has a "much more cordial relationship" with general chairman Sen. Paul Laxalt and RNC head Frank Fahrenkopf: "They are much more open than Richards." For himself, Fahrenkopf acknowledges that the independent PACs can be a "disruptive" influence in campaigns, but states flatly, "I am not one who is critical of independent groups. . . . They have the right to express themselves."

Yet beneath the placid surface of such diplomacy run the dangerous currents of tension and competition natural to relations between a party and this type of PAC. One of Fahrenkopf's party publications, *First Monday,* makes the point none too subtly. "Oceans of political direct mail fundraising letters promise to elect GOP candidates," the piece notes. "Some may prove helpful, some may not. Regardless, many people confuse this mail with Republican Party fundraising efforts."[37] As for the Democrats, it is no surprise that undisguised hatred for the conservative PACs is the order of the day. The DNC's Ann Lewis comments, "I'm personally content to let Jesse Helms and his friends choke in their own bile." But her distaste for independent PACs extends to the liberal side of the spectrum, suggesting again the contentious nature of a party's relations with even its PAC friends:

> I believe the independent PACs are a problem for two reasons. There's a finite pool of political money, and we simply can't afford this drain to them, gambling that they'll spend it wisely. . . . Second, unlike the parties, many of the independent PACs are essentially computer-driven mail-order operations that have no membership and are accountable to nobody.

Most PACs fall between the pro-party and antiparty poles; in fact most could perhaps best be described as indifferent to the parties. That does not mean the effects PACs have on party organization and development are neutral, of course. Overall, there is little evidence for the widespread claim that PACs have contributed greatly to the long-term decline of the political party system in the United States.[38] Rather, PACs may be one more manifestation of the atomizing forces which at a more general level have made the parties less appealing to Americans.[39] On the whole, general organizations such as the political parties, which represent broad-based interests and demand loyalties that cut across many different issues, seem to have less appeal today than compact units like ideological PACs, which attract adherents who share a single or well-defined set of emotional beliefs.

We will take up this subject again in the concluding chapter, but for now it is worth noting that though the rise of PACs has changed the relationship between a party and its candidates, the force and direction of that change are complex. On the one hand PACs provide an alternative source of funding and support services for a candidate, weakening his ties with the party and lessening his fear of severe electoral consequences if he is disloyal to his party. But at the same time the competition from PACs is one of many factors stimulating a dramatic surge in party organization, technology, programs, and fundraising that has drawn candidates much closer to the national parties. Parties can now do—or refuse to do—much more to elect their nominees than they could in the past. These party advances were occurring during the same years the PAC movement was maturing, and just as PACs have in some ways limited the parties' influence, so too have the invigorated parties acted as a check on PACs.

PARTY REGENERATION: OLD HATS, NEW FAVORS

The PACs have stolen the media spotlight, but the parties may be winning the long-run battle for political supremacy. Prematurely counted out by many political observers, the parties have surprised their critics by regenerating themselves at the national level through the use of direct mail and other tools of the new campaign technology.[40] The Republican party has led the way, spurred by the hope of breaking out of its minority status, and the Democrats have lately followed, prompted by the party's 1980 election disasters and the need to catch up with the GOP. Despite the press's focus on political action committees, the parties are financially healthier than the PACs. When the six national committees (DNC, RNC, DCCC, NRCC, DSCC, and NRSC) are taken together, the two parties raised $218 million in 1982, compared to about $190 million for all PACs.

The Democrats are clearly the junior partner in the new areas of campaign finance. Of the $218 million total in 1982, the Republicans raised more than 87 percent. The GOP has traditionally been more successful at fundraising, but the gap began to grow after 1968 and to accelerate rapidly in the mid-1970s. During this time the Republicans made an enormous success of their direct-mail program while the Democrats continued just to rely on large donors to whittle away accumulated campaign debts.[41] Table 5–1 displays the results of Republican initiative and Democratic lethargy. While the receipts of both parties have increased, the ratio has gone from 2.5 to 1 in 1976 to 5.5 to 1 in 1982 in favor of the GOP. Similarly, the contributions and expenditures parties make to and for their candidates show a startling Republican gain in relation to the Democrats; the $2.4-million gap of 1976 became a $14.8-million gulf by 1982.

The Democrats have taken steps since 1981 to begin to make up the difference, including instituting a direct-mail program. "It'll take a while, but they'll catch up," claims the RNC chairman Frank Fahrenkopf. But the GOP mail efforts began when postage and production costs were much lower, and while the Democrats' edge in sheer numbers can be transformed into dollars through the use of direct mail, the Republicans' technological lead of a decade will make it difficult for the Democrats to catch up for many years, if ever. "They're just not going to do it," says Joe Gaylord of the National Republican Congressional Committee. His Democratic adversaries realistically agree. "They got in during the golden era of direct mail and we'll never see it again," remarks the DCCC's Marty Franks ruefully. "They're always going to have more money to invest than we are. On the other hand there are far more Democrats than Republicans out there, so we don't need as much money. We can achieve functional parity without matching them dollar for dollar." Ann Lewis of the DNC agrees: "Our goal is to get to the point where we're not crisis ridden and have a regular flow of money." Adds the DSCC's Brian Atwood, perhaps wishfully in light of the growing financial divide: "Besides, the Republicans waste more money than we spend."

If the Republicans waste much money—a dubious assertion—they seem to waste it on the right candidates: those in close races in which additional resources can spell the difference between winning and losing. In 1982, 143 defeated House candidates received more than $10,000 each in help from their parties. Of those, 123 were Republicans and only 20 were Democrats. By contrast, there were 28 House contenders who received more than 45 percent of the vote in 1982 yet were given less than $10,000 by their parties. Every one of these candidates, who might have won with additional financial assistance, was a Democrat.[42]

The Republicans gave their winners as well as their losers far more cash. Under FECA, a party can give each House candidate direct contributions

Table 5–1.
Political Party Finances, 1976–1982[a]

	TOTAL RECEIPTS (MILLION $)		TOTAL CONTRIBUTIONS TO AND EXPENDITURES FOR PARTY CANDIDATES[b] (MILLION $)	
YEAR	DEMOCRATS	REPUBLICANS	DEMOCRATS	REPUBLICANS
1976	18.2	45.7	3.9	6.3
1978	26.4	84.5	2.3	8.9
1980	37.2	169.5	6.6	17.0
1982	39.3	215.0	5.1	19.9

SOURCE: Federal Election Commission.
[a]Includes total for the national senatorial and congressional committees as well as all other reported national and state/local spending.
[b]All presidential, Senate, and House candidates are included.

of up to $30,000 ($10,000[43] apiece from the national party committee, the national congressional campaign committee, and the state party). In addition, both the national and state parties are permitted to make "coordinated expenditures"[44] for their candidates up to a certain amount, which is adjusted for inflation in every election year. In 1982 the national and state parties could *each* donate as much as $18,440 in coordinated expenditures to a House nominee, over and above their direct contributions. All in all, then, party committees could add $66,880[45] to the coffers of each House candidate in 1982—fully a quarter of the cost of a competitive House campaign.[46] The Republicans were able to give nearly the full amount to practically every competitive House nominee in 1982,[47] while the Democrats often made just token contributions.

Much the same occurred on the Senate side, where much more party money could be donated. Although direct contributions in a Senate race are limited to $17,500 per candidate for all national party committees combined, the national and state parties in 1982 could each spend the greater of $36,880 or two cents per voter in each state in coordinated expenditures. So depending on the size of the state, from $91,260 to almost $1.33 million (in California) could be spent by the party for its Senate candidates,[48] and in most cases the GOP contributed up to the maximum. In 1982 the Republican party gave its Senate nominees about 15 percent of all the money they raised, and over 21 percent to GOP Senate challengers seeking to oust incumbent Democrats.[49] By contrast, Democratic party gifts accounted for only about 4 percent of its Senate candidates' totals, and challengers garnered but 5 percent of their war chests from the party.[50] However, it is important to keep in mind that both parties are now contributing a greater proportion of their candidates' budgets than previously. Moreover, the parties tend to give their donations relatively early, when it can help to get their nominees' campaigns off the ground and to attract the attention of the PACs.

These party contributions are, if anything, understated in significance because the parties donate more than money to their candidates. Parties are increasingly making their gifts in the form of dollar-stretching in-kind services, of the type that only a very few PACs are equipped to provide.[51] Since parties (unlike political consultants) have no desire to turn a profit, they are able to make these services (polling, media production, time-buying) available at cut-rate prices, which in effect multiplies their contribution limit and saves their nominees the large fees charged by many independent political consultants.[52]

The Republican party here again has proven to be the pace-setter, and the in-kind offerings of the three national GOP committees are diverse, sophisticated, and impressive. Both the NRCC and the NRSC hold extensive training sessions for their candidates and campaign staffs in Washington and around the country; the participants receive instruction in everything from on-camera conduct to off-camera, nuts-and-bolts organizing. Through direct computer terminal hookups with data banks in Washington, selected GOP congressional candidates are given instant access to the party's staff and research holdings, which include detailed background information on Democratic incumbents' voting records and public statements. The Senatorial Committee, in fact, guarantees its nominees an answer to their inquiries within forty-eight hours. The NRCC specializes in the design and production of television advertisements for House candidates at its in-house media center. In 1982, 180 television spots were developed for 92 Republican House candidates (about half incumbents and half challengers or open-seat contenders), and for many of these candidates the NRCC staff also arranged the purchase of air time to show the spots. This saved the campaigns the substantial commissions and fees charged by professional media consultants and time-buyers. The NRSC has regularly taken surveys for its Senate nominees, including (in thirteen states in 1982) "tracking polls" that follow a campaign's progress on a daily basis. The information revealed by these surveys was of crucial value to a number of GOP candidates.[53]

The Republican party's national operations are by no means limited to these direct candidate services. Its nominees are assisted indirectly by a myriad of party programs. The RNC holds regional training conferences for party workers and candidates each year; during these workshops, two-way satellite communications sessions are held so that the participants can hear and question Republican officeholders wherever they may be in the country.[54] The party committees also frequently sponsor "institutional" television advertising which touts Republicans generically, as well as spots to boost popular support for the Reagan administration—support the committees believe "trickles down" to other party candidates. In 1982 the Republicans spent $15 million nationally on these institutional and pro-Reagan commercials, which struck such themes as "give the guy [Reagan] a chance" and then "stay the course" with the president.[55] While these advertisements were not always helpful to moderate Republicans attempting to put distance between themselves and a conservative chief executive, pre- and post-election surveys suggested that the GOP-sponsored media campaigns were, on the whole, useful.[56] Polls also showed that President Reagan's standing was boosted in the forty-five media markets where the GOP spent $1 million on spots supporting the administration's economic policies in March 1983.[57]

Additionally, the NRCC and the NRSC often conduct exhaustive survey research to determine the most vulnerable Democratic congressmen, and then find and convince good potential GOP nominees to run against the selected incumbents. At the same time the party committees attempt to weaken these targeted Democrats with publicity campaigns in their home districts attacking the congressmen's Capitol Hill records and votes.[58] At the level of basic organization, the Republican Senatorial Committee actually pays hundreds of thousands of dollars of its Senate incumbents' office expenses,[59] and the RNC selects key counties across the country for organizational overhauls and infusion of national funds for voter registration and canvassing.

These programs are supported mainly by direct-mail fundraising, and each of the three major committees of the national parties has its own massive list of donors. The NRCC's, for example, expanded from 24,000 names in 1975 to 1.5 million by 1984. New letters are issued to past and potential contributors about once a month, and new gimmicks appear regularly. In 1983, for instance, the NRCC launched its very own mail "sweepstakes," akin to the Publishers' Clearinghouse extravaganza: entrants, who did not need to make a donation, were eligible for $100,000 in cash prizes.[60] More than three-fourths of the total receipts of the national GOP committees are raised by direct mail of some kind.

The roster of Republican party activities has been daunting for the Democrats, who offer few services comparable in size and scope. But after 1980 a consensus emerged in the Democratic party that organizational renewal was overdue. Since then the Republican party has been paid the highest possible compliment by its rival—imitation.[61] "We're doing the best damn job of copying that we can," admits the DCCC's Marty Franks.[62] Using borrowed and rented lists from Democratic candidates and interest groups, the DNC and the DCCC began direct-mail programs in 1981. From 25,000 party donors at the start, the DNC's support base grew to 400,000 by 1984, and the DCCC's to 125,000. Most of the resulting profits have been reinvested in direct mail to prospect for more donors, ensuring a better payoff in the latter part of the 1980s. Accounting for just 2.5 percent of the DNC's receipts in 1980, direct mail began to comprise more than a tenth of the DNC's income by 1983.

With another glance over their shoulder, the Democrats have established national and regional "training academies" to impart campaign skills to party candidates and staff. A media center was constructed with the aid of a $390,000 loan from former New York Gov. and Mrs. Averell Harriman; opened in January 1984, it was expected to produce television and radio commercials for up to 75 Democratic House and Senate candidates before the November election. Already the Democrats have aired their first institutional advertising. In 1982 they focused in on a vulnerable spot of President Reagan's with a clever $1-million campaign which, though relatively little seen because of inadequate financing, was successfully keyed to the theme of "It Isn't Fair—It's Republican." The Democrats followed up in 1983 with radio ads that denounced the Reagan deficits while an announcer explained that a background noise was a faucet dripping "red ink."[63] The Democrats' new $7-million headquarters on Capitol Hill, which houses the three national party committees, will itself prove a financial boon since in some years the Democrats paid more in rent than they garnered in contributions from all their labor sources.

Party-building in the states has become a Democratic priority too. The Democrats are basing their expansion on an organizational model designed by the political consultant Matt Reese and first used (very successfully) in New Mexico in 1982. Besides relying on such time-tested activities as canvassing, voter registration, and get-out-the-vote drives, the Reese program aimed to coordinate the campaigns of all Democratic candidates in a state by using party resources as the carrot to accomplish efficiencies and secure cooperation. The Democrats are also following a GOP example in sending out negative press releases to the districts of incumbent Republican congressmen. According to Marty Franks, the Republican legislators did not like the taste of their own party's medicine:

> Tony [Coelho, DCCC chairman] would sit on the House floor with a tally sheet and look up at the voting board and then look across the aisle at the Republicans, and guys would just scurry for cover. We let 'em get a whiff of their own smoke. It was psychological warfare with an impact beyond my wildest dreams. It caused the Republican party to spend money on the defensive which they'd never had to do before.

As Democrats discover the benefits of the new campaign technology, they will help to bring better balance to a clearly out-of-kilter competition between the GOP and themselves. An even balance is probably not possible, given the Republicans' long lead and problems of poor planning and bad luck which still plague the Democrats. A seventeen-hour DNC telethon on the NBC network held in May 1983, for instance, was supposed to raise at least $8 million over costs and add 300,000 new names to the party's donor list. In fact the production lost $2.8 million after expenses were paid, and garnered only 100,000 additional givers, although syndication of parts of the show and future mailings to donors may erase the deficit and yield some additional money besides.[64] No one disputes that the Democrats have much ground to cover, but the progress already made is substantial.[65]

Both party organizations have been palpably strengthened in recent years, and this has had definite consequences for American politics. First, the centralization of party resources is helping to nationalize candidate recruitment, campaign technique, and to some degree, nominees' stands on the issues.[66] Institutional advertising, after all, clearly projects party positions on some issues—positions from which a candidate wearing the party label cannot easily separate himself. Second, party services and spending on behalf of candidates are having an electoral effect by helping to pull marginal candidates to victory on election day. Party expenditures cannot reverse landslides, of course, but in competitive circumstances they can certainly make a difference of 1 or 2 percent of the vote. While traditional estimates based on economic conditions and presidential popularity forecast a Republican loss of forty or more House seats in 1982, for instance, the GOP dropped only twenty-six, and Republican party spending was assigned much of the credit for the difference.[67] It is no accident that, of the twenty-three close Senate contests (decided by a winning proportion of less than 53 percent of the vote) in 1980 and 1982, all but four were won by the GOP. The Republicans have also used their financial and technological offerings to entice strong party candidates to run, even in "bad" Republican years such as recession-plagued 1982.[68] This represents a major change from the past when candidates were more responsive to economic and issue tides, and the refusal of good candidates to seek office in a "bad" year almost guaranteed a party disaster on election day.

Finally, some suggest that party money and services are also drawing candidates much closer to their parties, since the parties are contributing in tangible ways to their nominees' election. Whether or nor any gratitude or obligation to the party is created in this fashion, such services as training schools, party issue papers, and institutional advertising put officeholders through a "homogenizing" process that may predispose them more favorably to the "party line" in government. Party leaders and political observers I interviewed differed about whether such a development was really taking place, but all were agreed on one point: the parties remain less influential than they would be otherwise because alternative sources of funding are available to candidates. And the most available "alternative source" for incumbents, as we have seen, is in PACs—a somewhat hidden but nonetheless vital aspect of the symbiotic and competitive PAC-party relationship.

Overall, however, the parties are clearly meeting whatever challenge PACs pose to their authority and predominance in the political system, and are even gaining strength as they respond to the PACs' competition for the loyalty of their candidates. Both the Democratic and Republican organizations have capitalized on the offerings of the pro-party PACs, have skillfully channeled PAC funds to their marginal candidates, and have generally minimized the damage done by antiparty PACs.

Now that the "great PAC debate" can be viewed in the full light of the facts, the final chapter will offer a general assessment of political action committees and their place in the political system, and will suggest a reform agenda to improve on the current system of campaign finance in the United States.

CHAPTER 6

PACs and Electoral Reform

> We've got to limit the PACs as part of a comprehensive reform to restore sanity and balance to the system of campaign finance.
>
> —Fred Wertheimer, president, Common Cause

> What we don't need is another goddamn reform. It just screws things up and in ten years it has the public even more cynical about politics.
>
> —Peter Fenn, director, Center for Responsive Politics

The reformist impulse is quick to surface in American politics, and PACs have drawn the reformer's eye as nothing else has in recent years. Changes in the election laws have been proposed by the cartload; it is as though, said AMPAC's Peter Lauer, "all the ills of the country are due to PACs." We will take a look at the possibilities for PAC reform later in this chapter. First, though, we will focus on the general public's view of PACs, and then offer a broad assessment of the ways and means of political action committees.

PUBLIC OPINION ABOUT PACS

What is the view of PACs held by the public at large? How aware is the electorate of PACs, and how concerned are people about them? As is usually the case on complicated issues, public opinion is mixed, relatively uninformed, and various, depending on the wording of survey questions.[1] The "red flag" words and phrases that dot many polls about campaign finance make them suspect as true barometers of public opinion. Louis Harris, for example, asked his survey respondents in November 1982:

Do you feel that *excessive* campaign spending in national elections is a very serious problem, only somewhat serious, or not a serious problem at all? [emphasis added].[2]

With the use of the biased adjective "excessive," it is hardly surprising that 62 percent of the respondents saw campaign spending as a very serious problem.[3] Similarly, it is hardly unexpected that 71 percent would agree with the suggestion in a January 1980 ABC News/Harris survey that PACs "are pouring too much money into the whole political process."[4] On the other hand a 1983 survey commissioned by BIPAC and other business interests showed that 53 percent of a random sample of the population believed that PACs should be allowed to make contributions to political campaigns, while only 32 percent did not.[5] This positive result becomes more understandable when one reads the preface to the question, which defined a PAC as "*individuals* who contribute . . . as a committee and may be comprised, for example, of union *members,* corporations' *employees,* or *citizens concerned* about a particular cause or issue" (emphasis added). Few Americans favor limiting individual rights in politics, and the pollster was clever to cast PACs in the mold of the individual rather than as abstract, suspect organizations and institutions.

A much more balanced question about PACs than that of either the Harris or BIPAC polls was asked by the Roper Organization in December 1982:[6]

Political action committees, or "PACs" as they're called, are committees formed by corporations, labor unions, trade associations and other groups to raise money that is then donated to political parties or candidates for office. The members of these committees are elected by the employees and raise their money from employees. Unless an employee designates where his or her contribution is to go, the PAC committee decides which party or candidates will get how much. Some people think these PAC committees are a good thing because they involve corporations, labor unions and trade associations in the political process. Others think they are a bad thing because they give such groups too much influence over who is elected. All things considered, do you think political action committees are a "good" thing or a "bad" thing?

By a margin of 41 percent to 23 percent the respondents called PACs a "bad thing."[7] When another version of the question was tested in which PACs were described as being formed only by corporations, the reaction was even more negative (45 percent then saw PACs as a "bad thing" compared to just 17 percent who called them a "good thing"). Granted, even this more balanced question remains terribly simplistic and does not do justice to the arguments on either side, but it probably does give a rough estimate of public opinion on PACs.

How significant is that opinion, and how intensely felt is it? The BIPAC poll provides one clue. Not even a third of the respondents to that survey really knew what a PAC was. Only 32 percent chose a reasonably correct definition of PAC; 44 percent thought PACs were political party committees, candidates' committees, interest groups, or election units of the government,[8] and the remaining 25 percent were so unsure that they would not even hazard a guess. Among those who do know what PACs are and have a negative view of them, it is very likely that their outlook on PACs has been colored by the extensive critical coverage in the press PACs have received in recent years. In the election year of 1980, for example, the *New York Times* ran just four stories about PACs. But in the next election cycle, seventy-two stories were run (thirty-one in 1981 and forty-one in 1982), most of them revelations about "special-interest" money and the alleged connections between PAC gifts and votes in Congress.[9] Until very recently PAC opponents have had a virtual monopoly on discussion of the subject in the popular press. Common Cause issued a torrent of critical studies on PACs,[10] while the pro-PAC forces remained lethargic. "I tried to get our people moving on this [in 1982, but] their feeling was that all of it was going to blow over," reported Richard Armstrong, president of the business-oriented Public Affairs Council.[11] The one-sided picture of PACs that has often emerged in the news media almost certainly has affected the public's stance.

When pollsters probe further, however, a more differentiated attitude about PACs becomes apparent. The 1982 Harris Survey cited earlier also asked respondents about *particular* PACs:

> Now let me ask you about different groups and types of people who contribute money to political campaigns. Now for each, tell me if you feel it is a good or bad influence on politics and government.

It is clear from the results (shown in Table 6–1) that public prejudices about PACs are partly judgments about their sponsoring individuals and organizations. Citizens regard the influence of women and environmental groups as desirable, and so their PACs are rated favorably. Conversely, labor unions and corporations are regarded as undesirable participants in elections, and so are their PACs.[12] The residue of bad publicity for PACs is especially evident here. The term "PAC," in and of itself when applied to a group, is sufficient to add 4–6 percentage points to the "bad influence" column. Notice, though, that no PAC is as despised as are "rich people who want to protect their interests."

The proposition that the public is deeply hostile to all PACs is suspect also because so many Americans are members of groups sponsoring PACs.

Table 6–1.
Public Perceptions of PACs and Other Political Contributors

PAC/POLITICAL CONTRIBUTOR	GOOD INFLUENCE	BAD INFLUENCE	NOT SURE
Environmental PACs	54%	35%	11%
Women's PACs	53	40	7
Conservative PACs	40	46	14
Labor unions	34	60	6
Labor union PACs	27	64	9
Big companies	26	67	7
Big-company PACs	20	71	9
Firms that do business with the government	23	69	8
Rich people who want to protect their interests	16	77	6

SOURCE: Harris Survey, release 1983 No. 1, Jan. 3, 1983.

A 1981 Gallup poll found that fully 26 percent of the American population reported either belonging to one or more of sixteen "special-interest groups" or contributing money to them.[13] Interest groups also command more public affection than the political parties. In a 1983 Gallup Poll taken for the Advisory Commission on Intergovernmental Relations,[14] respondents were asked whether they believed their concerns were best represented by "organized special-interest groups" (this time including business and labor) or by the two major political parties. Interest groups won the contest by 45 percent to 34 percent.[15]

There is every indication that public participation in interest groups—especially those involved in politics—is on the increase, and the growth of political action committees is one important reason why. The proportion of the population reporting a gift of money to a political party or candidate grew from a steady 10 percent during the 1950s and 1960s to 16 percent in 1976 and 38 percent by 1980.[16] While the new income tax "checkoff" permitting taxpayers to contribute a dollar to the public financing fund for presidential candidates may have accounted for much of this increase in 1976 and 1980, the rise in PAC gifts also played a part.[17] By 1980 as many people were reporting donations to PACs as to all candidates combined, and PAC contributors outnumbered party contributors by a margin of nearly two to one.[18] In sum, then, the public may simply be reflecting the bad press PACs have received when they condemn PACs generically. In truth, people's evaluation of political action committees varies dramatically from group to group, and their own actions in joining and contributing to organizations sponsoring PACs suggest that the electorate's attitude toward PACs is far more ambivalent than the popular polls have frequently led us to believe.

PACS AND AMERICAN DEMOCRACY: REFLECTIONS ON THE PAST AND FUTURE

Predictions are usually ravaged by unforeseen events more brutally than beach houses are by hurricanes. Nevertheless we can now review the directions in which PACs and the PAC community seem to be heading. The growth in the sheer number of national PACs is clearly slowing. "We've reached a plateau," says BIPAC's Bernadette Budde. Most labor unions inclined to form PACs have probably already done so,[19] and while the *potential* for growth of corporate PACs remains great—over 40 percent of the *Fortune* 500 companies still do not have PACs—it is unlikely that many of the nonparticipants will be joining the PAC community soon. While peer pressure, the reputed legislative victories of PAC groups, and the news media's focus on PACs (and the chance to be heard that comes with it) can all be powerful inducements to PAC formation, large companies without PACs often have compelling, specialized reasons for remaining outside the PAC fold, while many smaller companies find operating a PAC to be "too much work, too many reports to file," as Richard Armstrong of the Public Affairs Council put it.[20]

On the other hand while existing PACs may occasionally disband,[21] most established PACs of any consequence will remain open for business because those who have tried it generally like it. A 1982 Harris survey for *Business Week,* for instance, found that 71 percent of all polled executives reported that their PACs had been working out well and meeting the goals set for them.[22] Once formed, PACs display the same institutional inertia as other organizations—bodies in motion tend to remain in motion—and with successful fundraising machinery in place, PACs can normally weather bad years. The "New Right" PACs certainly proved as much after their 1982 election losses. Some of their adversaries had hastily predicted their demise as a consequence of defeat,[23] but the health of the group's bank accounts was more robust than ever in 1983 and 1984.

Overall, then, PAC numbers will generally stabilize, with some growth continuing but at a moderate clip compared to the explosive years of the "PAC Decade." The area of expansion whose potential is most likely to be realized is at the state and local level. Many national PACs as well as regional groups are encouraging the establishment of state and local counterparts or affiliates, and state legislative, gubernatorial, mayoral, and ballot-issue campaigns are likely to see increased PAC activity in future years.

Presidential contenders are also certain to continue to use candidate PACs since the PAC vehicle is ideally suited for their preannouncement maneuverings.

While the growth in PAC numbers will probably not be as great as in the recent past, the increase in PAC receipts will be substantial as fundraising becomes more sophisticated, payroll deduction becomes more widespread, and the solicitation pool is gradually expanded to include twice-yearly permissibles, spouses, and in some cases shareholders. PACs are likely to be more discriminating in the use of their treasuries as well. Candidates and parties will be expected to provide more and better information to help PACs make their contribution decisions, and PACs may attach more strings to the use of their money, for instance, by specifying more frequently exactly what activities their money is to be spent for. In-kind gifts, which allow PACs more control over their donations and increase the prominence of their gifts, may become more popular, though only the larger PACs have sufficient staff to organize extensive in-kind efforts. Similarly, additional use of independent expenditures will probably be restricted to the major PACs, but a significant expansion may occur if legislation to restrict PACs is passed.

The most important single trend in PAC development is not the swelling of the committees' treasuries but their increased emphasis on political education and grassroots activism. "Voter registration and get-out-the-vote efforts, political education courses, legislative action training, Washington visitation programs where we bring people to D.C. to instruct and motivate them, issue forums—this is the wave of the future," proclaims MAPCO PAC's Don Cogman. "I'm a big believer in it because it's much more effective. If you get twenty or thirty of your people active in a candidate's campaign, why that's ten times more valuable than a contribution of money."

Political education, grassroots activism, and PAC formation itself are all manifestations of the quickened pace of interest groups' political involvement—a direct result of the growing power and scope of government. Despite recent advances in the deregulation of certain industries, staffing of the federal regulatory agencies has risen by two-thirds in the past decade.[24] (Regulation has grown even faster in many states.) Fully 65 percent of the chief executive officers of the 200 largest American companies now come to Washington at least once every two weeks, compared to only 15 percent ten years ago.[25] Political action committees are one of the means interest groups use to influence the crucial decisions being made in Washington and the state capitals. The Federal Election Campaign Act combined with new campaign technology produced the conditions that have enabled PACs to play such a role.

The rapid rise of PACs—easily charted because of FECA's disclosure provisions—has inevitably proven controversial, yet many of the charges made against political action committees are exaggerated and dubious. It is said that PACs are dangerously novel and have flooded the political system with money, mainly from business. While the widespread use of the PAC structure is new, the fact remains that special-interest money of all types has *always* found its way into politics, and before FECA it did so in less traceable and far more disturbing and unsavory ways.[26] And yes, in absolute terms PACs contribute a massive sum to candidates, but it is not clear that there is *proportionately* more interest-group money in the system than before FECA was passed. As Michael Malbin of the American Enterprise Institute has argued, we will never know the truth because the pre-FECA record is so incomplete.[27] The proportion of House and Senate campaign funds provided by PACs has certainly increased since the early 1970s, but *individuals,* most of whom are unaffiliated with PACs, have supplied, and *still* supply, about two-thirds of all the money raised by House candidates and more than three-quarters of the campaign budgets of Senate contenders.[28] So while the importance of PAC spending has grown, PACs clearly remain secondary to individuals as a source of election funding. PACs seem rather less awesome when considered within the entire spectrum of campaign finance.

Apart from the argument over the relative weight of PAC funds, PAC critics claim that political action committees are making it more expensive to run for office. There is some validity to this assertion. Money provided to one side funds the purchase of campaign tools which the other side must then counter in order to stay competitive. The political scientist Gary Jacobson has pointed out that the increase in campaign costs between 1980 and 1982 was more than twice the usual average and certainly outstripped the inflationary rise in the costs of running for office.[29] In the aggregate, American campaign expenditures seem huge. All 1982 general election congressional candidates taken together spent $318 million, and the campaign of the average House nominee[30] cost $228,000. Will Rogers's 1931 remark has never been more true: "Politics has got so expensive that it takes lots of money to even get beat with." Yet as the political analyst Herbert Alexander has observed, $318 million is half the annual advertising budget of Proctor and Gamble, or as FEC Commissioner Lee Ann Elliott put it, "less than we spent as a nation for candy in twenty-four days and soft drinks in five and a half days." These days it is expensive to communicate, whether the message is political or commercial. Television time, polling costs, consultants' fees, direct-mail investment, and other standard campaign expenditures have been soaring in price, over and above inflation.[31] PACs have been fueling the use of new campaign techniques, but a reasonable case can be made that such expenses are necessary, and that *more,* and better, communication is required between candidates and an electorate that often appears woefully uninformed about politics. PACs therefore may be making a positive contribution by providing the means to increase and refine the flow of information during elections.

PACs are also called incumbent biased, and accused of being in the market to buy congressional votes. Except for the ideological ones, PACs do display a clear bias for incumbents, but the same bias is apparent in contributions from individuals.[32] Facing all contributors is a rational, perhaps decisive, economic question: Why waste money on nonincumbents if incumbents almost always win? PACs do not favor incumbents any more than other contributors do. In fact the best challengers—those perceived as having fair to good chances to win—are generously funded by PACs. Well-targeted PAC challenger money clearly helped the GOP win a majority in the U.S. Senate in 1980, for instance. It is true that PACs limit the number of strong challengers by giving so much early money to incumbents, money that helps to deter potential opponents from declaring their candidacy. But the money that PACs channel to competitive challengers late in the election season may then increase the turnover of officeholders on election day.[33] PAC money also certainly increases the level of competitiveness in open-seat congressional races—races without an incumbent candidate. The charge that PACs are shopping for congressional votes seems overdrawn as well. While some PACs may in fact be doing so, they seem to be remarkably unsuccessful in most cases. PAC contributions do purchase access to officeholders, and they do so intentionally, but lobbying efforts rather than PAC money may be responsible for many of the legislative successes of interest groups. Moreover, a fear of "buying votes" should direct attention to the $4.5 million awarded in 1982 by interest groups directly to legislators, not as campaign contributions but as "speaking fees" and honoraria.[34] This 1982 sum was much more than double the 1980 total.

PACs have also been accused of nationalizing the system of campaign finance, of being monolithic, and of determining the results of American elections. While PACs do aid in the centralization of election fundraising and expenditure, certain aspects of their work pull in the opposite direction. These include grassroots political participation programs, the proliferation of state and local PACs, and the decentralized decision-making characterizing many committees. Such elements maintain the local, more representative types of fundraising. The view of PAC influence as monolithic is undermined by the tendency of every category of PAC except labor to split its contributions among candidates of both parties. Taken as a whole, PACs are a diverse lot with dissimilar interests and motives. Certainly not every economic and political interest is represented equally in the PAC community, but the system's elasticity and ability to accommodate new political needs is evident in the development after 1980 of liberal PACs to balance the existing conservative groups. Both kinds of ideological PACs have discovered, though, that PACs affect elections less than they are often given and claim credit for. PAC money is but one ingredient in an electoral goulash, and the simple act of voting can never be explained simply in the aggregate. Conservative PACs trumpeted impressive win/loss ratios in 1980—but how much credit was really due them in the year of the Reagan landslide, especially when the national Republican party's extraordinary efforts are considered as well? Liberal PACs claimed a mandate as a result of the 1982 midterm congressional elections—but was it the relatively small contribution total of these infant PACs or the deepest recession since the end of the Great Depression that elected so many Democrats?

One line of attack on PACs is more justified. These important components of a largely democratic political system seem themselves to be undemocratic in some respects. The undemocratic character of some PACs' candidate-selection processes completely severs the connecting link between contributor and candidate. This unhealthy condition is most apparent in many of the ideological nonconnected PACs, whose lack of a parent body and whose free-style organization makes them accountable to no one and responsive mainly to their own whims. Who decides which candidates the conservative National Congressional Club supports? According to its director Carter Wrenn, he makes the decisions, with advice from several others in his headquarters; recommendations from Republican Sens. Jesse Helms and John East, as well as the political consultants Charles Black and Arthur Finkelstein, are normally followed too. The director of the liberal PAC Independent Action admits that his group's political godfather, Rep. Morris Udall, can order up a campaign contribution as he wishes: "I would not be inclined to veto his request," was the way Ed Coyle diplomatically stated it.

Both Coyle and Wrenn insisted that their PACs were still democratic since contributors would simply stop giving if dissatisfied with the PACs' candidate choices. But these PACs, like most nonconnected committees, raise money by direct mail. Except for an occasional news article, if that, the average PAC donor's only source of information about the PAC's activities is the PAC's own direct mail which, not surprisingly, tends to be upbeat and selective in reporting the committee's work. Moreover, as the political scientist Frank Sorauf has stressed, since direct mail can succeed with only a 2–5 percent response rate, and since prospecting for new donors is continuous, decisions by even a large number of givers to drop out will have little impact on PAC fundraising.[35]

Ideological PACs are not alone in following undemocratic practices. When the AFL-CIO overwhelmingly endorsed Democrat Walter Mondale for president in 1983, making available to him the invaluable resources of most labor PACs, a CBS News / *New York Times* poll showed that less than a quarter of the union members they interviewed reported having had their presidential preferences solicited in any fashion.[36] If a democratic sampling had taken place, the AFL-CIO might not have been so pro-Mondale. The CBS/*Times* poll indicated that not only was Mondale not favored by a majority of the union respondents, he was in a statistical dead heat with Sen. John Glenn for a plurality edge.

Many corporate PACs can hardly be considered showcases of democracy either. In a few PACs the chief executive officers completely rule the roost, and in many the CEOs have inordinate influence on PAC decisions. Some corporate PAC officers frankly admit that they do not encourage suggestions about candidates from their PAC donors, preferring to leave the decisions to those "in the know" about politics.[37] Earmarking is permitted by only 37 percent of all PACs, and most of these do not advertise its availability and express great relief that it is not widely used. PAC leaders may criticize split giving as an "accounting nightmare" and a "mixed signal," but the practice also strips PAC leaders of their power and flexibility. The use of coercion, implied or overt, is always a threat when subordinate employees are solicited to give to a CEO-endorsed program. Finally, supervision of the PAC's activities rarely extends to the corporation's stockholders, theoretically the company's owners, because management often wishes to avoid accountability.[38]

Several points can be made in defense of "PAC democracy," however. First of all, in the general sense most PACs are certainly participatory. "PACs are the United Way of politics," asserts Sen. David Durenberger (R–Minn.).[39] PAC contributors number in the millions, and while most donations are small, "It's like a horse race," Richard Armstrong of the Public Affairs Council commented. "If you've got a couple of bucks down, it's something more interesting than a bunch of four-legged animals running around in a circle."[40] Many of these PAC contributors, according to one study,[41] were not particularly active in politics before, suggesting that political action committees are tapping and activating a pool of previously inert citizens—a welcome accomplishment in a democracy. Second, most PACs do go to considerable trouble to construct a governing board that is representative of their membership, since it is obviously in the interest of their fundraising efforts to do so. They also actively solicit suggestions on candidate selection, though most are careful to note that nominations will receive only "due consideration." Decentralization of candidate selection to state or even congressional district units is not uncommon either, especially in large trade associations, unions, and corporations with major plants scattered throughout the country.

Even if in many cases internally undemocratic, PACs are misrepresented and unfairly maligned as the embodiment of corrupt special interests. Contemporary political action committees are another manifestation of what James Madison called factions. Through the flourishing of competing interest groups or factions, said Madison in his *Federalist No. 10,* liberty would be preserved: "Liberty is to faction what air is to fire, an element without which it would instantly expire."[42] Another keen observer of American democracy, Alexis de Tocqueville, hailed "associations"—a category which certainly includes modern-day PACs—with the same fervor as Madison saluted factions: "There are no countries in which associations are more needed, to prevent . . . the arbitrary power of a prince, than those which are democratically constituted."[43]

In any democracy, and particularly in one as pluralistic as the United States, it is essential that groups be relatively unrestricted in advocating their interests and positions. Not only is unrestricted political activity by interest groups a mark of a free society, but it provides a safety valve for the competitive pressures that build on all fronts in a capitalistic democracy. It also provides another means to keep representatives responsive to legitimate needs. This is not to say that all groups' interests are legitimate, nor that vigorously competing interests alone ensure that the public good prevails. "The sum of all the PAC interests is not equal to the whole public interest," correctly notes the PAC critic and congressman Dan Glickman (D–Kans.).[44] The press, public, and valuable watchdog groups such as Common Cause must always be alert to instances in which narrow private interests can prevail over the commonweal—occurrences that generally happen when no one is looking.[45]

Besides the press and organizations like Common Cause, there are two major institutional checks on the evils of factions, associations, and now PACs. The most fundamental of these is regular free elections with general suffrage. As Tocqueville commented:

> Perhaps the most powerful of the causes which tend to mitigate the excesses of political association in the United States is Universal Suffrage. In countries in which universal suffrage exists, the majority is never doubtful, because neither party can pretend to represent that portion of the community which has not voted. The associations which are formed are aware, as well as the nation at large, that they do not represent the majority: this is, indeed, a condition inseparable from their existence; for if they did represent the prepondering power, they would change the law instead of soliciting its reform.[46]

Sen. Robert Dole (R–Kans.) has said, "There aren't any poor PACs or Food Stamp PACs or Nutrition PACs or Medicare PACs,"[47] and PAC critics frequently make the point that certain segments of the electorate are underrepresented in the PAC community. Yet without much support from PACs,[48] there are food stamps, poverty and nutrition programs, and Medicare. Why? Because the recipients of governmental assistance constitute a hefty slice of the electorate, and as we saw in Chapter 4, votes matter more than dollars to politicians. Furthermore, many citizens *outside* the affected groups have also made known their support of aid to the poor and elderly —making yet a stronger electoral case for these PAC-less programs.

The other major institution that checks PAC influence is the two-party system. While PACs represent particular interests, the political parties build coalitions of groups and attempt to present a national perspective on policy. They arbitrate among special-interest claims, and they seek to reach a consensus on matters of overriding importance to the nation. The parties are one of the few unifying forces in an exceptionally diverse country. If interest groups and their PACs are invaluable to a functioning democracy, then the political parties must be considered essential. Yet just as PACs have been gathering strength, the parties (until very recently) have been steadily declining in power.[49] We have seen that the rehabilitation of the party system has begun, but there is a long way to go. A central goal of the reform agenda should be to strengthen the political parties. Reforms to bolster the parties also have a useful side effect: they temper the excesses of PACs by reducing their proportional effect on the election of public officials.

THE REFORM AGENDA

My own thoughts on election law can be summed up in three little words: "It's time for a change."

—Sen. Roger Jepsen (R–Iowa)[50]

Jepsen is not the only one who has difficulty counting when it comes to campaign finance. There have been literally dozens and dozens of reform proposals just in the last several years. The laws and their interpretations are mind-bendingly complex and unendingly variable. Moreover, as Fred Wertheimer, a reform veteran of many years' standing, puts it: "There are no fights like campaign finance fights because they are battles about the essence of politics and power."

The need for campaign finance reform remains undeniable, however, and we can now use what we know about PACs to suggest appropriate measures. Several caveats are in order first. We will not undertake an exhaustive review of even the current collection of reform proposals.[51] This is not altogether regrettable, for a number of reform offerings are embarrassingly silly and thoughtless. Rep. Jim Courter (R–N.J.), for example, introduced a bill to make the Federal Election Commission a blind trust which would pass PAC contributions to candidates without revealing how much each PAC gave.[52] One suspects that the result would be a dramatic surge in $10 donations from PACs. One also suspects that a congressman would somehow get word of large PAC gifts from credit-seeking interest-group lobbyists, leaving only the press and the public in the dark.

Another caveat to bear in mind is that any set of proposed reforms is unlikely to be implemented. It is doubtful that any major changes in election law will be passed by Congress and signed by the president in the near future. It is not that congressmen are happy with the current system. The Center for Responsive Politics, a Washington-based campaign-reform "think tank," found that by 1983 more than three-quarters of the legislators surveyed believed the campaign laws were basically unsatisfactory and in need of overhaul.[53] But as Rep. Pat Schroeder (D–Colo.) admitted, "Nobody wants to take on the people financing their campaigns."[54] And though congressmen may be dissatisfied with the finance laws, they know for certain that they can be elected under them. New laws may introduce unforeseen obstacles, and we can rest assured, of course, that congressmen will make every effort to keep their path to reelection uncluttered. The temptation to turn campaign reforms into "incumbent reelection acts" by biasing the laws toward the haves is always great. This ever-present danger is one reason to be thankful that many reforms are *not* passed.

Beyond this, reformers themselves have achieved no ready consensus on the best changes to enact. Any modern-day Republican president is likely to veto laws incorporating PAC limitations or public financing. Those proposals, if considered desirable, will have to await a Democratic chief executive and a solidly Democratic Congress. Even then, passage is hardly assured. After all, public financing of congressional campaigns was defeated by a Democratic legislature under President Carter. Many political observers believe that it will take another scandal on the order of Watergate to create the climate for change. Alternatively, it might be possible for a bipartisan, blue-ribbon commission on campaign finance to fashion a compromise package of reforms with a chance of success. For now, though, a major realignment in the system of campaign finance, while not entirely a pipedream, remains highly unlikely.

We should keep in mind, too, that the apparent improbability of reform is not such a bad thing. Nowhere does the law of intended consequences operate with such force as in the area of campaign finance. An especially ironic example of this fact is that modern PACs themselves are in large part a product of campaign finance reforms. NCPAC's chairman Terry Dolan once offered this testimony before yet another set of campaign-reform hearings: "Mr. Chairman, I sit before you today as a creation of the federal election laws. If it weren't for them, you wouldn't even be listening to me."[55] And in a later interview, Dolan confidently asserted, "Whatever changes they make in the law, we'll turn them to our advantage. New election rules can make us even more powerful."

Reforms have a way of turning into loopholes, as NCPAC and groups like it have repeatedly proven. Loopholes seem to be created especially when lawmakers attempt such impossibilities as obstructing the flow of interest-group influence. "Those who think they're going to limit special-interest money are hopelessly naïve, and they may end up doing just the opposite," says the Democratic party's Marty Franks. "I've lost faith in our ability to actually reform the process; it's a little like the tax code." Conversely, reformers often have a better chance to succeed when they are cautious and prudent. "What you learn as a reformer is that you have to take it one step at a time," observes Russell Hemenway of the National Committee for an Effective Congress. "You shouldn't continually tinker with the system, and occasionally you have to stand back and take stock of the damage you've done before going any farther." Reformers have the obligation to make sure that their proposed remedies will improve rather than worsen the malady, and that the changes they offer will enhance public confidence in politics rather than reinforce the cynicism that comes when another well-meaning scheme goes awry. As the political scientist Austin Ranney has wisely suggested:

> There is a part of the Hippocratic oath that doctors have to swear that says the first obligation of the physician is to do no harm. Then after that, if he is sure he is doing no harm, he can start seeing if he can do a little good. Maybe not a bad rule for political reformers too.[56]

LIMITATIONS ON PACS

We will begin by looking at a currently popular proposal for campaign finance reform: limiting the amount of PAC money any congressman may accept. A number of legislative proposals have been made to restrict a congressional candidate's PAC total to a fixed amount ($70,000 in the case of the Obey-Railsback bill that passed the House in 1979) or a fixed percentage of the candidate's total receipts.[57] Like many reforms, it has a certain appeal—a 1980 ABC News/Harris survey showed the public in favor of a PAC limit by 68 percent to 29 percent[58]—but the hidden costs and consequences of the proposal are enormous and destructive.

Such a limitation on PAC gifts might well be unconstitutional as an infringement on the First Amendment guarantee of free speech,[59] but regardless, its effects make it a most undesirable innovation. The Center for Responsive Politics's poll of congressmen[60] showed a 66 percent to 31 percent majority favoring PAC donation limitations, and this is not surprising given the fact that such limits would aid incumbents. While incumbents as a group raise far more PAC money than do challengers, in *competitive* races (where there is a good chance for the incumbent to lose) challengers often match or outraise incumbents among PACs, and the extra PAC money is usually much more useful to a little-known challenger than to a well-known incumbent. A cap on PAC gifts would give additional insurance to incumbents that, should they find themselves in electoral difficulty, their challengers will have less chance to raise enough money to defeat them. Also attractive to incumbents is the fact that a PAC cap would probably apply only to the general election.[61] Since incumbents receive the vast majority of early, prenomination PAC gifts while challengers usually receive their PAC money late in the general election, incumbents in effect would be able to accumulate PAC funds far in excess of a limit applied to the general election. On the other hand the timing of PAC gifts to challengers would mean that almost all their PAC money would fall under the ceiling. The "PAC cap" would in reality be a "challenger cap."

Limitations on PAC gifts would also have other unintended consequences. Reducing the flow of PAC funds would help wealthy candidates. Currently, any candidate can spend unrestricted personal funds on his own election; to diminish his opponent's assets would obviously add to the power of the wealthy candidate's unchecked bank account. It is ironic, in light of the support for PAC limits by labor-oriented Democrats, that a PAC cap is likely to hurt labor and Democratic candidates more than the business interests and Republicans. Democratic candidates depend on PAC funds more heavily than do Republicans because the Democratic party cannot supply them with as much money as the healthy Republican party can offer its nominees. Moreover, as the DNC political director Ann Lewis points out, "Once labor bumps up against the ceiling they can't go back to their members and expect to channel large individual donations [to favored candidates]. Our people don't have that kind of money, whereas the corporate PAC people can double their contributions by going to their executives and asking them to send personal donations [to candidates] of $1,000 each." Some PAC-limitation proposals have also called for reducing the maximum gift of $5,000 per election. But this is another move sure to hurt labor disproportionately since labor PACs tend to "max out" far more frequently than corporate and trade committees. In addition, it is not often realized that this type of PAC limitation has already occurred as a result of inflation: the 1974 gift of $5,000 has now been reduced in value by almost half to about $2,600.

The most disturbing consequence of further limits on PAC contributions would be an inevitable increase in independent expenditures. NCPAC's Terry Dolan, the acknowledged master of independent spending, stated it bluntly:

> If Congress passes a limit on what a PAC can give directly to candidates, it will automatically encourage more independent expenditures. In fact it will probably

encourage an exponential growth in independent expenditures. I can assure you that I will look forward to conducting seminars for other political action committees telling them how to set up independent campaigns.[62]

Independent expenditure is the least accountable form of political spending, and combined with the unfortunate fact that it often tends to be viciously negative in tone, it is hardly something the system of campaign finance should encourage. As we have seen, it is mainly the large PACs that are in a position to use independent spending widely and effectively. So a PAC limit would bolster these few wealthy PACs at the expense of the many smaller PACs that preserve diversity in the PAC community. Peter Lauer of AMPAC predicted:

A PAC limit isn't going to knock out NCPAC, AMPAC, the Realtors, or COPE. We'll just do independent expenditures. But the smallfry are going to be hurt in relation to us, and we'll become more powerful. That's the scary part—a few gigantic PACs controlling the system. So much for federalism or Madisonian democracy.

Actually, Lauer's fears are probably overdrawn. The smaller PACs are not going to fade away completely. They are now established organizations with the proven ability to raise money, and they will find useful ways to spend their funds. Reformers may be able to squeeze PAC cash out of candidates' election accounts, but they will not succeed in forcing it out of the political system. Other activities will simply come to the fore: internal communications, "soft money" gifts to parties in states without restrictions on corporate or union treasury contributions, Washington lobbying campaigns, and political education and involvement programs galore.[63] No doubt "bundling" efforts—the collection of *individual* gifts from PAC-affiliated persons for delivery to each favored candidate as a PAC-endorsed package—would also become widespread. Bundled donations, of course, are not as easily traceable as PAC gifts are. The DCCC's Marty Franks speculated that "with a PAC limit, instead of getting one check from Lockheed corporation's PAC we'll get five $1,000 checks from housewives in the San Fernando Valley with no mention that their spouses are executives with Lockheed. In that sense PACs serve an efficient bookkeeping and disclosure purpose."

Finally, an overall PAC limit might increase the chances that legislative votes could be swayed by PAC gifts. If both the railroads and the trucking industry, for instance, tried to make a contribution to a congressman, but only the railroads succeeded before the incumbent's PAC limit was reached, might not the legislator be more beholden to railroad interests as a result of this PAC limitation scheme? Allowing the congressman to accept donations from both the railroads and their natural competitors maintains some balance among competing interests.[64]

One of the leading PAC critics, Rep. David Obey (D–Wis.), has dismissed the argument that limiting PACs is futile because there will always be ways to circumvent the restrictions. "To me that is like saying, 'Don't cure heart disease, because the guy might get cancer.' "[65] But considering all the problems that would be introduced by PAC limits, a better medical analogy might be: Don't use a carcinogenic drug on a cold.

STRENGTHENING THE POLITICAL PARTIES

As we have seen, one sure way to lessen the importance of PACs is to shore up competing institutions and to increase the pool of alternative money. To begin with, the $1,000 limit on an individual's contribution to each candidate per election should be raised to recover its loss to inflation since 1974. (A $1,000 gift of ten years ago is worth only about $525 today.) Both the $1,000 cap and the companion limit of $25,000 that an individual is permitted to donate to *all* candidates taken together in a calendar year should be permanently indexed to the inflation rate. Restoring the value of individual contributions will offset somewhat the financial clout of the PACs.

Much more vital is the need to enhance the financial flexibility of the political parties.[66] While individuals and PACs represent particular interests and further the atomization of public policy, the parties encompass more general concerns and push the system toward consensus. Their role is absolutely central to American democracy's future health and success, and for that reason if no other the parties should be accorded special, preferential treatment by the campaign finance laws. The original FECA was not especially generous to the parties, though neither was it especially injurious considering its provisions allowing coordinated expenditures (by the party on behalf of its candidates) and its more liberal contribution and expenditure limits for the parties. The 1979 amendments to FECA helped by allowing state and local parties to spend unlimited amounts on materials for volunteer activity and get-out-the-vote drives. The most useful party advantage of all under current law may be the greatly reduced postage rates allowed party mailings, funded by a congressional subsidy. It was this provision, among others, that reportedly encouraged NCPAC to consider becoming a political party in 1982.[67]

But parties can be aided still further, which would strengthen their crucial position in the American system and indirectly lessen the influence of PACs and interest groups. The current limits on contributions to party committees ($20,000 a year for an individual and $15,000 for a multicandidate PAC) should be substantially increased. Additionally, individuals as well as corporations, labor unions, and trade associations should be permitted to underwrite without limit the administrative, legal, and accounting costs parties incur. A modest level of public funding from general tax revenues should be provided each year to the national party committees for party-building activities, or alternatively, a tax credit should be enacted to enable taxpayers to deduct 100 percent of each gift to a party up to a maximum of $50 per individual or $100 for a joint return.[68] It would be wise too for Congress eventually to reclaim a portion of the public's airwaves and require that television and radio stations—among the most profitable corporate ventures in the country—turn over half a dozen to a dozen five-minute time blocks each year to the *parties* (rather than to individual candidates) so that more generic, institutional advertising can be aired even by the relatively underfinanced Democrats.[69]

The relative poverty of the Democrats' treasury actually stands in the way of more substantial pro-party reforms. The Republican National Committee chairman Frank Fahrenkopf is surely correct in wondering "why the United Auto Workers or NCPAC can spend an unlimited amount of money supporting or opposing candidates for federal office [by means of independent expenditures] and not the Republican or Democrat parties."[70] At some point in the future the amounts party committees can give or spend on behalf of their nominees should be considerably increased, but not until the Democratic party becomes better funded. Brian Atwood of the Democratic Senatorial Campaign Committee admits that expanded party expenditure limits are "the right approach. The party ought to be providing a lot more money and it's healthier that it comes from the parties than from the special-interest groups. But the simple fact is that for us the additional expenditure is theoretical while for the Republicans it's already possible." Adds the Democratic National Committee's Ann Lewis: "To increase the party limits now would widen the disparity at a time when we're just beginning to catch up. We're not whining and we're not complaining, but for God's sake, leave us alone and let us catch up." In the interests of establishing a reasonable balance in resources between the two major parties, many desirable pro-party changes in the campaign finance law must be deferred for now.[71] But the long-term objective is clear: beef up the parties so that PACs will be limited *indirectly.* Candidates and the political system will benefit from the infusion of more party funds and influence, while PACs will remain unshackled by unfair and unworkable restrictions.

PUBLIC FINANCING AND TAX CREDITS

President Theodore Roosevelt first proposed in 1907 that the cost of campaigns be borne by the federal treasury, and since 1976, as a result of the Watergate scandals, presidential campaigns have been publicly financed. But three major attempts in the late 1970s to extend the presidential system to congressional races fell short,[72] and there now is little chance, barring another major scandal, that public financing for congressional races will be enacted.

It is not that the proposal lacks respectable sponsorship. Organizations from the American Bar Association[73] to the National Grange[74] have backed the idea, and even some conservative journals such as *Business Week* have given their assent.[75] COPE and other labor groups have vigorously pushed for public financing as well. (COPE's director John Perkins is frank to say why: "We'd just like to stick to registration and voter contact; that's what we're best at, and if we could put all our resources there, we could make a far greater contribution to our candidates.") Common Cause and its president, Fred Wertheimer, have tirelessly lobbied for a number of ingenious legislative schemes that have drawn the endorsement of a substantial number of congressmen, mainly liberal Democrats. One 1983 survey of congressmen even showed a narrow 51 percent majority in favor of some form of public financing.[76]

But the obstacles blocking passage of this reform are substantial. As long as Republicans are in control of either house of Congress or the presidency, no such bill will be passed and signed into law since most members of the GOP are philosophically and practically (they do not need the money) opposed to the idea. With the antispending, antiregulatory mood prevailing on Capitol Hill and perhaps in the country at large in the deficit-filled 1980s, even a solidly Democratic Congress and administration would have great difficulty securing a public financing law—despite the fact that it is theoretically possible to cancel the current tax credits individuals take for political giving and thereby bring in enough money to fund public financing without additional cost.[77] Then, too, public financing of congressional campaigns has an imposing list of opponents, including some surprising ones. The DNC political coordinator Ann Lewis declares, "If we can't afford basic human services for children I don't think we can afford public financing." The liberal philanthropist Stewart Mott, the former senator and ideological maverick Eugene McCarthy (D–Minn.), and NCPAC's Terry Dolan have joined forces to form Free and Open Elections (FOE), an odd coalition which pledges to air negative advertisements in the congressional districts of key supporters of public financing.[78]

But the weightiest opposition to this reform, and the fundamental reason why public financing will not be passed until a tidal change occurs, is the electorate's refusal to pay for it. Dolan expressed these sentiments with his usual bluntness at a congressional hearing in 1983:

> Members of Congress should oppose this bill for one simple reason—there is an army of millions of fed-up taxpayers just waiting to see how you vote on this issue. They, like me, will be morally indignant to get the names of those congressmen who

will spend tens of millions of dollars getting themselves reelected when they cannot balance the federal budget.[79]

We have seen that the public is hostile in varying degrees to the participation of "special-interest" groups in elections, and that when survey questions are phrased in certain ways it is possible to produce majority backing for public financing.[80] A 1982 Gallup poll[81] asked a random sample of the population this question: "It has been suggested that the federal government provide a fixed amount of money for the election campaigns of candidates for Congress and that all private contributions from other sources be prohibited. Do you think this is a good idea or a poor idea?" A solid majority (55 percent) said it was a good idea, with 31 percent terming public financing a poor idea and 14 percent not sure. But when it is explained that the federal government provides money courtesy of the taxpayers, support for public financing plummets. When the Civic Service survey firm asked a random sample in 1983 whether they would "approve or disapprove of the proposal to use public funds, federal money, to pay the costs of congressional campaigns," 65 percent said no and only 25 percent were in favor.[82] Those opposed were also much more likely to hold their opinion intensely.[83] A number of recent state polls have reported similar findings,[84] and the Harris Survey has charted a decline from plurality approval of public financing shortly after Watergate to majority disapproval in the 1980s.[85]

Public financing, if passed, should be designed in ways that benefit the political system. Public funds should be given to candidates as *floors* rather than as *ceilings.* Under this system, each congressional nominee of a major party would receive a certain flat amount (a floor) in public funds to ensure that he reaches the minimal financial threshold necessary to conduct a modern campaign. Beyond that, he should be permitted to raise as much as he can in unrestricted fashion from PACs and individuals. This approach guarantees at least basic competition in each district and augments the ability of candidates to communicate with voters while preserving for individuals, PACs, and interest groups a rightful and legitimate role in elections. A ceiling on expenditures, by contrast, almost certainly benefits incumbents since challengers must usually spend a great deal more than average to upend an incumbent. Moreover, a ceiling restricts the flow of communications between candidates and voters, and unfairly minimizes the direct participation of PACs in the political process. And as is true of other limitations on PAC contributions, a public-funds ceiling would squeeze PAC money into less accountable and less desirable channels, such as independent spending. A beneficial public-funding scheme would also filter treasury money through the national or state political parties, permitting them to keep a certain percentage for their own administration and party-building activities, and perhaps also allowing them some degree of flexibility in allocating funds to their nominees.

But these reform measures have virtually no chance of enactment. Congressmen are not going to give their parties any additional leverage to use over them, nor are they going to do any favors for their opponents by enacting public-funding floors that favor challengers rather than ceilings that favor themselves. Rep. Richard Cheney (R–Wyo.) said it best: "If you think this Congress, or any other, is going to set up a system where someone can run against them on equal terms at government expense, you're smoking something you can't buy at the corner drugstore."[86]

Probably the best form of public financing with a reasonable chance of passage is the tax credit option. Currently there exists a 50 percent tax credit for all contributions to candidates, PACs, and political committees of up to $50 for an individual and $100 on a joint return. A useful and feasible reform would increase the 50 percent tax credit to 100 percent, but only for contributions to political parties, or to House and Senate candidates *from the contributor's own state.*[87] Gifts to PACs, which are included in the tax credit currently available, would be eliminated from such eligibility. PACs and interest groups should not be restricted as they go about fulfilling their legitimate purposes, but neither should their political activities be subsidized by the taxpayers. While only a tiny percentage of taxpayers takes the current 50 percent credit for PAC gifts, the resulting revenue loss is substantial—an estimated $89 million over just two years (1981 and 1982).[88] The money saved by eliminating the PAC credit can be used to compensate for the revenue lost in doubling the individual gift credit.

Reforming the tax credit in this way would decrease somewhat the incentive to give to PACs, and augment the motivation for party giving. It would also encourage candidates to expand their base of small, in-state contributors rather than simply concentrating on national PACs and large individual donors. And while challengers would benefit from a form of public financing that increases the electoral money supply without capping expenditures, incumbents would perhaps be in a better position to take advantage of the small-donor tax credit because of their superior resources and higher name recognition. Of course, we have repeatedly seen examples of the inventiveness of PACs, and some may attempt to turn a new individual tax credit to their advantage by sponsoring "bundling" operations similar to the one now used by the Council for a Liveable World.[89] It may be necessary to incorporate "antibundling" provisions into any tax credit law. These would prohibit a PAC (and perhaps individuals too—with direct-mail consultants in mind) from acting as a conduit for individual contributions.

DISCLOSURE: PACS IN THE SUNSHINE

Probably the most universally supported and certainly the most successful provision of FECA is disclosure, whereby PACs and candidates are required at various intervals to reveal their contributors and their expenditures. Not only do the disclosure provisions expose the motives and decisions of PACs and politicians, but they alert competing interests to the need for mobilization.[90] Disclosure is no cure-all, however. As the political scientist David Adamany has pointed out, the disclosure laws generate more information than can be mastered by the media or the voters.[91] The volume of financial disclosure reports filed with the Federal Election Commission is crushing: 1,171,000 pages in the 1982 election cycle alone. Despite inadequate funding, the FEC does an admirable job in making this information available to press and public, but it is usually well after election day before any thorough analysis of the data can begin—too late to affect the election results. Still, disclosure serves many useful purposes, from permitting post-election enforcement of the laws to allowing comparisons to be made between campaign contributions and votes cast on the floor of Congress. Disclosure itself generates pressure for more reform. When campaign finance was out of sight, it was out of most people's minds; now that the trail of money can be easily followed, indignation is only a press release away.

Disclosure is the single greatest check on the excesses of campaign finance, for it encourages corrective action, whether judicial (prosecution in the courts) or political (retribution by the voters at the polls). It is such an essential and welcome device in American democracy that it should be broadened to bring to light a number of abuses or perceived abuses in the PAC community. No PAC practice is so distasteful as the distortion and deception found in many direct-mail solicitations, especially from the ideological committees. PACs using any form of direct-mail fundraising should be required to enclose a copy of all letters with their periodic FEC reports. Ed Coyle of Independent Action explained the compelling reason for such a mandate:

> People should be able to read the direct-mail letters, then look at what you've done as shown by your FEC reports and make sure it matches what you *said* you'd do in the letters. A lot of organizations will write and say whatever they need to say in direct mail and then not do anything even close to what they promised to do.

These transgressions are not uncommon, for successful direct-mail fundraising is built in part on the principle of exaggeration and deceptive promise.[92] The journalist Robert Timberg of the *Baltimore Sun* documented a number of such cases in a newspaper series on PACs.[93] The Life Amendment PAC, an antiabortion organization, sent out a letter begging for money to save the seat of antiabortionist Rep. Henry Hyde (R–Ill.), who was described as being in mortal danger of defeat. In fact Hyde, who knew nothing of the letter and repudiated it, was in a safe Republican district.[94] Another antiabortion group calling itself "Stop the Baby Killers" promised in 1979 to give maximum contributions to candidates opposing a number of "Political Baby Killers" (liberal Democratic congressmen), and to pay for polls, in-kind campaign consultants, and campaign training seminars for volunteers. In truth, the group made not a single contribution of any size to a candidate in 1979 or 1980, conducted no polls, and held no campaign seminars. What happened to the $189,000 the group raised? About $146,000 was used to pay three for-profit direct-mail firms with ties to the organization itself. The FEC has received more than a dozen complaints about fraudulent political fundraising,[95] and this may be only the tip of the iceberg. Unless a reporter happens to receive a copy of a questionable solicitation or a contributor takes it upon himself to trace his money through the FEC, little is heard about most direct-mail pieces.

Just as private charities must do in many states, PACs using direct mail should also be forced to disclose in each letter and on each contributor card how much of all money raised is devoted to fundraising and administrative costs. PROPAC's Victor Kamber enthusiastically backs the idea: "Contributors should definitely have a right to that information. And you know, if ninety-six cents on every dollar is going toward fundraising costs, I doubt the PAC is going to raise much additional money." Terry Dolan of NCPAC somewhat reluctantly agreed: "I have no problem with that although I want no more rules." Granted, prospecting for direct-mail donors is a necessary and expensive first step in the process, but it takes only a couple of paragraphs to explain this to letter recipients. They may not like what they read and consequently may refuse to give, but they are entitled to know how their money will be spent if any degree of accountability is to exist. Furthermore, *all* PACs, not just those using direct mail, should be required to report their list of candidate selections to their contributors. Most PACs already do this, but the ideological PACs, which frequently use direct mail and are far removed from their donors, are usually exceptions.

The ideological PACs should not only disclose candidate choices and fundraising costs to potential donors, and direct-mail letters to the FEC, but they should also be required to *establish* (and disclose) a fully independent, active board of directors to oversee their operations. The individuals serving on such boards should be prohibited from having business ties to or materially benefiting from their association with the organizations they are charged with supervising.

The need for wider disclosure is not restricted to ideological PACs. Corporations and labor unions should be required to reveal how much in general treasury funds they spend to operate their PACs, as well as the *full* expenses they incur for internal communications, political education, lobbying, and other political activities. These costs are far greater for many groups than the amount in contributions their PACs make to candidates. While no limitation on these political expenditures is (or should be) proposed, the public has the right to know the extent to which its political system and representatives are being influenced or importuned. For similar reasons, corporations should have to disclose to shareholders—in theory, their owners—how much money they spend to support PAC operations.[96]

THE DILEMMA OF INDEPENDENT EXPENDITURES

The independent PACs operate outside of [the] framework of accountability and simply become hit artists on the political scene.

—Sen. Paul Sarbanes (D–Md.)[97]

I'm against independent expenditures. I do not think they help the political process . . . because they decrease accountability. . . . I think candidates should be accountable for charges that are brought up. . . .

—John "Terry" Dolan, chairman of NCPAC[98]

It is not easy for a liberal Democratic senator who was a prime NCPAC target in his 1982 reelection race and the chairman of NCPAC to find common ground, but the issue of accountability in independent spending is apparently an area on which they agree. Voters simply cannot hold any candidates accountable for the charges made about their opponents by an independent group, and that is only the beginning of the nettlesome problems caused by independent expenditures.[99] Since independent spending is unlimited, it undermines a basic intent of the campaign finance laws. The frequent use of negative, even vicious messages and tactics by independent groups makes any sort of civility in politics much more difficult to achieve. And the groups' lack of proper governance as well as minimal contact with their contributors leaves them unaccountable to their own donors in addition to the voters at large.

Despite these widely acknowledged difficulties, and the opposition to unlimited independent expenditures of political figures as diverse as Sen. Barry Goldwater (R–Ariz.) and former Sen. George McGovern (D–S. Dak.), every attempt to rein in the independent groups has so far failed. For instance, a concerted but unsuccessful try was made by the Federal Election Commission to enforce a key provision of the Presidential Campaign Fund Act that bars PACs from spending more than $1,000 each on behalf of a presidential nominee who has accepted public financing.[100] The proximate cause of the failure was the Supreme Court's 1976 decision in *Buckley v. Valeo.*[101] The Court held that PACs and individuals, acting completely on their own, could advocate a candidate's election or defeat without limit. But the real obstacle to this reform is the First Amendment to the U.S. Constitution guaranteeing free speech. So precious is this right that, however noxious the independent groups' spending may be, it would be a dangerous and blatantly unconstitutional error to stifle it. "I don't think we can or should do anything to limit independent spending," said the Democratic party's Marty Franks. "The constitutional issues are pretty clear."

Even though independent spending itself should not be restricted, its unfortunate effects can be tempered somewhat. Once again, strengthening the financial role of political parties in elections as well as increasing the pool of small individual givers through tax credits would indirectly help to reduce the importance of independent spending. Beyond that, requiring the disclosure of direct-mail letters, candidate selections, and fundraising costs (as proposed in the last section) might also take the wind out of the sails of some independent expenditure groups.

Other remedies have been proposed, but while they are desirable in theory they are probably unworkable in practice. For example, the law requires independent expenditures to be conducted without any consultation with the campaign or candidate being assisted.[102] Yet independent PAC leaders have shared campaign consultants with their chosen candidates, and have been seen in the company of individuals closely connected to favored campaigns. They have even used PAC money to convince candidates to run (by showing them encouraging polls, for instance) and then subsequently launched independent spending efforts on their behalf.[103] A number of legislative proposals have sought to tighten enforcement of the "no coordination" provision,[104] but all efforts in this area are probably doomed. The network of friends and associates among campaigns and PACs is so large and so informed that anyone seriously desiring to know a candidate's campaign needs or plans has very little trouble doing so. The news media may be the best source of all for campaign information, and it is supplemented by a candidate's own literature and advertising, which often clearly reveal his underlying strategy.[105]

It is probably up to the candidate himself to take the only effective step to shut off undesirable independent spending being made on his behalf. Russell Hemenway of the National Committee for an Effective Congress advised the 1982 Democratic Senate nominee in Utah, Ted Wilson, to short-circuit Victor Kamber's allegedly ill-advised plans for a PROPAC independent expenditure against Wilson's opponent, Republican Sen. Orrin Hatch: "I told Ted to call Kamber up, have a conversation about his campaign, and then telephone the FEC and tell them he had just talked to Kamber. PROPAC will be stopped dead in its tracks and won't be able to spend a dime."[106] The conversation never took place because Kamber on his own decided not to make the independent expenditure. For the ploy to have worked, however, Kamber would have to have had cooperated by listening. When President Reagan called Terry Dolan in 1983 to tell him how much he liked NCPAC's independently produced television program "Ronald

Reagan's America," Dolan politely informed the president that their conversation had to be limited lest coordination be implied.[107]

Several reform bills have also been introduced in Congress to provide candidates with free response time when they are attacked or their opponent is supported by independent groups. For example, Rep. David Obey (D–Wis.) has championed a provision granting an aggrieved candidate either free radio and television advertising (courtesy of broadcasters) or a grant equal to the amount of the independent expenditure whenever independent spending against him tops $5,000.[108] This is a popular idea among lawmakers: fully 60 percent supported it in the Center for Responsive Politics's 1983 survey of congressmen.[109] However, the proposal may be of questionable constitutionality because it in effect discourages broadcasters from accepting independent ads by forcing them to provide equal response time free of charge.[110] Moreover, proposals such as Obey's overlook the ingenuity, inventiveness, and the aggressiveness of the independent groups. Terry Dolan has actually welcomed the Obey idea, announcing that he will simply run $100,000 in ads "attacking" a favored candidate and urging that he be defeated for "lowering taxes, opposing busing, and standing for a strong defense."[111] Besides identifying his candidate with a litany of popular positions, Dolan's independent salvo would trigger another $100,000 in free time for his candidate. "We don't have a perfect solution," admits Common Cause's Fred Wertheimer, who backs the Obey proposal. "There's always going to be a problem with independent expenditures."

CONCLUSION

While the reforms suggested here will help to build a better system of campaign finance and to balance some of the influence now enjoyed by political action committees, they clearly will not radically alter a system whose current defects are serious but not a threat to the health of American democracy. The reforms I have put forward are moderate and feasible: they address the weaknesses in campaign finance without risking deleterious side effects. The medicine, I hope, fits the disease. PACs are not the chaste and innocent political cheerleaders or selfless civic boosters that their proponents often contend they are. Neither are they cesspools of corruption and greed, modern-day versions of Tammany Hall.[112]

PACs will never be popular with idealistic reformers because they represent the rough, cutting edge of a democracy teeming with different peoples and conflicting interests. Indeed, PACs may never be hailed even by natural allies; it was the business-oriented *Wall Street Journal,* after all, that editorially compared Washington, D.C., to "the mutants' saloon in 'Star Wars'—

a place where politicians, PACs, lawyers, and lobbyists for unions, business or you-name-it shake each other down full time for political money and political support."[113]

Peter Fenn of the Center for Responsive Politics was surely correct when he observed that "the root of the problem is not PACs, it's money." Americans have an enduring mistrust of the mix of money (particularly business money) and politics, as Finley Peter Dunne's Mr. Dooley revealed:

> I niver knew a pollytician to go wrong ontil he'd been contaminated be contact with a business man. . . . It seems to me that th' on'y thing to do is to keep pollyticians an' business men apart. They seem to have a bad infloonce on each other. Whiniver I see an alderman an' a banker walkin' down th' street together I know th' Recordin' Angel will have to ordher another bottle iv ink.[114]

As a result of the new campaign finance rules of the 1970s political action committees superceded the "fat cats" of old as the public focus and symbol of the role of money in politics, and PACs inherited the suspicions that go with the territory. Those suspicions are valuable because they keep the spotlight on PACs and guard against undue influence. It may be regrettable that such supervision is required, but human nature—not PACs—demands it. For Mr. Dooley's celestial ruminations recall an observation of James Madison in one of the *Federalist* papers: "If men were angels, no government would be necessary."[115] And no PACs, either. But there is no heaven on earth, and both government and PACs are here to stay.

AFTERWORD

The 1984 Elections

Political action committees not only help to shape elections, but they are themselves shaped by other election-year forces. The 1984 campaign provides yet another illustration, as PACs flocked to incumbents and Democrats in record numbers.

In 1984 PACs continued a more moderate growth compared to the mid-1970s, with 4,000 PACs in existence by the end of the year—about a 14 percent increase over 1983.[1] They raised $288 million and spent $265 million, of which $104.9 million went as actual contributions to 1984 Senate and House candidates. This represents less than a 26 percent rise in PAC gifts compared to the previous election cycle,[2] whereas increases of 51 percent and 62 percent had been recorded in 1982 and 1980. There was also only a modest gain in the proportion of PAC money found in the average candidate's war chest: PACs provided 17 percent of the money in Senate races and 34 percent of the funds raised for House campaigns.[3] This temperate PAC growth was matched by the smallest gain in congressional campaign spending in four election cycles—just a 9.3 percent rise over 1982 levels.[4] Spending for House contests actually *declined* by two-tenths of one percent, a rarity in modern times.[5] The Senate race in North Carolina between Republican Jesse Helms and Democrat Jim Hunt, an extravaganza that cost almost $26 million and was repeatedly cited in the press as an example of the high cost of 1984 campaigns, thus proved to be the exception rather than the rule.

INCUMBENT BIAS

If the shifts in overall PAC spending patterns can be termed relatively minor, the same cannot be said for the allocation of PAC money to certain categories of candidates. While they are almost always PAC favorites, incumbents have not had such a rewarding PAC year since the new era of campaign finance began in 1971. Fully 71 percent of all PAC contributions went to incumbents' coffers, while challengers garnered a miserly 17 percent, and open-seat candidates just 12 percent of the PAC largesse. Corporate and trade PACs gave 78 and 79 percent of their funds, respectively, to incumbents.[6] While labor was a bit more generous to challengers, almost two-thirds (64 percent) of its PAC cash also went to favored incumbents.[7] Alone among PAC groupings, only the challenger-inclined nonconnecteds were able to resist the siren song of incumbency, allocating about as much money to the "outs" as the "ins."[8] In every category of PACs except for nonconnecteds, incumbents fared considerably better in 1984 than in 1982.[9] So lavish were PACs with congressional officeholders that a record 44 percent of all the funds raised by incumbent House members were PAC-given.[10] House committee chairmen and party leaders were even more successful: Twenty of the twenty-seven congressmen in this exclusive club secured more than half of their 1984 campaign war chests from PACs.[11]

Why was there such a tilt to incumbents in 1984? First of all, PACs generally saw the dynamics of the election year as strongly favoring the reelection of sitting congressmen, thus predisposing them toward incumbent gifts. President Reagan was an odds-on favorite for another term, and, ironically, the combination of economic prosperity and peace abroad that was to produce a Republican presidential landslide created an "era of good feeling" that benefited all incumbents, Republican and Democratic alike. Compared to 1980 or 1982, when the voters were in a surly mood and determined to throw the rascals out, 1984 was seen early on by the PACs as likely to be relatively placid—a condition favoring the status quo and discouraging always-risky donations to challengers. (In fact, the predictions of PAC leaders proved accurate. Marginal races—those in which the winner received 55 percent or less—were in short supply on election day: Fifty-seven in 1984 as opposed to eighty-two in 1982. Of course, PAC prophecies may be self-fulfilling; if challengers had secured more PAC money, perhaps the number of marginal races would have been greater.) Secondly, there were simply fewer opportunities in 1984 for PACs to give to non-incumbents. In 1982, fifty-eight congressional districts hosted open-seat contests; two years later only twenty-seven such districts were available. Similarly, sixty-four House candidates ran unopposed[12] in 1984, compared to just forty-six in 1982.[13]

PAC TILT TO DEMOCRATS

Not only was there a pro-incumbent bias among PACs in 1984, but PACs favored Democratic candidates to a degree not seen since 1976. Overall, about 57 percent of PAC contributions was given to Democrats, 43 percent to Republicans. While corporate PACs still sided heavily with the GOP, the Democratic share of their gifts (38 percent) was the largest in eight years. Trade PACs split their money nearly evenly, with 51 percent going to Republican candidates and 49 percent to Democratic contenders, while nonconnecteds cast their lot with the Democrats by a margin of 53 percent to 47 percent. For both trade and nonconnected PACs, it was the largest Democratic proportion ever registered. Labor PACs continued their traditionally heavy Democratic tilt, with Republicans garnering only a paltry 5 percent of labor PAC gifts.

Clearly, Democrats benefited from the same trends that produced a pro-incumbent PAC year. But beyond that, Democratic candidates were well served by the aggressive courting of business PACs undertaken by the Democratic leadership, especially U.S. Rep. Tony Coelho, chairman of the Democratic Congressional Campaign Committee. Coelho and his party counterparts on the Senate side were more successful not only in attracting more PAC money for Democratic nominees but also in raising more cash from all sources. The Democrats spent $97.2 million in 1983–1984, a 143 percent increase over the previous election cycle. Fully $11.5 million of this amount was contributed directly or spent on behalf of Democratic candidates for the House and Senate, a dramatic rise from the $5 million expended in 1982. The Republicans, of course, could once again boast a much larger party was chest. The GOP spent $303.2 million in 1984, a 40 percent increase from 1982, and its congressional candidates benefited from $24.9 million in party contributions and expenditures. But at least the Democrats were able to raise $1 for every $3 the GOP secured, considerably more than the $1 to $5 ratio that prevailed in 1982. And for the first time the Democrats managed to channel much of their resources to the most competitive Democratic challengers. Whereas in 1982 losing Democratic challengers who came within ten percentage points of winning were able to raise only about $182,000 on average, in 1984 similar Democratic contenders amassed was chests exceeding $293,000—the largest gain for any category of congressional challengers.[14]

In reality, the Democratic advances are not as spectacular as they appear at first flush. For instance, the GOP intentionally diverts some of its potential party revenue to its candidates. In 1984 the National Republican Senatorial Committee encouraged members of its Inner Circle club ($1,000 annual fee) and its "Senate Trust" organization ($10,000 fee) to write their dues checks directly to GOP candidates rather than to the party.[15] But, however it compares with the technologically more advanced Republican party, the Democratic party has begun to compete with the GOP more vigorously, and that is a welcome development for strong, two-party competition. And both parties' enhanced activities are indirectly helping to limit the PAC's influence,[16] as well as to hold down the rise in campaign costs by providing excellent services at prices far below those of independent political consultants.

INDEPENDENT SPENDING

What of the problem child of campaign finance, independent spending? It took a turn toward the positive in 1984, reflecting both the pro-Reagan bias of many independent-expenditure PACs and the questionable success of recent negative independent campaigns (as well as the opprobrium they have generated, making many candidates and PACs leery of such efforts). All PACs together directed $22.2 million to independent expenditures in 1983–1984, with the lion's share ($17.3 million) devoted to the presidential race. Just $800,000 was spent on negative presidential materials, while $16.5 million was spent on ads of a positive nature, the vast majority of it pro-Reagan. On the congressional side, PACs spent $3.3 million independently promoting their Senate and House favorites, and only $1.5 million bashing selected targets. As usual, most of the spending occurred in Senate campaigns,[17] and Republicans benefited disproportionately, though the edge was not nearly as overwhelming as in the presidential race.[18] As usual, the National Conservative Political Action Committee towered above all other independent expenditure PACs. NCPAC spent $19.3 million in 1983–1984, more than any other PAC in history, and it ran a panoply of pro-Reagan independent projects. The most interesting pro-Reagan, anti-Mondale thrust, however, belonged not to NCPAC but to the conservative American Security Council, which sent a "Peace Through Strength" mailer to 300,000 supporters that included a "Russian-English Phrase Card . . . useful in the event Walter Mondale is elected President." The card listed questions in both languages such as, "Where do I apply for ration cards?" and "How do I enroll my children in the Young Communist League?"[19]

PROBLEMS ANEW IN CAMPAIGN FINANCE

In more congressional campaigns than ever before, PACs were portrayed in 1984 as the central corrupting evil in American politics. Candidates from Maine to California scored points by forswearing the acceptance of PAC gifts earlier and more fervently than their opponents. In Massachusetts, for example, all the major contenders for the U.S. Senate in both parties refused to take PAC money, and one Bay State candidate for the U.S. House badgered his Democratic primary foe to sign a statement pledging to resign his seat in Congress should he "ever knowingly accept and keep a campaign contribution from a political action committee."[20] Despite its aggressiveness in attracting PAC money to itself and its candidates, the Democratic party included in its national platform a call for banning PAC funds from all federal elections,[21] and newspapers such as the Boston *Globe* crusaded against the PACs.[22]

PAC-bashing may be a popular campaign sport, but not much good comes of it. More importantly, the "big PAC attack" is an opiate that pleasantly obsecures the real concerns and problems of campaign finance, as the 1984 elections suggested anew. Among the problems discussed earlier in this volume is the need to broaden disclosure. Once again in 1984, many millions of dollars—an exact tally will never be made—were spent on behalf of candidates but not reported to the Federal Election Commission. These hidden sums include often unlimited contributions channeled by the national parties to some of their state and local affiliates for "party-building" activities: sizable "internal communications" costs spent by corporations and labor unions in sending information to their members; national party "building funds" collected from corporate and labor union treasuries; the administrative expenses of PACs—which may be far larger than the amounts they report contributing directly to candidates; and the expenditures of tax-exempt educational foundations sponsored by a number of large PACs. If the press and voters are to be able to gauge fully the influence bearing upon their elected representatives, then these sources of campaign money must also be revealed, and the FEC should be funded at a much more generous level to accommodate the increased crush of paper.[23]

Similarly, the 1984 elections underline the need to stimulate more small, individual contributions. For example, gifts of under $100 to House candidates have declined from 38 percent of all campaign money in 1978 to 22 percent in 1982 and 20 percent in 1984.[24] As discussed in Chapter 6,[25] increasing the tax credit for small gifts would encourage participation from more citizens while providing another indirect check on PACs. This reform might also help to stem another unhealthy development, the aggregation of large personal debts accumulated by candidates (especially nonincumbents) during their campaigns. By 1984, 12 percent of all money raised by Senate candidates and 8 percent of all funds secured by House candidates were in the form of loans by the candidates themselves from their personal fortunes or from bank lending. These loans can place elected representatives under great pressure once in office, as they attempt to repay the banks or themselves with PAC money or individual contributions.[26]

Finally, election year 1984 saw more than two dozen congressmen retire. This would not be noteworthy in the area of campaign finance except for a scandalous and little-noted "grandfather" clause in federal election law[27] permitting any member of Congress who was in office on January 8, 1980, to keep any remaining campaign contributions for *personal* use after leaving office. Many congressmen have not been shy about converting cash given them by PACs and individuals for their reelection races into supplementary pensions or personal slush funds.[28] One former House member purchased a new Cadillac as a "going away" gift to himself; others have purchased everything from furniture to flowers, though interest-free loans are particularly popular.[29] Most of the honorables, however, have simply pocketed the money. "I used it to help tide me over," said one, while another only "wished it had been more."[30]

U.S. Representative Andrew Jacobs of Indiana, though "grandfathered," is actively seeking to abolish the loophole. Explained Jacobs: "These funds are given for a *purpose*—to get elected—not to provide a civil service retirement fund. We already have a very generous one. When I think of those who have engaged in this sort of practice, only the word 'sleazy' comes to mind."[31] Surely the clause deserves a cruel fate—with excess campaign funds returned *pro rata* to contributors[23] or donated to charity (preferably without congressmen receiving the charitable tax deduction). Of course, repeal of the provision will not come easily, since 251 current representatives—a substantial majority of the House—are beneficiaries of the clause, and these members of Congress reported an average campaign surplus of almost $107,000 at the end of 1984.[33] Moreover, many of Congress's leaders are among the twenty-eight "grandfathered" representatives with surpluses exceeding $250,000. Whatever the chances for repeal of this singularly seedy clause, this particular instance suggests again the dangers inherent in campaign finance reform. Repeatedly over the years, campaign finance laws have yielded "surprises," some intentional and some not. For when all is said and done, it is Congress—not PACs or campaign-finance academics or public-interest lobbyists—that passes revisions in campaign laws. And Congress is certain to take care of its own. In the field of political money, the best advice remains "caveat reformator": let the reformer beware.

Glossary of PACs and Party Committees

PACS

ADPAC	American Dental Association Political Action Committee
AMPAC	American Medical Association Political Action Committee
BANKPAC	American Bankers Association Political Action Committee
BIPAC	Business-Industry Political Action Committee
CALPAC	California Medical Association Political Action Committee
CFTR	Citizens for the Republic
COPE	Committee on Political Education (AFL-CIO)
CSFC	Committee for the Survival of a Free Congress
DRIVE	Democratic Republican Independent Voters Education (Teamsters International)
HCI-PAC	Handgun Control Inc. Political Action Committee
HRCF	Human Rights Campaign Fund
MNPL	Machinists Non-Partisan Political League
NCEC	National Committee for an Effective Congress
NCPAC	National Conservative Political Action Committee
NEA-PAC	National Education Association Political Action Committee
NRA-PVF	National Rifle Association Political Victory Fund
PROPAC	Progressive Political Action Committee
R-PAC	National Association of Realtors Political Action Committee
SMACPAC	Sheet Metal and Air Conditioning Contractors Political Action Committee
SunPAC	Sun Oil Company Political Action Committee
TARPAC	Television and Radio Political Action Committee

PARTY COMMITTEES

DCCC	Democratic Congressional Campaign Committee
DNC	Democratic National Committee
DSCC	Democratic Senatorial Campaign Committee
NRCC	National Republican Congressional Committee
NRSC	National Republican Senatorial Committee
RNC	Republican National Committee

List of Interviewees†

Mark Adams, Director, American Dental Association Political Action Committee (ADPAC), Washington, D.C., Aug. 17, 1983.

Richard Armstrong, President, Public Affairs Council, Washington, D.C., July 27, 1983.

J. Brian Atwood, Executive Director, Democratic Senatorial Campaign Committee (DSCC), Washington, D.C., July 18, 1983.

Robert Biersack, Statistician, Federal Election Commission (FEC), Washington, D.C., July 27, 1983.

Ed Blakely, Communications Director, National Republican Congressional Committee (NRCC), Washington, D.C., Jan. 1, 1983.

Bernadette Budde, Director of Political Education, Business-Industry Political Action Committee (BIPAC), Washington, D.C., July 6, 1983.

Donald Cogman, Vice-President for Governmental Affairs, MAPCO, Inc., Washington, D.C., Aug. 4, 1983.

Kent Cooper, Assistant Director of Public Disclosure, Federal Election Commission (FEC), Washington, D.C., Jan. 7, 1983.

Edward F. Coyle, Executive Director, Independent Action, Washington, D.C., Aug. 17, 1983.

Timothy Crawford, Director of PAC Program, Republican National Committee (RNC), Washington, D.C., July 11, 1983.

John T. Dolan, National Chairman, National Conservative Political Action Committee (NCPAC), Arlington, Va., July 6, 1983.

*Fred Eiland, Press Officer, Federal Election Commission (FEC), Washington, D.C., June 14, 1983.

Lee Ann Elliott, Commissioner, Federal Election Commission (FEC), Washington, D.C., Aug. 4, 1983.

Stephen Endean, Treasurer, Human Rights Campaign Fund, Washington, D.C., Aug. 17, 1983.

Frank Fahrenkopf, Chairman, Republican National Committee (RNC), Washington, D.C., July 11, 1983.

Peter Fenn, Director, Center for Responsive Politics, Washington, D.C., July 21, 1983.

* = Interview conducted by telephone.

†*Note:* This is not a complete list of interviewees, since some PAC officials and corporate spokesmen granted interviews only with a guarantee of anonymity.

Marty Franks, Executive Director, Democratic Congressional Campaign Committee (DCCC), Washington, D.C., Aug. 25, 1983.

Joe Gaylord, Executive Director, National Republican Congressional Committee (NRCC), Washington, D.C., Aug. 4, 1983.

*Harold Haverty, President, Deluxe Check Printers Corp., St. Paul, Minn., Oct. 4, 1983.

Russell Hemenway, Executive Director, National Committee for an Effective Congress (NCEC), Washington, D.C., July 11, 1983.

William Holayter, Director of Legislative and Public Affairs, Machinists' Non-Partisan Political League, Washington, D.C., July 27, 1983.

Helena Hutton, National Director of Public Affairs, National Association of Manufacturers (NAM), Washington, D.C., July 22, 1983.

Alfred Jackson, Political Director, National Committee for an Effective Congress (NCEC), Washington, D.C., July 27, 1983.

Victor Kamber, Treasurer, Progressive Political Action Committee (PROPAC), Washington, D.C., July 21, 1983.

John Kochevar, Manager of Public Affairs, U.S. Chamber of Commerce, Washington, D.C., July 18, 1983.

*Kay Kunz, Secretary-Treasurer, Communications Workers of America, Local 3122, DAMPAC, Miami, Fla., Aug. 31, 1983.

Margaret Latus, Political Scientist, Brookings Institution, Washington, D.C., July 21, 1983.

Peter Lauer, Director of Political Affairs Division, American Medical Association Political Action Committee (AMPAC), Washington, D.C., Aug. 8, 1983.

*Arnyn Lear, Assistant Executive Director for Government Affairs, Pennsylvania Dental PAC, Harrisburg, Pa., Sept. 15, 1983.

Ann Lewis, Political Director, Democratic National Committee (DNC), Washington, D.C., July 22, 1983.

Jackie Lowe, Assistant Director of Fundraising, National Republican Senatorial Committee (NRSC), Washington, D.C., July 22, 1983.

Michael Malbin, Political Scientist, American Enterprise Institute, Washington, D.C., July 11, 1983.

*Martin Manley, AFL-CIO Committee on Political Education (COPE), and Director, Central Labor Council of Santa Clara County, San Jose, Calif., Sept. 13, 1983.

*Bernard McKay, Secretary-Treasurer, Pan-Am Flight Engineers' PAC, Garden City, N.J., Sept. 13, 1983.

Kenneth Melley, Director of Political Affairs, National Education Association (NEA), Washington, D.C., Aug. 17, 1983.

Brian Meyer, Assistant Director for State Associations, American Bankers Association Political Action Committee (BANKPAC), Washington, D.C., Aug. 25, 1983.

Mike Milligan, PAC Liaison, National Republican Senatorial Committee (NRSC), Washington, D.C., July 22, 1983.

Charles Orasin, Director, Handgun Control Inc. Political Action Committee (HCI-PAC), Washington, D.C., July 27, 1983.

Terri D. O'Grady, Federal Liaison, National Rifle Association (NRA), Washington, D.C., Aug. 25, 1983.

John Perkins, Director, AFL-CIO Committee on Political Education (COPE), Washington, D.C., Aug. 17, 1983.

*John Pennington, Director of Public Relations, Genesco, Nashville, Tenn., Oct. 12, 1983.

Alan V. Reuther, Assistant General Counsel, United Auto Workers (UAW), Washington, D.C., Aug. 21, 1983.

*John Serumgard, Vice-President for Industrial Relations, Rubber Manufacturers Association Political Action Committee, Washington, D.C., Sept. 15, 1983.

Frank H. Simpson, Director of Public Relations, Armstrong World Industries, Lancaster, Pa., Oct. 11, 1983.

*Jerry Simpson, Executive Director, California Medical Association Political Action Committee (CALPAC), San Francisco, Calif., Aug. 9, 1983.

*John Singer, Vice-President for Public Relations, American Hoescht Corporation, Somerville, N.Y., Oct. 3, 1983.

Glenn Skovholt, Director of Federal Government Relations, Honeywell Political Action Committee, Minneapolis, Minn., June 30, 1983.

Steve Stockmeyer, Senior Vice-President for Governmental Relations, Television and Radio Political Action Committee (TARPAC), Washington, D.C., July 11, 1983.

David Sweeney, Executive Director, International Teamsters Democratic Republican Independent Voters Education (DRIVE), Washington, D.C., Sept. 21, 1983.

Gregg Ward, Director of Government Relations, Sheet Metal and Air Conditioning Political Action Committee (SMACPAC), Washington, D.C., July 10, 1983.

Richard Warden, Legislative Director, United Auto Workers (UAW), Washington, D.C., July 22, 1983.

Fred Wertheimer, President, Common Cause, Washington, D.C., Sept. 21, 1983.

Paul Weyrich, Executive Director, Committee for the Survival of a Free Congress (CSFC), Washington, D.C., Aug. 8, 1983.

*Cindi Williams, Director of Legislation, Federation of American Hospitals Political Action Committee, Washington, D.C., Sept. 15, 1983.

*R. E. Carter Wrenn, Executive Director, National Congressional Club, Raleigh, N.C., July 8, 1983.

Notes

INTRODUCTION

1. *Washington Post,* Feb. 22, 1983, p. A7.
2. *National Journal* 14 (Oct. 30, 1982): 1836.
3. From a direct-mail letter signed by Common Cause's president Fred Wertheimer (undated, mailed in March 1983).
4. Statement of Sen. Richard G. Lugar (R–Ind.), in U.S., Congress, Senate, Committee on Rules and Administration, *Hearing on the Federal Election Campaign Act of 1971, as Amended, and on Various Measures to Amend the Act: S. 85, S. 151, S. 732, S. 810, S. 1185, S. 1350, and S. 1684,* 98th Cong., 1st sess., S. HRG 98–588, May 17, 1983, p. 325.
5. From a direct-mail letter signed by Independent Action's chairman Morris K. Udall (undated, mailed during 1983).
6. From a column by Patrick J. Buchanan, "In Defense of PACs," *Richmond Times-Dispatch,* Feb. 12, 1983.
7. *Common Cause* 9 (March/April 1983): 44.
8. Glenn's remarks were contained in a film, *PACs: Making Government Our Business,* produced by the Public Affairs Council in 1981.
9. *Common Cause* 9 (March/April 1983): 43–45.
10. See note 5, above.
11. *PACs and Lobbies* 4 (July 6, 1983): 17.
12. The Moyers series was aired Feb. 22–26, 1982.
13. Walter Isaacson, "Running with the PACs: How Political Action Committees Win Friends and Influence Elections," *Time,* Oct. 25, 1982, pp. 20–26.
14. Elizabeth Drew, "Politics and Money, Part I," *The New Yorker* 58 (Dec. 6, 1982): 54–149; id., "Politics and Money, Part II," *The New Yorker* 58 (Dec. 13, 1982): 57–111.
15. The interviewees are listed at the back of this book. Most were in-person interviews, and the average duration exceeded one and one-half hours.
16. A computer-generated sample of 399 of the 2,200 multicandidate PACs existing during the 1981–1982 election cycle was used. A multicandidate PAC is a committee qualified to contribute up to $5,000 per candidate, per election; to qualify, a committee must have been registered for at least six months, must have received contributions from more than fifty persons, and must have made contributions to at least five federal candidates; see 11 CFR 100.5 (e) (3). Some

114 (or 29%) of the 399 PACs returned the lengthy questionnaire, which was separately designed for each of the six categories of PACs (labor, corporate, trade/membership/health, nonconnected, cooperative, and corporation without stock). The questionnaires (depending on the PAC category) requested between 95 and 101 items of information. Given the expected reluctance of PACs to return such lengthy and revealing questionnaires, extra efforts were undertaken: cover letters of endorsement from prominent PAC leaders were sent with the questionnaires, certain direct-mail techniques (such as personalization and multiple live stamps) were employed, and up to seven follow-ups were made by telephone instead of mail to increase the personalization. The final set of returned questionnaires matched the universe of multicandidate committees closely. For example, by category:

PAC CATEGORY	UNIVERSE OF MULTICANDIDATE PACS	RETURNED QUESTIONNAIRES
Corporate	47%	43%
Trade	21	26
Labor	17	16
Nonconnected	11	11
Cooperative	2	2
Corporation without stock	2	2

CHAPTER 1. THE GROWTH OF POLITICAL ACTION COMMITTEES

1. Personal interview with Donald Cogman, executive director of MAPCO, Inc.
2. Alexis de Tocqueville, *Democracy in America* (New York: Vintage Books, 1954), 2 : 114.
3. See George Thayer, *Who Shakes the Money Tree?* (New York: Simon and Schuster, 1973), pp. 48–52.
4. Act of Jan. 26, 1907, Chap. 420, 34 Stat. 864 (1907).
5. The Federal Corrupt Practices Act is found in Chap. 368, Title III, §313, 43 Stat. 1074 (1925). The act was mainly a response to *Newberry v. United States,* 256 U.S. 232 (1921), which invalidated portions of the existing campaign finance law.
6. Herbert E. Alexander, *Financing Politics* (2nd ed.; Washington, D.C.: Congressional Quarterly, Inc., 1980), p. 68; see also Michael J. Malbin, "The Problem of PAC-Journalism," *Public Opinion* 5 (December/January 1983): 15–16, 59.
7. Alexander Heard, *The Costs of Democracy* (Chapel Hill, N.C.: University of North Carolina Press, 1969), pp. 133–34; Joseph E. Cantor, *Political Action Committees: Their Evolution and Growth and Their Implications for the Political System* (Washington, D.C.: Library of Congress Congressional Research Service Report No. 82–92 GOV, Nov. 6, 1981; updated May 7, 1982), pp. 28–32.

8. Paul Taylor, "Lobbyists' Success," *Washington Post,* Aug. 2, 1983, p. A9.
9. Louise Overacker, *Money in Elections* (New York: Macmillan, 1972), Chap. 6.
10. Heard, *The Costs of Democracy,* p. 130.
11. Michael J. Malbin, "Looking Back at the Future of Campaign Finance Reform: Interest Groups and American Elections," in *Money and Politics in the United States: Financing Elections in the 1980s,* edited by Michael J. Malbin (Washington, D.C.: American Enterprise Institute / Chatham House, 1984), pp. 246–47.
12. David W. Adamany and George E. Agree, *Political Money: A Strategy for Campaign Financing in America* (Baltimore, Md.: Johns Hopkins University Press, 1975), p. 39.
13. Murray Seeger, quoted in an Associated Press dispatch, Feb. 10, 1983.
14. Heard, *The Costs of Democracy,* p. 169.
15. Cantor, *Political Action Committees,* p. 23; Overacker, *Money in Elections,* pp. 50–58.
16. War Labor Disputes Act (Smith-Connally Act), Chap. 144, §9, 57 Stat. 167 (1943).
17. Alexander, *Financing Politics* (2nd ed.), p. 68.
18. Labor Management Relations Act (Taft-Hartley Act), Chap. 120, Title III, §304, 61 Stat. 159 (1947).
19. Herbert E. Alexander, *Financing the 1976 Election* (Washington, D.C.: Congressional Quarterly Press, 1979), pp. 64–65; id., *Financing the 1968 Election* (Lexington, Mass.: Heath Lexington Books, 1971), pp. 195, 200–2.
20. Herbert E. Alexander, *Financing the 1972 Election* (Lexington, Mass.: D. C. Heath, 1976), pp. 461, 504.
21. Edward Handler and John R. Mulkern, *Business in Politics: Campaign Strategies of Corporate Political Action Committees* (Lexington, Mass.: Lexington Books, 1982), pp. 58–59.
22. See Introduction, note 16, above.
23. In the Handler and Mulkern study (*Business in Politics,* p. 58), 48% of the 71 companies they investigated had had a pre-PAC contribution program of some type.
24. See Cantor, *Political Action Committees,* pp. 1–8.
25. See Introduction, note 16.
26. See Cantor, *Political Action Committees,* pp. 36–48. See also Michael J. Malbin (ed.), *Parties, Interest Groups and Campaign Finance Laws* (Washington, D.C.: American Enterprise Institute, 1980), pp. 3–5; and Edwin M. Epstein, "An Irony of Electoral Reform," *Regulation* 3 (May/June 1979), pp. 35–37.
27. 86 Stat. 3 (1971); Public Law 92–225.
28. Corporations were also made equal partners in the FECA bill in order to attract Republican support.
29. 88 Stat. 1263 (1974); Public Law 93–443.
30. This limit applies only to multicandidate PACs; other PACs can only give $1,000 per candidate per election.
31. Public funding of presidential general election campaigns had been provided for by the Revenue Act of 1971, a companion law to the 1971 FECA, but the

1974 amendments extended public funding in some respects to the preconvention presidential elections. Public financing is reviewed in the concluding Chapter 6.

32. FECA had continued a prohibition in effect since the Hatch Act of 1940 (54 Stat. 772).
33. *Congressional Quarterly Almanac* 29 (1973): 742.
34. FEC Advisory Opinion 1975–23 (Nov. 24, 1975).
35. Epstein, "An Irony," p. 36.
36. 90 Stat. 475 (1975); Public Law 93–443.
37. 93 Stat. 1339 (1979); Public Law 96–187. See *Congressional Quarterly Weekly,* Jan. 5, 1980, pp. 33–34.
38. One 1979 amendment required PACs to include in their titles the name of their connected or sponsoring group, thus helping to identify the PAC's source of funding. Most of the other 1979 amendments dealt with the political parties and will be reviewed in Chapters 5 and 6.
39. Cantor, *Political Action Committees,* pp. 55–59.
40. The classifications are sometimes arbitrary and occasionally wrong. The Citizens' Research Foundation, for example, found that a number of party-related committees (that were not PACs) had been incorrectly assigned by the FEC to the nonparty PAC totals. See Herbert Alexander, *Financing the 1980 Elections* (Lexington, Mass.: D. C. Heath, 1983), pp. 128–29. Some of the classifications, while logical, are misleading as well. For example, some corporate PACs (such as Dart and Kraft, Inc.) are highly ideological, at least as much as most PACs classified as "nonconnected," the category associated with ideological PACs.
41. The decrease in the trade/membership/health category in 1977 was due to a reclassification by the FEC, which added three new categories of PACs (nonconnected, cooperative, and corporate without stock) previously included in the trade/membership/health total.
42. See Margaret Ann Latus, "Assessing Ideological PACs: From Outrage to Understanding," in *Money and Politics in the United States: Financing Elections in the 1980s,* edited by Michael J. Malbin (Washington, D.C.: American Enterprise Institute / Chatham House, 1983), pp. 143–44.
43. See *PACs and Lobbies* 6 (Mar. 16, 1983): 5. Some of the paltry PACs do not even attempt to raise money. Many are merely vehicles "in place" should their sponsors decide they are needed.
44. See Theodore J. Eismeier and Philip H. Pollock, "Political Action Committees: The Shaping of Strategy and Influence," prepared for the annual meeting of the Midwest Political Science Association, Chicago, Ill., Apr. 20–23, 1983, p. 4. See also Frank J. Sorauf, "Accountability in Political Action Committees: Who's in Charge?" prepared for the annual meeting of the American Political Science Association, Denver, Colo., Sept. 2–5, 1982, pp. 4–5.
45. 1980 = 1.00.
46. PAC contributions at the federal level are focused almost entirely on congressional contests, with individual gifts and matching funds from the national treasury filling the coffers of presidential candidates in the preconvention period, and public funds alone in the general election for president. In 1980,

for example, PAC gifts to presidential candidates amounted to just $1.6 million (only 1.4% of the primary campaign receipts). See Alexander, *Financing the 1980 Election,* p. 50.

47. "Business-related" PAC spending was calculated as Edwin M. Epstein did in his "An Irony of Electoral Reform," p. 37. One-half of all noncorporate, nonlabor PAC spending was added to corporate PAC contributions. As Epstein noted, this yields a conservative estimate of corporate PAC spending.
48. While labor has consistently declined since 1974 in the proportion of PAC funds that it constitutes, the gains by other PAC categories have fluctuated somewhat from year to year, as the following table indicates:

	PROPORTION OF PAC CONTRIBUTIONS				
TYPE OF PAC	1974	1976	1978	1980	1982
Labor	50%	36%	29%	24%	24%
Corporate	20	31	28	35	33
Trade/membership/health	18	20	33	29	26
Other	11	12	10	12	17

49. Figures compiled by Common Cause. See *Common Cause News,* Feb. 1, 1983, p. 1.
50. Ibid. Twelve of the thirty-three raised more than half a million dollars from PACs.
51. Gary C. Jacobson, "Money in the 1980 and 1982 Congressional Elections," in *Money and Politics in the United States,* edited by Michael J. Malbin (Washington, D.C.: American Enterprise Institute / Chatham House, 1983), Table 1, p. 39. See also Cantor, *Political Action Committees,* pp. 73 81.
52. Growth of PAC money as a proportion of all contributions has been more uneven in Senate races than in House races. PAC gifts actually declined slightly as a proportion of the total Senate campaign funds in both 1978 and 1982. But like their House counterparts, the long-term trend still appears to be upward for Senate candidates.
53. The comparable figure for nonconnected PACs is 36% and for cooperative and corporation without stock PACs is 78%. The largest corporate PACs are clearly in a class by themselves.
54. This listing of "concerns" is taken from *National Journal* 14 (Dec. 11, 1982): 2108–11.
55. Ibid.
56. See Elizabeth Bartz, "Campaign Newsline," *Campaigns and Elections* 3 (Spring 1982): 57.
57. See *PACs and Lobbies* 4 (Apr. 6, 1983): 6.
58. See Margaret Latus, "Mobilizing Christians for Political Action: Campaigning with God on Your Side," prepared for presentation at the annual meeting of the Society for the Scientific Study of Religion, meeting jointly with the Religious Research Association and the Association for the Sociology of Religion, Providence, R.I., Oct. 22–24, 1982, p. 2.

CHAPTER 2. PACS AT WORK: ORGANIZATION AND FUNDRAISING

1. As quoted in Robert Timberg, "The PAC Business," *Baltimore Sun* reprint of articles which ran July 11–19, 1982, pp. 6–7.
2. Ibid., p. 4.
3. See Edward Handler and John R. Mulkern, *Business in Politics: Campaign Strategies of Corporate Political Action Committees* (Lexington, Mass.: Lexington Books, 1982), p. 50; and Bernadette A. Budde, "The Practical Role of Corporate PACs in the Political Process," *Arizona Law Review* 22, no. 2 (1980): 559–60.
4. See Thomas L. Gais, "On the Scope and Bias of Interest Group Involvement in Elections," prepared for the annual meeting of the American Political Science Association, Chicago, Ill., Sept. 1–4, 1983, pp. 13–14; and Edwin M. Epstein, "Business and Labor under the Federal Election Campaign Act of 1971," in *Parties, Interest Groups, and Campaign Finance Laws,* edited by Michael J. Malbin (Washington, D.C.: American Enterprise Institute, 1980), pp. 127–29.
5. Handler and Mulkern, *Business in Politics,* pp. 59–60.
6. See Introduction, note 16.
7. Lee Ann Elliott, "Political Action Committees—Precincts of the 1980's," *Arizona Law Review* 22, no. 2 (1980): 546–47.
8. Epstein, "Business and Labor under the Federal Election Campaign Act of 1971," pp. 132–36.
9. Bernadette A. Budde, "Business Political Action Committees," in *Parties, Interest Groups, and Campaign Finance Laws,* edited by Michael J. Malbin (Washington, D.C.: American Enterprise Institute, 1980), p. 11. See also Daniel Esty, "The Moneyed Interests: An Empirical Analysis of the Relationship between Economic Power and Political Influence," Bachelor of Arts Honors Thesis presented to the Department of Economics, Harvard University, Mar. 18, 1981. Esty found (p. 83) that, on average, for every million dollars spent in politics, an industry has twenty-nine bills filed that relate to it.
10. David Biaz, "Who and Why of Big-Buck Politics: Spend Money to Make Money," *Wall Street Journal,* Nov. 15, 1983, p. 34.
11. See, for example, Gais, "On the Scope and Bias." See also Carl L. Swanson, *A Framework for Evaluating and Planning Corporate PAC Strategies for Political Campaign Contributions* (Richardson, Tex.: Center for Research in Business and Social Policy, University of Texas at Dallas, 1982), pp. 9–14.
12. FEPAC employee newsletter, circulated in 1981.
13. This subject will be explored in greater detail in Chapter 3.
14. Donald Cogman of MAPCO, in a personal interview.
15. Gais, "On the Scope and Bias," p. 17.
16. As quoted in Congressional Quarterly's *Dollar Politics* (3rd ed.; Washington, D.C.: Congressional Quarterly, Inc., 1982), p. 46.
17. Ronald Brownstein, "When Powerful Interests Can't Agree, Members of Congress Prefer to Duck," *National Journal* 15 (Nov. 5, 1983): 2305.
18. William A. Hunter, *The "New Right": A Growing Force in State Politics,* edited

by Thomas W. Bennett (Washington, D.C.: The Conference on Alternative State and Local Policies, and the Center to Protect Workers' Rights, 1980), p. 32.

19. A mail survey with a sample size of 913 groups with 564 responses. See Gais, "On the Scope and Bias," pp. 8–14.
20. Epstein, "Business and Labor under the Federal Election Campaign Act of 1971," p. 127.
21. A random sampling (N = 29) was made of the 206 corporations (listed in the 1982 *Fortune* 500 ranking of the largest U.S. industrial corporations) which had not formed a PAC as of Dec. 31, 1982. Each was contacted by telephone between September and November 1983, and interviews were conducted with representatives of fifteen of the twenty-nine. In most cases the individual interviewed was a corporate officer in public relations or governmental affairs, although some interviews were conducted with higher corporate executives.
22. As quoted in Nina Easton, "Swimming against the Tide," *Common Cause* 9 (September/October 1983): 13.
23. See Herbert Alexander, *Financing the 1980 Election* (Lexington, Mass.: Lexington Books, 1983), p. 374.
24. See the example of the Food Marketing Institute's FoodPAC in Robert E. Bradford, "FoodPAC: Effectiveness and Efficiency," in *The PAC Handbook: Political Action for Business,* Fraser Associates (Cambridge, Mass.: Ballinger Publishing Company, 1980), p. 101.
25. Handler and Mulkern, *Business in Politics,* p. 66.
26. As quoted in Diane Granat, "Scientists Divided on Value of PAC Activity," *Congressional Quarterly Weekly* 41 (Mar. 19, 1983): 552.
27. Donald Cogman of MAPCO, Inc., in a personal interview.
28. See the example of the National Federation of Independent Business in Dick Fisher, "Starting a National Association PAC," in *The PAC Handbook: Political Action for Business,* Fraser Associates (Cambridge, Mass.: Ballinger Publishing Company, 1980), p. 118.
29. The Singer Corporation was included in this study's *Fortune* 500 survey (see note 21, above). The individual contacted by telephone cannot be identified here under the terms of the interview.
30. Telephone interview, Oct. 11, 1983. The individual cannot be identified here under the terms of the interview.
31. Telephone interview, Oct. 4, 1983. The individual cannot be identified here under the terms of the interview.
32. Telephone interview, Oct. 4, 1983. The individual cannot be identified here under the terms of the interview.
33. Telephone interview, Oct. 3, 1983. The individual cannot be identified here under the terms of the interview.
34. John R. Bolton, "Constitutional Limitations on Restricting Corporate and Union PACs," *Arizona Law Review* 22, no. 2 (1980): 411–12.
35. See Curtis C. Sproul, "Corporations and Unions in Federal Politics: A Practical Approach to Federal Election Law Compliance," *Arizona Law Review* 22, no. 2 (1980): 493–94. See also 11 CFR §102.7(a).

36. See Handler and Mulkern, *Business in Politics,* pp. 73–78. Interviews of PAC officers conducted for this study are also the basis for the statements made here about the operation of each PAC category.
37. A similar observation was made by Handler and Mulkern, *Business in Politics,* p. 69.
38. Handler and Mulkern (*Business in Politics,* p. 76) found the CEO on the PAC board in 16% of their corporate sample.
39. Stockholders are rarely solicited by corporate PACs for contributions, however, so their exclusion from the governing board may be on these grounds. As Chapter 6 will discuss, some PAC critics believe that corporate officers deliberately exclude stockholders to avoid any accountability to them for the actions of their PAC.
40. 2 United States Congress §441 a(a)(5)(1976).
41. See Joseph E. Cantor, *Political Action Committees: Their Evolution and Growth and Their Implications for the Political System* (Washington, D.C.: Library of Congress Congressional Research Service Report No. 82–92 GOV, Nov. 6, 1981; updated May 7, 1982), pp. 108–9.
42. Michael J. Malbin, "Looking Back at the Future of Campaign Finance Reform: Interest Groups and American Elections," in *Money and Politics in the United States: Financing Elections in the 1980s* edited by Michael J. Malbin (Washington, D.C.: American Enterprise Institute / Chatham House, 1984), p. 260.
43. Cantor, *Political Action Committees,* p. 24.
44. Malbin ("Looking Back at the Future of Campaign Finance Reform," p. 258) cites James Q. Wilson, *Political Organizations,* (New York: Basic Books, 1973), Chap. 7, on this point.
45. Frank J. Sorauf, "Accountability in Political Action Committees: Who's in Charge?" prepared for the annual meeting of the American Political Science Association, Denver, Colo., Sept. 2–5, 1982, pp. 21–22. See also Theodore J. Eismeier and Philip H. Pollock, "Political Action Committees: The Shaping of Strategy and Influence," prepared for the annual meeting of the Midwest Political Science Association, Chicago, Ill., Apr. 20–23, 1983, pp. 8–9.
46. Timberg, "The PAC Business."
47. Terry Dolan of NCPAC, in a personal interview.
48. Timberg, "The PAC Business," and my personal interview with Victor Kamber of PROPAC, during which he explained, "There is no structure [to PROPAC] purposely to show the absurdity of independent expenditures."
49. Personal interview with Paul Weyrich of the Committee for the Survival of a Free Congress (CSFC).
50. See Introduction, note 16.
51. Gifts to the lobby are *not* tax deductible, however.
52. See Hunter, *The "New Right,"* pp. 6–9.
53. Handler and Mulkern (*Business in Politics,* pp. 66–67) found that in about 30% of the corporate PACs they studied, a separate selection committee was operating under the parent governing board. In some of those cases, however, the selection committee was merely a subcommittee of the parent body.
54. The findings of this study about corporate PACs parallel in most cases data

collected by the Business-Industry Political Action Committee (BIPAC) and the National Association of Business Political Action Committee (NABPAC) [Civic Service, Inc., "Attitudes toward Campaign Financing" (St. Louis, Mo.: Civic Service, Inc., February 1983); and *NABPAC Newsletter* 6 (January/February 1983): 1–2].

55. See Handler and Mulkern, *Business in Politics,* pp. 70–71.
56. However, surveys are conducted as a standard direct-mail fundraising technique. They are used as "participation devices": letter recipients indicate their favorite candidates or preferred targets for defeat, and thus feel more "involved" and therefore more likely to contribute. See Larry Sabato, *The Rise of Political Consultants: New Ways of Winning Elections* (New York: Basic Books, 1981), pp. 238–39. Nonconnected PACs frequently employ surveys in their direct-mail programs, but the survey results are generally not even tallied, much less used to determine the PAC's allocation of funds.
57. Under terms of the interview, this example cannot be attributed.
58. This statistic was provided by the Federal Election Commission. About 16% of the multicandidate PACs in the random sample prepared for this study were Washington based; when PACs located in northern Virginia and southern Maryland were added, the Washington PAC proportion rises to about 19%. Other regions of the country are, of course, represented in the PAC world, but with somewhat of a southern and eastern bias.

REGION	% OF ALL MULTICANDIDATE PACS
Washington, D.C.	16
Northeast	16
South	24
Border states	7
Midwest	20
West	16

For geographical definitions of regions listed in the table, see Larry Sabato, *Goodbye to Good-Time Charlie: The American Governorship Transformed* (2nd ed.; Washington, D.C.: Congressional Quarterly, 1983), p. 17.

59. See Introduction, note 16.
60. See especially Eismeier and Pollock, "Political Action Committees," pp. 5–8, 19–21; Handler and Mulkern, *Business in Politics,* pp. 26–27; and Sorauf, "Accountability in Political Action Committees," pp. 8, 19, 455.
61. From results of this study's survey of multicandidate PACs. "No preference" in the hypothetical choice posed in the survey question was chosen by 27% of the Washington-office PACs and 50% of the non–Washington-office PACs. See also Handler and Mulkern, *Business in Politics,* pp. 26–27.
62. The fascinating relationship between PACs and lobbyists will be explored more fully in Chapter 4.

63. Unless otherwise noted, the statistics cited in the rest of this section are drawn from the results of the multicandidate PAC survey.
64. See Eismeier and Pollock, "Political Action Committees," pp. 19–21.
65. This subject will be taken up again in Chapter 3.
66. Sorauf, "Accountability in Political Action Committees," p. 19.
67. "Working with PACs," National Republican Congressional Committee, 1982.
68. Quoted in Thomas B. Edsall, "PACs Bankrolling GOP Challengers," *Washington Post,* Sept. 14, 1982, p. D7.
69. Results from the survey of multicandidate PACs conducted for this study; see Introduction, note 16.
70. Ibid. The exact percentages for trade PACs were: 29% in BIPAC, 36% in the Chamber, 4% in the Public Affairs Council.
71. Ibid.
72. The parties' activities in dispensing information to the PACs will be examined in Chapter 5.
73. See Elizabeth Drew, "Politics and Money, Part I," *The New Yorker* 58 (Dec. 6, 1982): 71–72.
74. The U.S. Chamber of Commerce and the National Association of Manufacturers were two others.
75. Public Affairs Council, *IMPACT,* May 1983, p. 1.
76. Eismeier and Pollock, "Political Action Committees," p. 5.
77. Herbert E. Alexander, *Financing the 1980 Election* (Lexington, Mass.: Lexington Books, 1983), pp. 130–31.
78. See, for example, *Political Finance/Lobby Reporter,* Oct. 28, 1981, p. 276.
79. Corporate PACs were especially well treated by their parents; 84% of the corporate PACs in the multicandidate PAC survey conducted for this study had all or nearly all of their expenses paid by the company.
80. FEC, Advisory Opinion 1980–59.
81. There is considerable dispute about whether such gifts are tax deductible, and the IRS has recently ruled in one particular case that they are not. See *Political Finance/Lobby Reporter,* Jan. 27, 1982, p. 15; and *Campaign Practices Reports* 9 (Feb. 1, 1982): 3.
82. See Chapter 1, p. 000. As was noted there, the other PAC categories contribute between 52% and 63% of their budgets directly to candidates.
83. Timberg, "The PAC Business."
84. Ibid.
85. Personal interviews with Dolan and Kamber.
86. Personal interview with Dolan.
87. See Sabato, *The Rise of Political Consultants,* pp. 220–65.
88. See, for example, the case of the Christian Voice PAC in Margaret Ann Latus, "Mobilizing Christians for Political Action: Campaigning with God on Your Side," prepared for the annual meeting of the Society for the Scientific Study of Religion, meeting jointly with the Religious Research Association and the Association for the Sociology of Religion, Providence, R.I., Oct. 22–24, 1982, p. 4.
89. As quoted by Timberg, "The PAC Business," p. 7.

90. D. Craig Yesse, "Loctite Corporation: The Making of a PAC," in *The PAC Handbook: Political Action for Business,* Fraser Associates (Cambridge, Mass.: Ballinger Publishing Company, 1980), p. 80.
91. For a detailed presentation of the rules of PAC solicitation, see Sproul, "Corporations and Unions in Federal Politics," pp. 483–92.
92. The rules listed here for corporate PACs also apply to PACs of corporations without stock, except that the latter category has no stockholders to solicit.
93. Granting solicitation rights to a trade association in no way restricts the right of the corporation to solicit its own executive and administrative personnel and stockholders. Of course some corporations view trade PAC solicitation of their employees as competition for their own PACs, which hampers the efforts of trade PACs to secure prior approvals from the corporations.
94. The rules listed here for trade association PACs do *not* apply to membership organizations also classed in the trade/membership/health category. A membership organization can solicit, without limit, all formal members of the group. "Member" is defined as anyone who currently satisfies the group's requirements for membership, as long as those requirements entail more than merely making a contribution to the group's PAC. See Sproul, "Corporations and Unions in Federal Politics," pp. 480–81, 487–88. Incidentallv, the membership organizations may *not* solicit the *families* of members, while corporate, trade, and labor PACs are permitted to do so (though, in fact, few ever do).
95. See Introduction, note 16.
96. As quoted in Bradford, "FoodPAC," p. 103.
97. Survey results contained in BG&E PAC's 1982 Annual Report.
98. Under FEC regulations, just about any otherwise legal fundraising gimmick can be used, though the PAC must raise at least $3 for every $1 it spends on the actual fundraising event.
99. Investment income in excess of $100 must be reported to the FEC, but there are no other restrictions except that all PAC funds must be channeled first through a checking account.
100. See *PACs and Lobbies* 4 (May 18, 1983): 7.
101. From my survey of multicandidate PACs; see Introduction, note 16.
102. See also Handler and Mulkern, *Business in Politics,* pp. 45–46.
103. The chapter on direct mail in Sabato, *The Rise of Political Consultants,* pp. 220–65, serves as the basis for much of the discussion that follows, as well as the many dozens of PAC direct-mail solicitations collected during the course of this study.
104. The response rate was around 8% and more than $100,000 was grossed in each of 1981 and 1982 from the retirees' letter.
105. See Dale Russakoff, "Getting Out the 'Green Vote' for Friends of Nature," *Washington Post,* Oct. 5, 1982, p. A1; and Jeff Dionne, "With Their Man in the White House, Conservative Legal Groups Are Hurting," *National Journal* 15 (Nov. 5, 1983): 2316.
106. The letter-writer, Rep. Morris K. Udall (D–Ariz.), dubbed Independent Action "the anti-PAC PAC." This characterization was no accident. According to Edward F. Coyle, executive director of Independent Action, liberals had

become suspicious of PACs and hesitant to give to any, liberal or not. Giving to an "anti-PAC PAC" was presumably easier for this PAC's mail constituency.

107. See *PACs and Lobbies* 4 (May 4, 1983): 1; and *Washington Post,* June 5, 1983, p. A8.
108. Alan Green, *Communicating in the 80's: New Options for the Nonprofit Community* (Washington, D.C.: Benton Foundation, 1983), pp. 11–12.
109. See Cantor, *Political Action Committees,* pp. 68–70, 111–12; and Alexander, *Financing the 1980 Election,* p. 400.
110. See *Campaigns and Elections* 3 (Spring 1982): 49.
111. Timberg, "The PAC Business," p. 3; also see Alexander, *Financing the 1980 Election,* pp. 393–94.
112. Estimate provided by Carter Wrenn, executive director of the Club, in a telephone interview.
113. See, for instance, Richard Viguerie, *The New Right: We're Ready to Lead* (Falls Church, Va.: The Viguerie Company, 1980), p. 123.
114. As an example, some corporate PACs solicit only the top company officers, others include middle management, and still others solicit every employee allowable under FECA. See Handler and Mulkern, *Business in Politics,* p. 35.
115. The figures cited here are all medians, not averages.
116. See also Handler and Mulkern, *Business in Politics,* p. 44.
117. See also Anne H. Hopkins and Ruth S. Jones, "Individual Contributors to State Elections: Arizona and Tennessee," prepared for the annual meeting of the American Political Science Association, Chicago, Ill., Sept. 1–4, 1983, p. 14.
118. Ruth S. Jones and Warren E. Miller, "Financing Campaigns: Modes of Individual Contribution," prepared for the annual meeting of the Midwest Political Science Association, Chicago, Ill., Apr. 21–23, 1983, pp. 33–34. Frank Sorauf has suggested, however, that the public's tendency to overreport personal political activity, as well as survey question wording, may have inflated the 7 percent figure by half or even more. See Frank J. Sorauf and the Twentieth Century Fund Task Force on Political Action Committees, *What Price PACs?* (New York: Twentieth Century Fund, 1984), pp. 81–82.
119. See pp. 52–53.
120. From the results of the survey of multicandidate PACs conducted for this study; see Introduction, note 16. Handler and Mulkern, in *Business in Politics,* reported similar findings for corporate PACs.
121. See Sproul, "Corporations and Unions in Federal Politics," pp. 483–85.
122. From the survey of multicandidate PACs conducted for this study; see Introduction, note 16. Other surveys, using different corporate PAC samples, have yielded similar findings. See Herbert E. Alexander, *Financing Politics* (2nd ed.; Washington, D.C.: Congressional Quarterly, 1980), pp. 83–84; Alexander, *Financing the 1980 Election,* p. 373; and Handler and Mulkern, *Business in Politics.*
123. Stockholders can also be given a similar PAC contribution option called "dividend deduction."
124. Orlando B. Potter, "The Disposition of Compliance Cases and Penalties Incurred in the Enforcement of the Federal Election Campaign Act: An Analysis

of Persuasion and Punitive Action," *Campaigns and Elections* 3 (Summer 1982): 13–15.

125. About half the amount was recovered by NEA-PAC when some contributors returned their donations in a legal fashion. See also Alexander, *Financing the 1980 Election,* pp. 385–86.
126. All these figures are from the survey of multicandidate PACs conducted for this study; see Introduction, note 16. See also *Political Finance/Lobby Reporter,* Dec. 2, 1981, p. 314; and Handler and Mulkern, *Business in Politics,* pp. 47–49.
127. Richard B. Berman, "The Corporate PAC Experience," in *The PAC Handbook: Political Action for Business,* Fraser Associates (Cambridge, Mass.: Ballinger Publishing Company, 1980), p. 50.
128. See the cases of Pfizer, Inc., and American Telephone and Telegraph discussed in *PACs and Lobbies* 4 (July 6, 1983): 5.
129. This is in cases where the company does not use payroll deduction itself; if it does do so, it is required to make the system available to labor automatically.
130. National Education Association, "How to Raise Money for NEA-PAC-Education's Defense Fund," p. 4.
131. Congressional Quarterly, Inc., *Dollar Politics* (1st ed.; Washington, D.C.: Congressional Quarterly, 1982), p. 44.
132. See, for example, the practice of the Council for a Liveable World in Stephen W. Thomas's commentary in *Parties, Interest Groups and Campaign Finance Laws,* edited by Michael J. Malbin (Washington, D.C.: American Enterprise Institute, 1980), pp. 84–85. See also Margaret Ann Latus, "Assessing Ideological PACs: From Outrage to Understanding," in *Money and Politics in the United States: Financing Elections in the 1980s,* edited by Michael J. Malbin (Washington, D.C.: American Enterprise Institute / Chatham House, 1984), p. 164.
133. Only if the PAC retains some of the decision-making in selecting recipients does the gift count against the PAC contribution limit. The example concerning generic designation of the recipient (mentioned above in the text) *would* therefore count against the PAC limit.
134. Sometimes the PAC actually deposits all individual gifts in its own account and forwards the total of all such gifts for each candidate in a check from its own account. The covering letter, however, lists the individual contributors.
135. See *Campaign Practices Reports* 10 (Jan. 31, 1983): 10. The advice may not be acceptable to the IRS, which has issued two technical advisory memoranda bringing into doubt all corporate deductions for PAC administration expenses.
136. From the survey of multicandidate PACs conducted for this study; see Introduction, note 16. Two different surveys of corporate PACs alone have yielded roughly similar conclusions, though major differences in sample composition, and in one case question wording, make exact comparisons impossible. See Handler and Mulkern, *Business in Politics,* pp. 79–80; Civic Service, Inc., Survey for BIPAC, p. 26.
137. From chapter manual of the Sheet Metal and Air Conditioning Contractors' PAC (SMACPAC), p. 37.
138. As quoted in Stephen J. Sansweet, "Political-Action Units at Firms Are Assailed by Some over Tactics," *Wall Street Journal,* July 24, 1980, pp. 1, 12.

139. As quoted in Congressional Quarterly, Inc., *Dollar Politics* (3rd ed.), p. 44.
140. As quoted in *Campaign Practices Reports* 10 (Apr. 25, 1983): 7.
141. Nicholas Goldberg, "Shakedown in the Boardroom," *Washington Monthly* 15 (December 1983): 14.
142. Malbin, editor's discussion, *Parties, Interest Groups, and Campaign Finance Laws,* p. 226; and Alexander, *Financing the 1980 Election,* p. 376.
143. See, for example, the Eton Corporation's letter in Goldberg, "Shakedown in the Boardroom," p. 16.
144. Louise Overacker, *Money in Elections* (New York: Macmillan, 1972), pp. 60–61.
145. For a recent case, see Goldberg, "Shakedown in the Boardroom," p. 17.
146. Easton, "Swimming against the Tide," p. 14.
147. Remarks by Edward C. Joullian III of the Mustang Fuel Corporation, Oklahoma City, Okla., June 20, 1980, taken from the mimeographed text of his speech.
148. In such cases a third party, possibly an accounting firm, acts as a conduit for the PAC gifts. Actually, if a company has payroll deduction, complete anonymity is usually impossible; at least some employees in the payroll division will have knowledge of, or access to, contributions information.
149. See Alexander, *Financing the 1980 Election,* pp. 74–75.
150. *Pipefitters Local No. 562 v. United States,* 407 U.S. 385 (1972).
151. See Sproul, "Corporations and Unions in Federal Politics," pp. 499–500.
152. **In the SunPAC decision in 1975, the FEC had forbidden solicitation of employees by their supervisors, but this rule was reversed by the 1976 Amendments to FECA.**
153. Epstein, "Business and Labor under the Federal Election Campaign Act of 1971," p. 150.
154. Results from the survey of multicandidate PACs conducted for this study; see Introduction, note 16.
155. In large companies, unions, and trade associations, the PAC is usually one part of a "governmental affairs" or "political" division. The political education programs are frequently sponsored by these divisions rather than by the PAC.
156. The $2,000 limit applies *only* to materials expressly advocating the election or defeat of a clearly identified candidate. Also excluded from the limit are any materials where more than half is devoted to noncandidate news of general interest to employees or members (such as a union newspaper).
157. *FEC Record* 9 (October 1983): 6.
158. In 1979–1980 almost $4 million was actually spent on communications but only $1.3 million of that was related to House and Senate races. Most of the rest was spent on the presidential contest. See also Alexander, *Financing the 1980 Election,* pp. 380, 416–20.
159. Hunter, *The "New Right,"* p. 15.
160. Sproul, "Corporations and Unions in Federal Politics," p. 472. Under new and significant regulations preliminarily approved by the FEC in 1983, corporations and unions would be permitted to hold registration and get-out-the-vote drives in conjunction with a nonpartisan, nonprofit group aimed at the general public, not just their stockholders, members, or employees. They would also be al-

lowed to publish "voter guides" (showing the voting records of House and Senate candidates) for distribution to the general public. See *Washington Post,* Nov. 9, 1983, p. A17.

161. Malbin, "Looking Back at the Future of Campaign Finance Reform," p. 264.
162. Haynes Johnson and Nick Kotz, *The Unions* (New York: Pocket Books, 1972), p. 81.
163. Estimate by Michael J. Malbin writing in *National Journal* 9 (Mar. 19, 1977): 412. See also Herbert Alexander, *Financing the 1976 Election* (Washington, D.C.: Congressional Quarterly Press, 1979), p. 623; and Edwin M. Epstein, "An Irony of Electoral Reform," *Regulation* 3 (May/June 1979): 38.
164. See *National Journal* 15 (Sept. 24, 1983): 1938. See also Kathy Sawyer, "In Iowa Chill, Warming to Mondale," *Washington Post,* Dec. 14, 1983, p. A6.
165. Dues were raised from 19¢ per member per month to 27¢ by 1983—a tiny sum for an individual but a mighty cumulative war chest.
166. William Serrin, "Once-Robust Labor Publications Show Signs of Making Comeback," *New York Times,* Dec. 12, 1983, p. B18.
167. See Cantor, *Political Action Committees,* pp. 28–29; and David Jessup, "Can Political Influence Be Democratized? A Labor Perspective," in *Parties, Interest Groups, and Campaign Finance Laws,* edited by Michael J. Malbin (Washington, D.C.: American Enterprise Institute, 1980), pp. 31–32.
168. Stephen K. Gilpin, formerly of General Electric PAC, as quoted in Congressional Quarterly's *Dollar Politics* (3rd ed.), p. 49. The figures on reported internal communications costs (note 158, above) confirm that Gilpin's view predominates.
169. Julian Scheer, "LTV PAC: Part of a Total Political Focus," in *The PAC Handbook: Political Action for Business,* Fraser Associates (Cambridge, Mass.: Ballinger Publishing Company, 1980), p. 67.
170. Yesse, "Loctite Corporation," p. 79.
171. See Latus, "Assessing Ideological PACs," pp. 162–63.

CHAPTER 3. PACS IN THE PUBLIC EYE: THEIR CANDIDATES AND CONTRIBUTIONS

1. As quoted in *Association Management* 35 (July 1983): 57.
2. As quoted in Richard Viguerie, *The New Right: We're Ready to Lead* (Falls Church, Va.: The Viguerie Company, 1980), pp. 58–59.
3. See Joseph E. Cantor, *Political Action Committees: Their Evolution and Growth and Their Implications for the Political System* (Washington, D.C.: Library of Congress Congressional Research Service Report No. 82–92, Nov. 6, 1981; updated May 7, 1982), pp. 73–76. The 1981–1982 proportion, for instance, was 73% to 27% in favor of the House. In my study, about 13% of all multicandidate PACs surveyed reported giving exclusively to House races, compared to just 2% for Senate contests. Corporate PACs tend to be a bit more Senate oriented, while labor PACs focus more heavily on the House.
4. Cantor, *Political Action Committees,* pp. 76–77.
5. Michael J. Malbin, "Of Mountains and Molehills: PACs, Campaigns, and

Public Policy," in *Parties, Interest Groups, and Campaign Finance Laws,* edited by Michael J. Malbin (Washington, D.C.: American Enterprise Institute, 1980), p. 157. See also Cantor, *Political Action Committees,* p. 172.

6. Yet it is also true that a lack of money is one reason why so many congressional campaigns look hopelessly behind.
7. See Theodore J. Eismeier and Philip H. Pollock, "Political Action Committees: The Shaping of Strategy and Influence," prepared for the annual meeting of the Midwest Political Science Association, Chicago, Ill., Apr. 20–23, 1983, p. 4.
8. See Richard P. Conlon's commentary in Michael J. Malbin (ed.), *Parties, Interest Groups, and Campaign Finance Laws* (Washington, D.C.: American Enterprise Institute, 1980), p. 187. For example, in 1982 there were seven key congressional races where challengers were seriously threatening incumbents, and did indeed defeat the incumbents. In all seven cases the challengers raised more PAC money than the incumbents, most of whom had easily outdistanced their opponents among PACs in the past. See *National Journal* 14 (Dec. 18, 1982): 2150–51.
9. The reelection rates for House incumbents who seek reelection consistently range in the low 90s; Senate incumbents have fared much less well since 1976, though in 1982 only two incumbents were defeated.
10. See Kirk F. Brown, "Campaign Contributions and Congressional Voting," prepared for the annual meeting of the American Political Science Association, Chicago, Ill., Sept. 1–4, 1983; William P. Welch, "The Allocation of Political Monies: Economic Interest Groups," *Public Choice* 35 (1980): 97–120; and Diana Evans Yiannakis, "PAC Contributions and House Voting on Conflictual and Consensual Issues: The Windfall Profits Tax and the Chrysler Loan Guarantee," prepared for the annual meeting of the American Political Science Association, Chicago, Ill., Sept. 1–4, 1983.
11. See pp. 52–60.
12. Eismeier and Pollock, "Political Action Committees," pp. 5–8; Frank J. Sorauf, *Party Politics in America* (4th ed.; Boston: Little, Brown and Company, 1980), p. 8; and Edward Handler and John R. Mulkern, *Business in Politics: Campaign Strategies of Corporate Political Action Committees* (Lexington, Mass.: Lexington Books, 1982), pp. 26–27. In my survey of multicandidate PACs conducted for this study, 61% of those with a Washington office preferred to support incumbents, while only 6% tilted toward challengers; by comparison, among PACs without a D.C. base just 38% preferred incumbents and 10% placed a priority on challengers.
13. Handler and Mulkern, *Business in Politics,* p. 26; Eismeier and Pollock, "Political Action Committees," pp. 9–10, 17–19.
14. Handler and Mulkern, *Business in Politics,* pp. 29–31.
15. See *National Journal* 14 (Aug. 7, 1982): 1371.
16. "Facts about CALPAC," a CALPAC mimeograph, p. 1.
17. See, for example, Robert J. Wager, "Toward an Effective PAC: What to Do and How to Do It," in *The PAC Handbook: Political Action for Business,* Fraser Associates (Cambridge, Mass.: Ballinger Publishing Company, 1980), p. 162; *Association Management* 35 (July 1983): 55; Carl L. Swanson, *A Frame-*

work for Evaluating and Planning Corporate PAC Strategies for Political Campaign Contributions (Richardson, Tex.: Center for Research in Business and Social Policy, University of Texas at Dallas, 1982), pp. 18–21; and Yiannakis, "PAC Contributions and House Voting," pp. 16–22.

18. See Elizabeth Drew, "Money and Politics, Part I," *The New Yorker* 58 (Dec. 6, 1982), pp. 119–20.
19. Steve Lilienthal, "Oklahoma I: Feeling the Tulsa Heat," *The Political Report* 6 (Sept. 2, 1983): 3.
20. As quoted in the *Washington Post,* Aug. 21, 1983, p. A16.
21. Larry Light, "The Game of PAC Targeting: Friends, Foes and Guesswork," *Congressional Quarterly Weekly* 39 (Nov. 21, 1981): 2270.
22. Frank J. Sorauf, "Accountability in the Political Action Committees: Who's in Charge?" prepared for the annual meeting of the American Political Science Association, Denver, Colo., Sept. 2–5, 1982, p. 19.
23. Light, "The Game of PAC Targeting," p. 2267.
24. Congressional Quarterly, Inc., *Dollar Politics* (3rd ed.; Washington, D.C.: Congressional Quarterly, Inc., 1982), p. 46.
25. Quoted in *Association Management* 35 (July 1983): 57. See also Light, "The Game of PAC Targeting," p. 2267.
26. Margaret Ann Latus, "Assessing Ideological PACs: From Outrage to Understanding," in *Money and Politics in the United States: Financing Elections in the 1980s,* edited by Michael J. Malbin (Washington, D.C.: American Enterprise Institute / Chatham House, 1984), p. 143. See also Edward Roeder, *PACs Americana: A Directory of Political Action Committees (PACs) and Their Interests* (Washington, D.C.: Sunshine Services Corporation, 1982).
27. Stuart Rothenberg and Richard R. Rolden, *Business PACs and Ideology: A Study of Contributions in the 1982 Elections* (Washington, D.C.: The Institute for Government and Politics of the Free Congress Research and Education Foundation, 1983), pp. 9–11.
28. Eismeier and Pollock, "Political Action Committees," pp. 10–11, 24–26.
29. From "Author's Replies," in Malbin (ed.), *Parties, Interest Groups, and Campaign Finance Laws,* p. 96.
30. Paul Weyrich of CSFC.
31. Drew, "Money and Politics, Part I," pp. 142–46.
32. There were nine items in this index, with topics ranging from the Equal Rights Amendment to gay rights.
33. Dick Fisher, "Starting a National Association PAC," in *The PAC Handbook: Political Action for Business,* Fraser Associates (Cambridge, Mass.: Ballinger Publishing Company, 1980), p. 121.
34. In many states, however, state legislators are rated by interest groups, and these scores can be used when higher office is sought.
35. See Larry Sabato, "Parties, PACs and Independent Groups," in *The American Elections of 1982,* edited by Thomas E. Mann and Norman J. Ornstein (Washington, D.C.: American Enterprise Institute, 1983), pp. 93–94.
36. Political Resources Director Randall Moorhead, as quoted in Mark Green, "Political PAC-Man," *The New Republic* 187 (Dec. 13, 1982): 21.
37. Light, "The Game of PAC Targeting," p. 2270.

38. As quoted in the *Washington Post,* Oct. 30, 1982, p. A5.
39. Light, "The Game of PAC Targeting," p. 2268.
40. Under terms of the interview, no attribution can be made. The congressman in question was defeated for reelection in 1982, though his loss had nothing to do with his alleged extracurricular activities.
41. From this study's random-sample survey; see Introduction, note 16.
42. Since $5,000 could also be given for the nomination, a maximum of $10,000 ($15,000 if there were a runoff) was possible.
43. Prepared statement of Bradley S. O'Leary, P/M Consulting, Inc., in U.S., Congress, Senate, Committee on Rules and Administration, *Hearing on the Federal Election Campaign Act of 1971, as Amended, and on Various Measures to Amend the Act: S. 85, S. 151, S. 732, S. 810, S. 1185, S. 1350, and S. 1684,* 98th Cong., 1st sess., S. HRG 98–588, Jan. 26, 1983, p. 143.
44. Eismeier and Pollock, "Political Action Committees," p. 12.
45. See Rothenberg and Rolden, *Business PACs and Ideology,* pp. 8–9.
46. In the survey of multicandidate PACs conducted for this study, the average number of candidates receiving money from a PAC in 1981–1982 was 47. The median number was 20.
47. Sorauf, "Accountability in the Political Action Committees: Who's in Charge?"
48. News from the Public Affairs Council, May 20, 1983; from a survey of corporate PACs conducted by the Public Affairs Council.
49. Brown, "Campaign Contributions and Congressional Voting," p. 29.
50. "NEA Congressional Endorsement Procedures," p. 3.
51. See Dennis Farney and John J. Fialka, "His Ability as Fund-raiser Enhances the Power of California Democratic Rep. Henry Waxman," *Wall Street Journal, Nov.* 10, 1983, p. 58. This practice may well be illegal under current regulations. (See 2 U.S.C. s441f and 11 CFR 110.6(d).)
52. See Paul D. Kamenar, "PACs, the Taxpayer, and Campaign Finance Reform," The Heritage Foundation *Backgrounder* 257 (Apr. 14, 1983): 9.
53. See Karen Feld, "Special Event Fundraisers: The Which, the When, and the How, Part I," *Campaigns and Elections* 1 (Winter 1981): 14–15.
54. From the survey of multicandidate PACs conducted for this study; see Introduction, note 16.
55. See Ronald Brownstein, "When Powerful Interests Can't Agree, Members of Congress Prefer to Duck," *National Journal* 15 (Nov. 5, 1983): 2305; and Paul Taylor, "Lobbyists' Success at Raising Funds Proves Costly," *Washington Post,* Aug. 2, 1983, p. A9.
56. Bernadette A. Budde, "Business Political Action Committees," in *Parties, Interest Groups, and Campaign Finance Laws,* edited by Michael J. Malbin (Washington, D.C.: American Enterprise Institute, 1980), p. 22.
57. Handler and Mulkern (*Business in Politics,* p. 84), interviewing only corporate PACs, found even fewer cases per PAC—around 3% of the total number of candidate decisions. See also Lee Walczak, "Business 'Double Dips' for Candidates," *Business Week,* Aug. 16, 1982, p. 113.
58. "Objectives and Guidelines of the Honeywell Employees' Political Action Committee," number 5.

59. Brown, "Campaign Contributions and Congressional Voting," p. 17.
60. See Herbert E. Alexander, *Financing the 1980 Election* (Lexington, Mass: D. C. Heath, 1983), p. 378.
61. See Chapter 2, pp. 63–64.
62. Congressional Quarterly, Inc., *Dollar Politics* (3rd ed.), p. 48.
63. Cantor, *Political Action Committees,* p. 72.
64. See the *New York Times,* Nov. 6, 1983, p. A1.
65. From the survey of multicandidate PACs conducted for this study; see Introduction, note 16. See also the NABPAC corporate PAC survey, which has some similar findings, in *NABPAC Newsletter* 6 (January/February 1983): 1–2.
66. See, for example, Paul M. Weyrich, "The New Right: PACs and Coalition Politics," in *Parties, Interest Groups, and Campaign Finance Laws,* edited by Michael J. Malbin (Washington, D.C.: American Enterprise Institute, 1980), p. 74.
67. See Swanson, *A Framework for Evaluating and Planning,* pp. 21–23; and Latus, "Assessing Ideological PACs," p. 37.
68. Fisher, "Starting a National Association PAC," p. 125.
69. Under FECA disclosure rules no contribution under $1,000 received less than 20 days before the election need be reported to the FEC until after the election, and contributions of over $1,000 do not have to be reported before election day if received in the last 48 hours of the campaign.
70. See Budde, "Business Political Action Committees," p. 24.
71. Prepared statement of Jay Angoff, staff attorney, Public Citizen's Congress Watch, in U.S., Congress, Senate, Committee on Rules and Administration, *Hearing on the Federal Election Campaign Act of 1971, as Amended, and on Various Measures to Amend the Act: S. 85, S. 151, S. 732, S. 810, S. 1185, S. 1350, and S. 1684,* 98th Cong., 1st sess., S. HRG 98–588, Jan. 27, 1983, p. 230; see also the *Washington Post,* Aug. 21, 1983, p. A16. Some House members returned these contributions.
72. See "Trial Lawyers Group Contributes Almost Quarter of a Million Dollars to 1976 Congressional Candidates, According to Common Cause; No-Fault Legislation Pending in Congress," Common Cause press release, Feb. 28, 1978.
73. From the survey of multicandidate PACs conducted for this study; see Introduction, note 16. See also *Political Finance/Lobby Reporter,* Dec. 2, 1981, p. 314; and *NABPAC Newsletter* 6 (January/February 1983): 1–2.
74. Figures compiled and provided by Common Cause, Washington, D.C.
75. The services are assessed at some approximation of their value and charged against the PAC's maximum allowable contribution to any candidate. Many advisory opinions issued by the Federal Election Commission set standards for assessing certain in-kind gifts. One such example, concerning a PAC's transfer of polling data to a candidate, will be discussed later in this section.
76. From the survey of multicandidate PACs conducted for this study; see Introduction, note 16.
77. Donald Cogman of MAPCO, Inc., in a personal interview.
78. See Dom Bonafede, "Interest Groups Pressing for Earlier, More Active Role in Electoral Process," *National Journal* 15 (May 14, 1983): 1005–6; *Campaign*

Practices Reports 10 (Mar. 28, 1983): 5; and Paul Taylor, "AMA Finds It Can Use Polling Data to Boost Election Donations Legally," *Washington Post,* Oct. 6, 1982, p. A14.

79. This premise is questionable, because the "benchmark" surveys conducted by AMPAC are meant to measure underlying public sentiments not subject to drastic alteration overnight. A benchmark survey—even one a year old—provides invaluable information to a campaign. See Larry Sabato, *The Rise of Political Consultants: New Ways of Winning Elections* (New York: Basic Books, 1981), pp. 75–81.
80. The contribution price of an AMPAC survey is often well under the $5,000 maximum thanks to this amortization plus the sixty-one-day rule. As a result AMPAC can sometimes supplement the in-kind poll gift with an additional cash contribution to a candidate.
81. See Dale Russakoff, "Getting Out the 'Green Vote' for Friends of Nature," *Washington Post,* Oct. 5, 1982, p. A1; and *The Political Report* 6 (Mar. 4, 1983): 2–6.
82. Terry Dolan of NCPAC, as quoted by "Money and Politics: Campaign Spending Out of Control," Center for Responsive Politics, 1983, p. 23.
83. Terry Dolan of NCPAC, from an interview on KUTV, Salt Lake City, Utah, Mar. 23, 1980, as quoted in Democrats for the '80s, "The New Right: A Threat to America's Future," 1983 pamphlet.
84. Terry Dolan of NCPAC, from Myra MacPherson, "The New Right Brigade," *Washington Post,* Aug. 10, 1980, p. F1.
85. Ibid.
86. If there is any consultation or coordination, the expenditure is treated as an "in-kind" contribution subject to the $5,000-per-election limit.
87. For a background discussion of independent expenditures, see Rodney Smith, "Federal Election Law, Part II: What You Can Get Away With," *Campaigns and Elections* 3 (Fall 1982): 22. See also Alexander, *Financing the 1980 Election,* pp. 129, 168, 370, 378, 387–90.
88. From the survey of multicandidate PACs conducted for this study; see Introduction, note 16.
89. Ibid.
90. See Alexander, *Financing the 1980 Election,* p. 387.
91. Ibid., p. 168.
92. Latus, "Assessing Ideological PACs," p. 149.
93. Seven individuals and seventeen non-PAC groups also made independent expenditures in 1981–1982.
94. See William A. Hunter, *The "New Right": A Growing Force in State Politics,* edited by Thomas W. Bennett (Washington, D.C.: The Conference on Alternative State and Local Policies, and the Center to Protect Workers' Rights, 1980); Latus, "Assessing Ideological PACs"; Alexander, *Financing the 1980 Election,* pp. 397–402; Robert Timberg, "The PAC Business," *Baltimore Sun,* July 11–19, 1982; and Viguerie, *The New Right.*
95. See L. Patrick Devlin, "Contrasts in Presidential Campaign Commercials of 1980," *Political Communications Review* 7 (1982): 18–24.
96. As quoted in the *Washington Post,* Sept. 2, 1983, p. A16.

97. *Washington Post,* Apr. 5, 1983, p. C3.
98. Ibid., June 21, 1983, p. A4.
99. See Viguerie, *The New Right,* pp. 84–87.
100. As quoted in *The Political Report* 6 (Apr. 1, 1983): 6.
101. See *Campaigns and Elections* 3 (Fall 1982): 46; and Democrats for the '80s, "The New Right: A Threat to America's Future."
102. Alexander, *Financing the 1980 Election,* p. 464. The Justice Department held that the offer was not a bribe, but would have been if it had caused Neal to change his mind and vote for the tax cut. (Neal had voted against the cut.)
103. Albert R. Hunt of the *Wall Street Journal* first investigated and reported the ruse. See the *Washington Monthly* 15 (April 1983): 11; *Congressional Quarterly Weekly* 41 (Mar. 19, 1983): 573; and the *Washington Post,* Mar. 4, 1983, p. A5.
104. As quoted in *The Political Report* 6 (July 8, 1983): 9.
105. That is, more poll respondents indicate that they dislike the incumbent and can mention specific reasons why.
106. MacPherson, "The New Right Brigade."
107. Testimony of Sen. Lloyd Bentsen (D–Tex.), in U.S., Congress, Senate, Committee on Rules and Administration, *Hearing on the Federal Election Campaign Act of 1971, as Amended, and on Various Measures to Amend the Act: S. 85, S. 151, S. 732, S. 810, S. 1185, S. 1350, and S. 1684,* 98th Cong., 1st sess., S. HRG 98–588, Jan. 26, 1983, p. 57.
108. See survey results by the NCPAC pollster Arthur Finkelstein in *Campaigns and Elections* 3 (Fall 1982): 36–41; and also Lance Tarrance, *Negative Campaigns and Negative Votes: The 1980 Elections* (Washington, D.C.: Free Congress Research and Education Foundation, 1982).
109. Ibid. Dolan disputes that any real backlash takes place because those respondents who tell pollsters they resent NCPAC's attacks are, claims Dolan, "blacks or liberal Democrats who never once considered voting for our candidate." Many Democratic pollsters disagree with Dolan, however; particularly as NCPAC becomes prominent, they insist that resentment is transferred from NCPAC to the challenger among some undecided, nonliberal voters.
110. See, for example, *National Journal* 14 (Aug. 7, 1982): 1373; *Congressional Quarterly Weekly* 40 (Oct. 9, 1982): 257; *The Political Report* 5 (Dec. 16, 1982): 3–6; *The New Republic* 187 (Oct. 11, 1982): 15; *Washington Post,* Sept. 24, 1982, p. A6; and ibid., Oct. 23, 1982, p. A9.
111. Such a tie was not always unfair. As Dolan once admitted, "Publicly [the candidates helped by NCPAC] continue to badmouth us, but privately we have had no negative reactions." As quoted in Devlin, "Contrasts in Presidential Campaign Commercials," p. 20.
112. See *Washington Post,* Oct. 7, 1982, p. A11; *Campaigns and Elections* 3 (Fall 1982): 46; and Alexander, *Financing the 1980 Election,* p. 464.
113. See, for example, *The New Republic* 187 (Oct. 11, 1982): 15.
114. *Political Finance/Lobby Reporter,* Dec. 30, 1981, p. 342; and *Campaign Practices Reports* 10 (May 23, 1983): 3.
115. Gregg Ward of SMACPAC, in a personal interview.
116. Peter Lauer of AMPAC.
117. See, for example, Xandra Kayden, "Independent Spending," Chap. 7 in *Fi-*

nancing Presidential Campaigns: An Examination of the Ongoing Effects of the Federal Election Campaign Laws upon the Conduct of Presidential Campaigns, prepared for the U.S. Congress, Senate Committee on Rules and Administration, by the Institute of Politics, John F. Kennedy School of Politics, Harvard University, 1982, pp. 7–31, note 6.

118. Dolan hotly disputes that NCPAC had a bad record in 1982: "Ninety-five percent of incumbents return to office. We keyed in on four [Senate] races and won one [i.e., defeated an incumbent]. That's 25 percent, five times better than the average." But as David Broder has shown [*Washington Post,* Nov. 10, 1982], Dolan is putting the best possible face on disappointing election returns. See Sabato, "PACs, Parties and Independent Groups," pp. 100–2.

119. See Maxwell Glen, "Independent Spenders Are Gearing Up, and Reagan and GOP Stand to Benefit," *National Journal* 15 (Dec. 17, 1983): 2627–29.

120. Cited in Latus, "Assessing Ideological PACs," p. 165.

121. See *Campaign Practices Reports* 10 (May 9, 1983): 4; and *PACs and Lobbies* 4 (July 6, 1983): 6.

122. See *Campaigns and Elections* 3 (Fall 1982): 38–39; and *The Political Report* 6 (Mar. 4, 1983): 6–10.

123. Irwin B. Arieff, Nadine Cohodes, and Richard Whittle, "Senator Helms Builds a Machine of Interlinked Organizations to Shape Both Politics, Policy," *Congressional Quarterly Weekly* 40 (Mar. 4, 1982): 479–505; and Paul Taylor, "Helms Modernizes GOP Political Machine for the Electronic Age," *Washington Post,* Oct. 15, 1982, p. A2.

124. See Helen Dewar, "Battle for Black King Holiday May Hurt Helms at Home," *Washington Post,* Oct. 23, 1983, p. A2.

125. For examples of FCM's presidential commercials see Devlin, "Contrasts in Presidential Campaign Commercials," pp. 18–24.

126. See the *Washington Post,* July 3, 1982, p. A2.

127. Another gun PAC which makes independent expenditures is the Gun Owners of America Campaign Committee. See Latus, "Assessing Ideological PACs," p. 20.

128. Testimony of Wayne LaPierre, National Rifle Association Institute for Legislative Action, in U.S., Congress, Senate, Committee on Rules and Administration, *Hearing on the Federal Election Campaign Act of 1971, as Amended, and on Various Measures to Amend the Act: S. 85, S. 151, S. 732, S. 810, S. 1185, S. 1350, and S. 1684,* 98th Cong., 1st sess., S. HRG 98–588, pp. 734–35.

129. See Dan Nimmo, *The Political Persuaders* (Englewood Cliffs, N.J.: Prentice-Hall, 1970), pp. 42–43.

130. Margaret Ann Latus, "Mobilizing Christians for Political Action: Campaigning with God on Your Side," prepared for the annual meeting of the Society for the Scientific Study of Religion, meeting jointly with the Religious Research Association and the Association for the Sociology of Religion, Providence, R.I., Oct. 22–24, 1982, p. 23.

131. See Jack Erickson, "The Democrats: Rebuilding with Support Groups," *Campaigns and Elections* 3 (Spring 1982): 4–14.

132. Still other liberal groups spend their energies monitoring the independent expenditures of the conservative PACs, rather than making their own. George

McGovern's Americans for Common Sense and the Committee for American Principles (founded by Bob Blaemire, 1980 campaign manager for defeated Democratic Sen. Birch Bayh of Indiana) are examples. See Erickson, ibid., pp. 8, 13; see also Alexander, *Financing the 1980 Election,* pp. 470–74.

133. As quoted in *The Political Report* 6 (July 8, 1983): 8.
134. Victor Kamber of PROPAC, in a personal interview.
135. *The Political Report* 6 (July 8, 1983): 9.
136. From a PROPAC-produced circular in 1982.
137. Alexander, *Financing the 1980 Election,* p. 469.
138. See Maxwell Glen, "Independent Spenders Are Gearing Up," pp. 2627–30.
139. See *Washington Post,* June 12, 1983, p. L1; see also Erickson, "The Democrats," pp. 5–6; and Alexander, *Financing the 1980 Election,* p. 468.
140. Most of Democrats for the '80s' money is spent for direct contributions to candidates and the Democratic party, however. This independent expenditure was unusual for the PAC.
141. See *The Political Report* 6 (Mar. 4, 1983): 2–6.
142. Alexander, *Financing the 1980 Election,* p. 401.
143. David Jessup, "Can Political Influence Be Democratized? A Labor Perspective," in *Parties, Interest Groups, and Campaign Finance Laws,* edited by Michael J. Malbin (Washington, D.C.: American Enterprise Institute, 1980), p. 36.
144. Prepared statement of Fred C. Rainey, M.D., chairman of the Board of Directors of the American Medical Association Political Action Committee, in U.S., Congress, Senate, Committee on Rules and Administration, *Hearing on the Federal Election Campaign Act of 1971, as Amended, and on Various Measures to Amend the Act: S. 85, S. 151, S. 732, S. 810, S. 1185, S. 1350, and S. 1684,* 98th Cong., 1st sess., S. HRG 98–588, Jan. 26, 1983, p. 75.
145. See Sabato, "Parties, PACs and Independent Groups," p. 96.
146. This 30-second spot was produced by the Campaign Group, a political consulting firm.
147. See Matthew MacWilliams, "Introducing the New Filthy Five," *Environmental Action* 12 (May 1981): 10–16; and Gail Robinson, "Many Happy Returns," *Environmental Action* 12 (December 1980): 28–32.
148. See, for examples, *The Political Report* 6 (Sept. 9, 1983): 6; and ibid., Sept. 16, 1983, p. 4.
149. See Steven Pressman, "The Gay Community Struggles to Fashion an Effective Lobby," *Congressional Quarterly Weekly* 41 (Dec. 3, 1983): 2546–47.
150. The letter reads, in part, "Your support for individual rights, personal privacy, and more importantly, your support for civil rights for gay people, has been greatly appreciated by the Human Rights Campaign Fund."
151. Pressman, "The Gay Community," p. 2547.
152. See the *Washington Post,* Feb. 9, 1983, p. A1.
153. See Alexander, *Financing the 1980 Election,* p. 150.
154. As quoted in *The Political Report* 6 (Sept. 9, 1983): 6.
155. See *Political Finance/Lobby Reporter* 3 (May 5, 1982): 118. Railsback was defeated for renomination in the 1982 GOP primary by a more conservative candidate.

156. See, for example, Steve Lilienthal, "Pennsylvania 4: Steel Valley Blues," *The Political Report* 6 (Oct. 21, 1983): 5.
157. See Taylor, "Lobbyists' Success at Raising Funds Proves Costly," p. A9.
158. Quoted in the *Washington Post,* Aug. 21, 1983, p. A16.
159. As quoted in Light, "The Game of PAC Targeting," p. 2270.
160. Paul Taylor, "For Business PACs This Year, Suitable Targets Are in Short Supply," *Washington Post,* July 27, 1982, p. A6.
161. NRCC mimeograph, "Working With PACs," 1982.
162. See Deborah Baldwin, "From Outsider to Insider," *Common Cause* 9 (September/October 1983): 29. See also Tom Hamburger, "How to Fleece the PACs," *Washington Monthly* 15 (July-August, 1983): 29.
163. See Feld, "Special Event Fundraisers," p. 16–17.
164. Under FECA, presidential candidates, once announced and qualified for public funding, must adhere to an overall spending limit for all preconvention activities, and must abide by individual limits for each state primary or caucus as well.
165. Alexander, *Financing the 1980 Election,* pp. 146–48.
166. See Charles R. Babcock, "Citizen Mondale's Transition Made Him a Conglomerate," *Washington Post,* Nov. 6, 1983, p. A6; see also *National Journal* 15 (Jan. 22, 1983): 165.
167. The list could not be directly donated to the campaign because its worth clearly exceeded the $5,000 limitation on contributions. So the Mondale PAC sold it to a list broker for $23,000 and the broker in turn rented it to the Mondale campaign.
168. Babcock, "Citizen Mondale's Transition." Mondale's campaign manager lamely explained that the no-PAC-money pledge was meant to be applied only to the campaign committee.
169. See *National Journal* 15 (Feb. 12, 1983): 325–26.
170. The North Carolina Campaign Fund was in existence for only a year, disbanding in 1983. Hunt was not an organizer, though his friends manned it and the governor benefited from the Fund's $724,000 in expenditures.
171. *Campaign Practices Reports* 10 (Mar. 14, 1983): 1.
172. Leon Billings, as quoted in Farney and Fialka, "His Ability as Fund-raiser."
173. See Tom Sherwood, "Robb Says Controversial PAC Will Be Going Out of Business," *Washington Post,* Nov. 2, 1983, p. C1.
174. From the survey of multicandidate PACs conducted for this study; see Introduction, note 16; see also *Political Finance/Lobby Report,* Dec. 2, 1981, p. 314.
175. See Ruth S. Jones, "Financing State Elections," in *Money and Politics in the United States: Financing Elections in the 1980s,* edited by Michael J. Malbin (Washington, D.C.: American Enterprise Institute / Chatham House, 1984) p. 186.
176. Ibid., p. 187.
177. *Campaign Practices Reports* 10 (Mar. 14, 1983): 2.
178. Ibid.
179. Wallace Turner, "Cap on Interest Group's Campaign Influence Urged on Coast," *New York Times,* Sept. 6, 1983, p. A20. These eight PACs were: California Medical Political Action Committee, California Trial Lawyers, the

Fund for Insurance Education, the California State Employees Association, the California Real Estate PAC, the California Teachers Association, Operating Engineers Local No. 3, and the California Cable Television Association.

180. From the survey of multicandidate PACs conducted for this study; see Introduction, note 16.
181. See Council on Governmental Ethics Laws, *The Blue Book: 1980–81 Edition* (Sacramento, Calif.: Council on Governmental Ethics Laws, 1981), p. 2.
182. Cantor, *Political Action Committees,* p. 24.
183. Once funds in any amount (even as little as a dollar) are transferred from a state PAC to a federal PAC, the two committees become affiliated by law and are subject to a joint $5,000-per-election contribution limit. See *PACs and Lobbies* 4 (Mar. 2, 1983): 6.
184. FEC PAC registration is dotted with committees that give very meager sums to federal candidates and reserve almost all funds for state and local candidates. Some of the state PACs register with the FEC as a contingency, in case they should choose to contribute to a congressional candidate at some point.
185. See Bernadette A. Budde, "The Practical Role of Corporate PACs in the Political Process," *Arizona Law Review* 22, no. 2 (1980): 564–65. Budde applies these two models only to corporate and trade PACs, but in some respects union PACs can also be similarly classified.
186. *Campaign Practices Reports* 10 (Mar. 14, 1983): 3.
187. Ibid.
188. "Facts About CALPAC," p. 1.
189. There have been a few exceptions over the years, but the separation is "98 percent" consistent, said AMPAC's Lauer.
190. See Hunter, *The "New Right,"* pp. 81–83.
191. The Council's PAC, formed in 1980, is called the Citizen Action Non-Partisan PAC (or CANPAC).
192. See Jones, "Financing State Elections," pp. 186–93.
193. Budde, "The Practical Role of Corporate PACs," pp. 566–67.
194. See Council on Governmental Ethics Laws, *The Blue Book: 1980–81 Edition;* Herbert E. Alexander, *Campaign Money: Reform and Reality in the States* (New York: The Free Press, 1976); Herbert E. Alexander and Jennifer W. Frutig, *Public Financing of State Elections* (Los Angeles, Calif.: Citizens' Research Foundation, 1983); National Conference of State Legislatures, *State Legislative Report* [on campaign finance]; Candice Romig, "Placing Limits on PACs," *State Legislatures* 10 (January 1984): 19–22; and David S. Alperin, *State Political Action Regulations: Index and Directory of Organizations* (Westport, Conn.: Quorum Books, 1984).
195. *Campaign Practices Reports* 10 (May 23, 1983): 7; and Jones, "Financing State Elections," p. 27.
196. See Robert E. Mutch, "Corporate Money and Elections: The New Look of State Law," *State Legislatures* 9 (February 1983): 22–25; Budde, "The Practical Role of Corporate PACs," p. 565; and *Campaign Practices Reports* 10 (Mar. 14, 1983): 3.
197. See Alexander, *Financing the 1980 Election,* p. 66; and *Campaign Practices Reports* 10 (Mar. 14, 1983): 10.

198. See, for example, the case of Maryland in *Comparative State Politics Newsletter* 4 (April 1983): 4.

CHAPTER 4. AFTER THE ELECTION: PACS AND LOBBYING

1. As filmed in a 1983 Common Cause anti-PAC television advertisement.
2. Personal interview, Aug. 4, 1983.
3. Personal interview, July 11, 1983.
4. As quoted in the *Wall Street Journal,* Aug. 15, 1978, p. 1.
5. The following examples are cited in *Common Cause News,* July 29, 1983, p. 3.
6. The overall growth of PAC congressional contributions from 1980 to 1982 was 51%. See Table 1–3, p. 15.
7. Kenneth B. Noble, "Political Action Groups' Gifts Focus on New Areas in House," *New York Times,* Sept. 18, 1983, p. B13.
8. From "The Next Move Is Up to You . . . ," a SMACPAC brochure.
9. From "Facts about CALPAC," CALPAC mimeograph, p. 1.
10. From the survey of multicandidate PACs conducted for this study; see Introduction, note 16. A large majority in each category of PACs with a parent organization has a Washington lobbying office or representative: 67% of corporate PACs, 62% of trade PACs, and 77% of labor PACs. About 58% of the corporate PACs and 44% of the labor PACs were divisions of larger governmental affairs departments.
11. See Chapter 2, pp. 36–37. See also William A. Hunter, *The "New Right": A Growing Force in State Politics,* edited by Thomas W. Bennett (Washington, D.C.: The Conference on Alternative State and Local Policies, and the Center to Protect Workers' Rights, 1980), pp. 7–9.
12. See Michael J. Malbin, "Looking Back at the Future of Campaign Finance Reform: Interest Groups and American Elections," in *Money and Politics in the United States: Financing Elections in the 1980s,* edited by Michael J. Malbin (Washington, D.C.: American Enterprise Institute / Chatham House, 1984), p. 257; and Theodore J. Eismeier and Philip H. Pollock, "Political Action Committees: The Shaping of Strategy and Influence," prepared for the annual meeting of the Midwest Political Science Association, Chicago, Ill. Apr. 20–23, 1983, pp. 5–8.
13. See Thomas L. Gais, "On the Scope and Bias of Interest Group Involvement in Elections," prepared for the annual meeting of the American Political Science Association, Chicago, Ill., Sept. 1–4, 1983, p. 14.
14. See Bernadette A. Budde, "The Practical Role of Corporate PACs in the Political Process," *Arizona Law Review,* 22, no. 2 (1980): 561. The National Association of Manufacturers is one example.
15. From the survey of multicandidate PACs conducted for this study; see Introduction, note 16. Of those PACs with a D.C. lobbying office, only 26% express a preference for the Republican candidate in a congressional contest when all other considerations are equal; of PACs without such a lobbying office, 35% prefer the GOP contender.

16. From BANKPAC brochure "You Can Make a Difference."
17. See Steven Pressman, "Reported Lobby Spending Understates Capitol Efforts," *Congressional Quarterly Weekly,* 41 (Aug. 27, 1983): 1729–32. Ironically, Common Cause is usually at or near the top of the lobby expenditure list (the organization spent $1.5 million in 1983 on lobbying). But partly this is due to strict disclosure by Common Cause and loose reporting by most other lobbying groups. See the text discussion below, and also Richard Cohen, "Controlling the Lobbyists," *National Journal* 15 (Dec. 31, 1983): 269.
18. Cited by Michael J. Malbin, "Of Mountains and Molehills: PACs, Campaigns, and Public Policy," in *Parties, Interest Groups, and Campaign Finance Laws,* edited by Michael J. Malbin (Washington, D.C.: American Enterprise Institute, 1980), p. 179.
19. See the *Wall Street Journal,* June 25, 1981, p. 29.
20. See *National Journal* 15 (Nov. 26, 1983): 2459. For additional examples, see Malbin, "Looking Back at the Future," p. 251.
21. FEC Advisory Opinion 1983–4. See *PACs and Lobbies* 4 (Mar. 2, 1983), p. 1. Use of PAC funds for lobbying can jeopardize the political contribution tax credit for individuals, however. See also *Political Finance/Lobby Reporter* 3 (Feb. 25, 1982): 41–42.
22. See *Political Finance/Lobby Reporter,* (Dec. 9, 1981), p. 320. The contributors to the lobby must be given an opportunity to request a refund of their money before the PAC can gain use of a lobby's dollars.
23. John Perkins of COPE, in a personal interview.
24. As quoted in the *Washington Post,* Aug. 21, 1983, p. A16.
25. As quoted in *Congressional Quarterly Weekly* 41 (Mar. 12, 1983): 505.
26. As quoted in Paul Taylor, "Lobbyists' Success," *Washington Post,* Aug. 2, 1983, p. A9.
27. As quoted in the *Washington Post,* Aug. 21, 1983, p. A16.
28. As quoted in the *Washington Post,* Aug. 2, 1983, p. A9.
29. As quoted in "Corporate PAC Newsmemo No. 3," Public Affairs Council, June 17, 1983, p. 2.
30. See, among others, David Truman, *The Governmental Process: Political Interests and Public Opinion* (New York: Knopf, 1951); Lester Milbrath, *The Washington Lobbyists* (Westport, Conn.: Greenwood Press, 1976); Norman J. Ornstein and Shirley Elder, *Interest Groups, Lobbying and Policymaking* (Washington, D.C.: Congressional Quarterly, Inc., 1978), p. 54; and James F. Herndon, "Access, Record, and Competition as Influences on Interest Group Contributions to Congressional Campaigns," *Journal of Politics* 44 (1982): 997.
31. As quoted by Walter A. Zelman, executive director of California Common Cause, in the transcript of "Political Action Committees" videotape, published by the Center for the Study of Business in Society, California State University, Los Angeles, 1982, p. 11. See also David Adamany, "PACs and the Democratic Financing of Politics," *Arizona Law Review* 22, no. 2 (1980): 572 note 22.
32. Attribution cannot be made under terms of the interview.
33. Herbert E. Alexander, *The Case for PACs* (Washington, D.C.: Public Affairs Council, 1983), pp. 16–17.

34. See Kirk F. Brown, "Campaign Contributions and Congressional Voting," prepared for the annual meeting of the American Political Science Association, Chicago, Ill., Sept. 1–4, 1983, pp. 12–13; and Herndon, "Access, Record, and Competition," p. 997.
35. Albert R. Hunt, "Teachers Tie Election Cash to Single Issues," *Wall Street Journal,* Oct. 17, 1980, p. 33.
36. James M. Perry, "How Realtors' PAC Rewards Office Seekers Helpful to the Industry," *Wall Street Journal,* Aug. 2, 1982, pp. 1, 13.
37. David W. Adamany and George E. Agree, *Political Money: A Strategy for Campaign Financing in America* (Baltimore, Md.: The Johns Hopkins University Press, 1975), pp. 39–40.
38. Testimony of Wayne LaPierre, National Rifle Association Institute for Legislative Action, in U.S., Congress, Senate, Committee on Rules and Administration, *Hearing on the Federal Election Campaign Act of 1971, as Amended, and on Various Measures to Amend the Act: S. 85, S. 151, S. 732, S. 810, S. 1185, S. 1350, and S. 1684,* 98th Cong., 1st sess., S. HRG 98–588, pp. 734–35.
39. Congressional Quarterly, Inc., *Dollar Politics* (3rd ed.; Washington, D.C.: Congressional Quarterly, Inc., 1982), p. 48.
40. As quoted in Ornstein and Elder, *Interest Groups, Lobbying, and Policymaking,* p. 62.
41. Quoted in Larry Light, "The Game of PAC Targeting: Friends, Foes and Guesswork," *Congressional Quarterly Weekly* 39 (Nov. 21, 1981): 2269–70.
42. Ibid.
43. Elizabeth Drew, "Politics and Money, Part I," *The New Yorker,* 58 (Dec. 6, 1982): 72; *Washington Post,* Mar. 18, 1983, p. A19; and personal interviews.
44. Cited in Herbert E. Alexander, "The Obey-Railsback Bill: Its Genesis and Early History," *Arizona Law Review* 22, no. 2 (1980): 662; original account contained in the *Washington Post,* Oct. 18, 1979, p. A4.
45. See Herbert E. Alexander, *Financing the 1980 Election* (Lexington, Mass.: Lexington Books, 1983), p. 462. See also NCPAC's threat to air advertising concerning votes on the Reagan tax package in Chapter 3 (pp. 100–101).
46. Brown, "Campaign Contributions and Congressional Voting," p. 16.
47. Quoted in the *Washington Post,* Aug. 21, 1983, p. A16.
48. Quoted in Taylor, "Lobbyists' Success," p. A9. See also Mark Green, "Political PAC-Man," *The New Republic* 188 (Dec. 13, 1982): 18–24.
49. *Campaigns and Elections* 3 (Spring 1982): 48.
50. Ibid.
51. Prepared statement of Jay Angoff, staff attorney, Public Citizen's Congress Watch, in U.S., Congress, Senate, Committee on Rules and Administration, *Hearing on the Federal Election Campaign Act of 1971, as Amended, and on Various Measures to Amend the Act: S. 85, S. 151, S. 732, S. 810, S. 1185, S. 1350, and S. 1684,* 98th Cong., 1st sess., S. HRG 98–588, Jan. 26, 1983, p. 230.
52. Ruth S. Jones, "Financing State Elections," in *Money and Politics in the United States: Financing Elections in the 1980s,* edited by Michael J. Malbin (Washington, D.C.: American Enterprise Institute / Chatham House, 1984), p. 191.
53. Telephone interview with CALPAC's Jerry Simpson, Aug. 9, 1983.
54. See the *Washington Post,* Aug. 21, 1983, p. A16.

55. Quoted in Herbert E. Alexander, *Campaign Money: Reform and Reality in the States* (New York: The Free Press, 1976), p. 313.
56. Noble, "Political Action Groups' Gifts."
57. Green, "Political PAC-Man," p. 20.
58. Dennis Farney and John J. Fialka, "His Ability as a Fund-raiser Enhances the Power of California's Democratic Rep. Henry Waxman," *Wall Street Journal,* Nov. 10, 1983, p. 58. See *Congressional Quarterly Weekly* 41 (Mar. 12, 1983): 505.
59. Edward Roeder, "Catalyzing Favorable Reactions: A Look at Chemical Industry PACs," *Sierra Club Bulletin* 66 (March/April 1981): 23.
60. *Common Cause* 9 (March/April 1983): 44. AMPAC strongly objects to Common Cause's classification of state and national associations together, correctly pointing out that the governing and candidate-selection structures are entirely separate for each state association, and independent of the national group. However, the legislative interests of the disparate medical associations would surely be similar in most cases. See Herbert E. Alexander, *Financing Politics* (2nd ed.; Washington, D.C.: Congressional Quarterly, Inc., 1980), pp. 148–49; and Fred Wertheimer, "The PAC Phenomenon in American Politics," *Arizona Law Review* 22, no. 2 (1980): 612–13.
61. See Wertheimer, "The PAC Phenomenon," pp. 612–13; and Alexander, *Financing Politics* (2nd ed.), pp. 148–49.
62. There are many strong correlations that are nonsensical. One example cited by Edward R. Tufte, *Data Analysis for Public Policy* (Englewood Cliffs, N.J.: Prentice-Hall, 1974), pp. 88–91, is the nearly perfect positive correlation between the number of radios in Great Britain and the incidence of mental illness there in the 1924–1937 period.
63. See ibid. for a general discussion of these techniques.
64. These studies, only a few of which are discussed in the text because of space limitations, include Michael B. Binford, "PAC Campaign Contributions and the State Legislature: Impact on Legislators and the Legislative Agenda," prepared for the meeting of the Southern Political Science Association, Memphis, Tenn., Nov. 5–7, 1981; Brown, "Campaign Contributions and Congressional Voting"; Henry W. Chappell, Jr., "Campaign Contributions and Congressional Voting: A Simultaneous Probit-Tobit Model," *Review of Economics and Statistics* 64 (February 1982): 77–83; Henry W. Chappell, Jr., "Campaign Contributions and Legislative Voting on the Cargo Preference Bill: A Comparison of Simultaneous Models," *Public Choice* 36 (1981): 301–12; James Eisenstein and Roger Karapin, "The Relationship between Political Action Committee Contributions and Roll Call Votes in the Pennsylvania House of Representatives: A Preliminary Analysis," prepared for the meeting of the Pennsylvania Political Science Association, University Park, Pa., Mar. 28, 1981; John P. Frendreis and Richard W. Waterman, "PAC Contributions and Legislative Behavior: Senate Voting on Trucking Deregulation," prepared for the annual meeting of the Midwest Political Science Association, Apr. 20–22, 1983; Herndon, "Access, Record, and Competition"; James B. Kau and Paul Rubin, *Congressmen, Constituents, and Contributors* (Boston: Studies in Public Choice Service, Martinus Nijhoff, 1982), pp. 105–13; Dickinson McGaw and Richard McCleary, "The Corporate-Labor PAC Struggle: A Vector ARIMA

Time Series Analysis," prepared for the annual meeting of the American Political Science Association, Denver, Colo., Sept. 2–5, 1982; Candice J. Nelson, "Counting the Cash: PAC Contributions to Members of the House of Representatives," prepared for the annual meeting of the American Political Science Association, Denver, Colo., Sept. 2–5, 1982; Jonathan I. Silberman and Garey C. Duider, "Determining Legislative Preferences on Minimum Wage: An Economic Approach," *Journal of Political Economy* 84 (April 1976): 317–29; William P. Welch, "Campaign Contributions and Legislative Voting: Milk Money and Dairy Price Supports," *Western Political Quarterly* 35 (December 1982): 478–95; William P. Welch, "Patterns of Contributions: Economic Interest and Ideological Groups," in *Political Finance,* edited by Herbert E. Alexander (Beverly Hills: Sage, 1979), pp. 199–220; Diana Evans Yiannakis, "PAC Contributions and House Voting on Conflictual and Consensual Issues: The Windfall Profits Tax and the Chrysler Loan Guarantee," prepared for the annual meeting of the American Political Science Association, Chicago, Ill., Sept. 1–4, 1983.

65. Welch, "Campaign Contributions and Legislative Voting."
66. Chappell, "Campaign Contributions and Congressional Voting." The one positive case involved contributions from Rockwell International that influenced the B-1 bomber appropriation. There was also a positive, but not significant, relationship in five of the other cases.
67. Yiannakis, "PAC Contributions and House Voting."
68. Frendreis and Waterman, "PAC Contributions and Legislative Behavior."
69. The weakest relationship was observed for those senators whose elections were the farthest away, in 1984.
70. Brown, "Campaign Contributions and Congressional Voting."
71. Ibid. p. 49.
72. Only the influence exerted by PACs over the legislative branch is discussed in this chapter, but some have contended that PACs have an impact, albeit a lesser one, on the executive branch. President Reagan, for example, who received about $285,000 from PACs in the 1980 prenomination campaign and benefited from large independent expenditures in the fall, held a private White House reception for $5,000 contributors to NCPAC in February 1983, and appointed Lee Ann Elliott, who served for sixteen years as associate executive director of AMPAC, to the Federal Election Commission. Elliott not only was appointed, she received a full six-year term, bumping an incumbent Republican member up for reappointment into a two-year unexpired term of another commissioner who had resigned.
73. Incumbent senators at the time of the vote had received a collective total of over $770,000 from AMPAC and the American Dental Association's ADPAC since 1978.
74. Malbin makes this point in "Looking Back at the Future," p. 248.
75. This much is conceded even by vociferous PAC opponents on the Hill. See ibid.
76. Fred Wertheimer's commentary in *Parties, Interest Groups and Campaign Finance Laws,* edited by Michael J. Malbin (Washington, D.C.: American Enterprise Institute, 1980), pp. 199–200. See also Edwin M. Epstein, "An Irony of Electoral Reform," *Regulation* 3 (May/June 1979): 35–44; and Christopher

Madison, "Federal Subsidy Programs under Attack by Unlikely Marriage of Labor and Right," *National Journal* 15 (Dec. 31, 1983): 2682–84.

77. Malbin, "Author's Replies," in *Parties, Interest Groups and Campaign Finance Laws,* edited by Michael J. Malbin (Washington, D.C.: American Enterprise Institute, 1980), p. 214.
78. See Wertheimer, "The PAC Phenomenon," pp. 613–14; also Richard P. Conlon's commentary in *Parties, Interest Groups and Finance Laws,* edited by Michael J. Malbin (Washington, D.C.: American Enterprise Institute, 1980), p. 197.
79. Obey, Federal Election Campaign Act of 1971 Amendments, H9276, as quoted in Joseph E. Cantor, *Political Action Committees: Their Evolution and Growth and Their Implications for the Political System* (Washington, D.C.: Library of Congress Congressional Research Service Report No. 82–92 GOV, Nov. 6, 1981; updated May 7, 1982), p. 168.
80. Light, "The Game of PAC Targeting," p. 2269.
81. *Congressional Record,* Dec. 20, 1982, p. S15071. NADA used the same technique in its push to veto the "lemon rule." See Brown, "Campaign Contributions and Congressional Voting," pp. 4 note 9, 40 note 78.
82. Green, "Political PAC-Man," p. 21.
83. Malbin, "Looking Back at the Future," p. 265.
84. Drew, "Politics and Money, Part I," pp. 38–43.
85. Alexander, *Financing the 1980 Election,* p. 379.
86. Robert J. Samuelson, "The Campaign Reform Failure," *The New Republic* 189 (Sept. 5, 1983): 32–33.
87. See BIPAC's *Politikit* (November 1981): 31.
88. Testimony of Sen. David Durenberger (D–Minn.), in U.S., Congress, Senate, Committee on Rules and Administration, *Hearing on the Federal Election Campaign Act of 1971, as Amended, and on Various Measures to Amend the Act: S. 85, S. 151, S. 732, S. 810, S. 1185, S. 1350, and S. 1684,* 98th Cong., 1st sess., S. HRG 98–588, Jan. 26, 1983, pp. 131–32.
89. As quoted in *Campaign Practices Reports* 10 (May 9, 1983): 5–6.
90. See, for example, Gary C. Jacobson, *The Politics of Congressional Elections* (Boston, Mass.: Little, Brown and Company, 1983), p. 194.
91. See Paul Taylor, "Lobbyists Lose the Game," *Washington Post,* July 31, 1983, p. A12; Simon Lazarus, "PAC Power? They Keep on Losing," *Washington Post,* Mar. 27, 1983, pp. B1–B2; David Jessup, "Can Political Influence Be Democratized? A Labor Perspective," in *Parties, Interest Groups and Campaign Finance Laws,* edited by Michael J. Malbin (Washington, D.C.: American Enterprise Institute, 1980), p. 41; and Daniel Esty, "The Moneyed Interests: An Empirical Analysis of the Relationship between Economic Power and Political Influence," Bachelor of Arts Honor Thesis, Department of Economics, Harvard College, Cambridge, Mass., Mar. 18, 1981, p. 87.
92. From the NRCC publication "Working with PACs" (1982).
93. See Paul D. Kamenar, "PACs, the Taxpayer, and Campaign Finance Reform," The Heritage Foundation *Backgrounder* 257 (Apr. 14, 1983): 8.
94. As quoted in the *Washington Post,* Aug. 21, 1983, p. A16.
95. As quoted in the *Washington Post,* Nov. 9, 1982, p. A3.

96. See also *SMACPAC Reports* 4 (May 1983): 2; *ADPAC Communicator* (Spring-June 1983): 2; and Herndon, "Access, Record, and Competition," p. 999.
97. See Chapter 1, pp. 3–5. See also Adamany, "PACs and the Democratic Financing of Politics," p. 39.
98. As quoted in the *Washington Post,* Aug. 21, 1983, p. A16.

CHAPTER 5. PACS AND THE POLITICAL PARTIES

1. See also the Harris Survey in *Business Week,* Oct. 4, 1982, p. 16; and Lee Walczak, "Business 'Double Dips' for Candidates," *Business Week,* Aug. 16, 1982, p. 113.
2. As quoted in *Campaign Practice Reports* 10 (Apr. 25, 1983): 7.
3. Gary C. Jacobson, "Money in the 1980 and 1982 Congressional Elections," in *Money and Politics in the United States: Financing Elections in the 1980s,* edited by Michael J. Malbin (Washington, D.C.: American Enterprise Institute / Chatham House, 1984), p. 43.
4. Ibid.
5. See Chapter 3, pp. 90–92.
6. MNPL solicitation brochure, 1983.
7. These independent expenditure totals include money spent by *all* ideological PACs, not just those found in the nonconnected category.
8. From the survey of multicandidate PACs conducted for this study; see Introduction, note 16. The median contribution was a hefty $3,875. Almost exactly this proportion was found in a BIPAC survey of 275 corporate PACs in 1979–1980. See BIPAC, "The Truth about Business Employee PACs" (1981), a brochure summarizing BIPAC's post-1980 election survey.
9. The $6-million overall sum does not include contributions to state and local parties by nonfederal PACs. Inexplicably, the parties themselves reported lower totals of PAC gifts in 1981–1982: the GOP said it received $1.2 million and the Democrats listed $3.1 million in their FEC statements. The Federal Election Commission could not explain the discrepancy, but an examination of PAC reports confirms the $6-million figure.
10. For example, from the survey of multicandidate PACs conducted for this study: of those PACs that go to GOP briefings, 29% prefer the Republican candidate and only 16% the Democrat in a race in which all other factors are equal. Of those PACs that do not attend GOP briefings, 24% prefer the Republican candidate and 29% the Democrat. A similar finding was made for those PACs that attend Democratic briefings: 17% prefer the GOP candidate and 31% the Democrat. Of those that do not go to Democratic briefings, 33% prefer the Republican and only 16% the Democrat.
11. Party clubs of various sorts have long been in existence. See Joseph E. Cantor, *Political Action Committees: Their Evolution and Growth and Their Implications for the Political System* (Washington, D.C.: Library of Congress Congressional Research Service Report No. 82–92 GOV, Nov. 6, 1981; updated May 7, 1982), p. 30.

12. See *Campaign Practices Reports* 10 (May 23, 1983): 3.
13. Maxwell Glen, "At the Wire, Corporate PACs Come Through for the GOP," *National Journal* 11 (Feb. 3, 1979): 174.
14. As quoted in the *Washington Post,* Dec. 22, 1983, p. A6. See also Thomas B. Edsall, "PACs Bankrolling GOP Challengers," *Washington Post,* Sept. 14, 1982, p. D8; and *Political Finance/Lobby Reporter,* Dec. 23, 1981, p. 334.
15. As quoted in Paul Taylor, "For Business PACs This Year, Suitable Targets Are in Short Supply," *Washington Post,* July 27, 1982, p. A6. See also *National Journal* 14 (Aug. 7, 1982): 1368–73.
16. As quoted in Thomas B. Edsall, "Hard Times: Independent Gas Industry Loses Power," *Washington Post,* Apr. 26, 1983, p. A8.
17. See also Thomas B. Edsall, "Democrats Woo Big Business with Prospect of Senate Takeover," *Washington Post,* Oct. 16, 1983, p. A3.
18. Partial transcript of Coelho's filmed remarks.
19. See Xandra Kayden, "The Nationalizing of the Party System," in *Parties, Interest Groups and Campaign Finance Laws,* edited by Michael J. Malbin (Washington, D.C.: American Enterprise Institute, 1980), pp. 257–81.
20. See *Business Week,* Feb. 15, 1982, pp. 122–23.
21. See Ruth S. Jones, "Financing State Elections," in *Money and Politics in the United States: Financing Elections in the 1980s,* edited by Michael J. Malbin (Washington, D.C.: American Enterprise Institute / Chatham House, 1984), p. 197.
22. See Brown Carpenter, "Democratic Campaign Letter Assails Helms," *Washington Post,* July 11, 1983, p. C5.
23. See the *Washington Post,* Jan. 19, 1983), p. A3; ibid., Apr. 25, 1983, p. A-1; and ibid., Apr. 26, 1983, p. A1.
24. Juan Williams, "Lugar Urges Republican Women to Run for Congress, Statehouses," *Washington Post,* Oct. 9, 1983, p. A4.
25. Evans had been appointed to the seat of the late Henry Jackson, a Democrat, and was seeking election for the remaining five years in the term.
26. To be truly "independent" an expenditure must be made without consultation or cooperation with any candidate or campaign. See Chapter 3, pp. 000–000.
27. See the *Washington Post,* Nov. 16, 1983, p. A2.
28. As quoted in *Time,* Aug. 20, 1979, p. 21.
29. As quoted in James Conaway, "Righting the Course," *Washington Post,* Mar. 22, 1983, p. D1.
30. See Margaret Ann Latus, "Assessing Ideological PACs: From Outrage to Understanding," in *Money and Politics in the United States: Financing Elections in the 1980s,* edited by Michael J. Malbin (Washington, D.C.: American Enterprise Institute / Chatham House, 1984), pp. 157–59.
31. See *Congressional Quarterly Weekly* 40 (Mar. 6, 1982): 499–505.
32. See Paul M. Weyrich, "The New Right: PACs and Coalition Politics," in *Parties, Interest Groups, and Campaign Finance Laws,* edited by Michael J. Malbin (Washington, D.C.: American Enterprise Institute, 1980), p. 81.
33. See *Political Finance/Lobby Reporter* 3 (July 21, 1982): 188. In response to the GOP charges, the FEC forbade NCPAC from soliciting Republican donors NCPAC had copied from financial disclosure reports. NCPAC had not yet

solicited them, though the FEC agreed with the GOP that NCPAC's intent to solicit eventually was clear.

34. See *Political Finance/Lobby Reporter* 3 (Sept. 22, 1982): 252.
35. *Los Angeles Times,* Apr. 28, 1981, and cited in Herbert E. Alexander, *Financing the 1980 Election* (Lexington, Mass.: D. C. Heath, 1983), p. 473.
36. See *Political Finance/Lobby Reporter* 1981 (Nov. 25, 1981): 306.
37. *First Monday* 13 (November/December 1983): 9.
38. Herbert E. Alexander, *The Case for PACs* (Washington, D.C.: Public Affairs Council, 1983), pp. 22–23.
39. See, for example, Frank J. Sorauf, "Political Parties and Political Action Committees: Two Life Cycles," *Arizona Law Review* 22, no. 2 (1980): 449–50.
40. Generally on this subject, see Larry Sabato, *The Rise of Political Consultants: New Ways of Winning Elections* (New York: Basic Books, 1981), pp. 284–300; and Larry Sabato, "Parties, PACs, and Independent Groups," in *The American Elections of 1982,* edited by Thomas E. Mann and Norman Ornstein (Washington, D.C.: American Enterprise Institute, 1983).
41. Rhodes Cook, "Democrats Develop Tactics: Laying Groundwork for 1984," *Congressional Quarterly Weekly* 40 (July 3, 1982): 1595.
42. *National Journal* 15 (Dec. 31, 1983): 2702.
43. The $10,000 includes $5,000 for the primary and $5,000 for the general election. Where runoff primaries are held, another $5,000 for each committee can be added.
44. 2 U.S.C. §441 a(d); 11 CFR 110.7. Coordinated expenditures differ from direct contributions in that the party, as well as the candidate, must exercise some control over the spending of coordinated funds, whereas direct money can be spent at the sole discretion of the candidate.
45. That is, $30,000 (direct gifts) + $18,440 (state party coordinated) + $18,440 (national party coordinated) = $66,880.
46. See Gary C. Jacobson, "Money in the 1980 and 1982 Congressional Elections," in *Money and Politics in the United States: Financing Elections in the 1980s,* edited by Michael J. Malbin (Washington, D.C.: American Enterprise Institute / Chatham House, 1984), p. 47. Incidentally, parties cannot make independent expenditures for candidates.
47. In most cases the national GOP paid the state party's share as well, which is permitted as long as the state party agrees to let the national party act as its agent.
48. These figures combine the maximums for both direct contributions and coordinated expenditures.
49. Testimony of Dr. Michael J. Malbin, American Enterprise Institute for Public Policy Research, *Hearings Held before the Task Force on Elections,* in U.S., Congress, House, Committee on House Administration, 98th Cong., 1st sess., June 16, 1983, p. 258.
50. Ibid.
51. See pp. 93–95.
52. See Sabato, *The Rise of Political Consultants,* pp. 290–300; and id., "Parties, PACs, and Independent Groups," pp. 76–79.
53. Sabato, "Parties, PACs, and Independent Groups," p. 76.

54. Alan Green, *Communicating in the '80s: New Options for the Non-Profit Community* (Washington, D.C.: Banton Foundation, 1983), p. 13.
55. Sabato, "Parties, PACs, and Independent Groups," pp. 77–79.
56. Ibid., pp. 78, 107 notes 25–26.
57. See the *Washington Post,* Apr. 15, 1983, pp. A1, A9.
58. See Phil Duncan, "Wealthy and Well Organized GOP Panel Eyes 1984 Elections," *Congressional Quarterly Weekly* 41 (July 2, 1983): 1350–51.
59. See Bill Hogan et al., "The Senate's Secret Slush Fund," *The New Republic* 188 (June 20, 1983): 17–20. This article claims that the NRSC subsidized the operations of Republican U.S. senators by at least $760,000 in 1981 and the first half of 1982. The correct total as provided by the FEC is actually $673,000, but the author's description of the NRSC practice is otherwise substantially correct.
60. See *PACs and Lobbies* 4 (July 6, 1983): 1.
61. See Sabato, "Parties, PACs, and Independent Groups," pp. 82–86.
62. As quoted in Dan Balz, "Parties Switch Roles for '84 Hill Races," *Washington Post,* Aug. 30, 1983, p. A6.
63. George Lardner, "Demo's to Rap Reagan as Big Spender," *Washington Post,* Sept. 30, 1983, p. A3.
64. See the *Washington Post,* May 21, 1983, p. A4; ibid., Aug. 20, 1983, p. A4; and ibid., Dec. 17, 1983, p. A11. The Democrats claim that an organized Republican attempt to call in and jam the telethon's contribution lines was a major factor in the event's disappointing balance sheet, but no hard evidence exists to confirm or refute their charges.
65. See Dom Bonafede, "Democratic Party Takes Some Strides Down the Long Comeback Trail," *National Journal* 15 (Oct. 8, 1983): 2053; and Rob Gurwitt, "Democratic Campaign Panel: New Strategy and New Friends," *Congressional Quarterly Weekly* 41 July 2, 1983): 1348. The DNC's 105 staffers are little more than a third of the RNC's total, for instance, yet the 1983 DNC staff roster was double its 1981 size.
66. See Alan Ehrenhalt, "Campaign Committees: Focus of Party Revival," *Congressional Quarterly Weekly* 41 (July 2, 1983): 1345.
67. See Sabato, "Parties, PACs, and Independent Groups," pp. 80–82.
68. Jacobson, "Money in the 1980 and 1982 Congressional Elections," p. 66–67.

CHAPTER 6. PACS AND ELECTORAL REFORM

1. For an examination of the effect of question wording on poll results, see Larry Sabato, *The Rise of Political Consultants: New Ways of Winning Elections* (New York: Basic Books, 1981), pp. 92–96.
2. The Harris Survey, release 1983 No. 1, Jan. 3, 1983.
3. Other responses: 29% responded "only somewhat serious"; 8% said "not serious at all"; 1% were not sure.
4. Other responses: 19% disagreed; 10% were not sure. Cited in *Public Opinion* 5 (August/September 1982): 53.

5. Another 15% were not sure. The poll was taken in January and February 1983. It was a random-sample, in-person survey of 1,503 adults.
6. A random-sample, in-person survey of 1,007 adults. See S. Prakash Sethi and Nemiki Nobuaki, *Public Perception of and Attitude toward Political Action Committees (PACs): An Empirical Analysis of Nationwide Survey Data—Some Strategic Implications for the Corporate Community* (Richardson, Tex.: Center for Research in Business and Social Policy, University of Texas at Dallas, 1982), pp. 1–15. See also William Schneider, "Campaign Financing: Curb Special-Interest Giving But Don't Go Public," *National Journal* 15 (Feb. 26, 1983): 472.
7. Interestingly, conservatives as well as liberals, and executives as well as blue-collar workers were inclined to see PACs as a "bad thing." The response was relatively undifferentiated by political philosophy or occupation, although women and older people tended to be more critical of PACs than other demographic groups.
8. The exact percentages: 9% political party committee; 14% candidate committee; 19% special-interest organization; 2% government elections committee.
9. Jeremy Gaunt, "The PAC Wars," *Election Politics* 1 (Winter 1983–1984): 22. See also Michael J. Malbin, "The Problem of PAC-Journalism," *Public Opinion* 5 (December/January 1983): 15–16, 59.
10. Some of these studies are mentioned in Chapter 4. Common Cause, incidentally, has benefited from the publicity given it for its anti-PAC attacks, with both membership and income on the increase. See Jeff Dionne, "With Their Man in the White House, Conservative Legal Groups Are Hurting," *National Journal* 15 (Nov. 5, 1983): 2316.
11. Gaunt, "The PAC Wars," p. 23. The PAC community did begin a counter-offensive in 1983. See Chapter 1, pp. 25–26.
12. Margaret Ann Latus, in "Mobilizing Christians for Political Action: Campaigning with God on Your Side" (prepared for the annual meeting of the Society for the Scientific Study of Religion, meeting jointly with the Religious Research Association and the Association for the Sociology of Religion, Providence, R. I., Oct. 22–24, 1982, p. 28), gives another example, noting that the "Christian Right" PACs (such as Jerry Falwell's Moral Majority and the Christian Voice Moral Government Fund) were rated negatively by the public because of concern about the separation of church and state, and the distaste the public had for their sponsoring organizations.
13. Joseph E. Cantor, *Political Action Committees: Their Evolution and Growth and Their Implications for the Political System* (Washington, D.C.: Library of Congress Congressional Research Service Report No. 82–92 GOV, Nov. 6, 1981; updated May 7, 1982), p. 217, regarding a Gallup Poll released Aug. 16, 1981.
14. See Advisory Commission on Intergovernmental Relations, "Changing Public Attitudes on Governments and Taxes, 1983, A Commission Survey" (Washington, D.C.: Advisory Commission on Intergovernmental Relations, 1983), p. 3. The random-sample, in-person survey of 1,517 adults was conducted in April and May 1983.
15. Other political parties were selected by 3%, and 17% were undecided.

16. From Ruth S. Jones and Warren E. Miller, "Financing Campaigns: Modes of Individual Contribution," presented at the annual meeting of the Midwest Political Science Association, Chicago, Ill., Apr. 21–23, 1983, pp. 9–12. The figures are derived from the University of Michigan Center for Political Studies' National Election Studies.
17. Herbert E. Alexander, *Financing the 1980 Election* (Lexington, Mass.: D. C. Heath, 1983), p. 421.
18. Jones and Miller, "Financing Campaigns," pp. 13–14. Almost 7% of the respondents in the 1980 Election Study gave to PACs, the same proportion donated money to candidates, and slightly under 4% gave to political parties. (See, however, Frank J. Sorauf's reservations about the accuracy of these figures as noted in Chapter 2, note 118, above; and Frank J. Sorauf and the Twentieth Century Fund Task Force on Political Action Committees, *What Price PACs?* [New York: Twentieth Century Fund, 1984], pp. 81–82.) Of the group reporting PAC contributions, 6% gave to a business PAC, 17% to a union PAC, 17% to a professional (trade) PAC, 7% to an "ideological" PAC, 18% to the National Rifle Association, and 34% to another group. The NRA percentage *may* be inflated because the organization was given as an example of a PAC in the survey question. PAC contributors tended to come from the middle-income bracket rather than upper or lower income groups, and PAC givers were much younger, on average, than party donors. Not unexpectedly, party contributors were Republicans by a three-to-one margin (76% to 24%). The national parties received 48% of the reported gifts, the state parties 2%, and the local parties 20%. See also John C. Green and James Guth, "Partisans and Ideologues: A Profile of Contributors to Party and Ideological PACs," prepared for the annual meeting of the Southern Political Science Association, Birmingham, Ala., Nov. 3–6, 1983, pp. 2–3, 16–17.
19. Edwin M. Epstein, "An Irony of Electoral Reform," *Regulation* 3 (May/June 1979): 39–40.
20. See Chapter 2, pp. 32–34.
21. One recent example was the National Asphalt Pavement Association's PAC, which was dismantled in 1983 after its leadership became disillusioned about congressmen's use of their money. See *Washington Post,* Feb. 28, 1983, p. A1; and *U.S. News and World Report* Mar. 7, 1983, p. 35. The group is continuing to encourage members to make individual gifts, however.
22. The poll was conducted in September 1982 among leaders of 600 of the 1,200 companies included in *Business Week*'s "Corporate Scoreboard." See *Business Week,* Oct. 4, 1982, p. 16.
23. See Larry Sabato, "Parties, PACs and Independent Groups," in *The American Elections of 1982,* edited by Thomas E. Mann and Norman Ornstein (Washington, D.C.: American Enterprise Institute, 1983), pp. 72, 100–2.
24. David Boaz, "Who and Why of Big-Buck Politics: Spend Money to Make Money," *Wall Street Journal,* Nov. 15, 1983, p. 34.
25. Ibid.
26. See, for example, David W. Adamany and George E. Agree, *Political Money: A Strategy for Campaign Financing in America* (Baltimore, Md.: The Johns Hopkins University Press, 1975), p. 39.

27. Malbin, "The Problem with PAC-Journalism."
28. Gary C. Jacobson, "Money in the 1980 and 1982 Congressional Elections," in *Money and Politics in the United States: Financing Elections in the 1980s,* edited by Michael J. Malbin (Washington, D.C.: American Enterprise Institute/Chatham House, 1984), p. 41.
29. Ibid.
30. Republicans and Democrats only; independents are excluded from this calculation.
31. See Sabato, *The Rise of Political Consultants;* see also *National Journal* 15 (Apr. 16, 1983): 780–81.
32. See Herbert E. Alexander, *The Case for PACs* (Washington, D.C.: Public Affairs Council, 1983), pp. 18–21.
33. Michael J. Malbin, "Looking Back at the Future of Campaign Finance Reform: Interest Groups and American Elections" in *Money and Politics in the United States: Financing Elections in the 1980s,* edited by Michael J. Malbin (Washington, D.C.: American Enterprise Institute/Chatham House, 1984), p. 263.
34. *Washington Post,* May 27, 1983, p. A2; ibid., May 18, 1983, p. A2.
35. Frank J. Sorauf, "Accountability in the Political Action Committees: Who's in Charge?" prepared for the annual meeting of the American Political Science Association, Denver, Colo., Sept. 2–5, 1982, pp. 21–22. See also Jones and Miller, "Financing Campaigns," p. 43.
36. The random-sample telephone poll of 1,587 adults was taken in September 1983 at about the time of the AFL-CIO endorsement.
37. Personal interviews. See also Edward Handler and John R. Mulkern, *Business in Politics: Campaign Strategies of Corporate Political Action Committees* (Lexington, Mass.: Lexington Books, 1982), p. 79.
38. See David Jessup, "Author's Replies" in *Politics, Interest Groups, and Campaign Finance Laws,* edited by Michael J. Malbin (Washington, D.C.: American Enterprise Institute, 1980), p. 96; Alexander, *Financing the 1980 Elections,* p. 413.
39. As quoted in *Intergovernmental Perspective* 9 (Nov. 3, 1983): 18.
40. As quoted in Paul Taylor, "Don't Pick on PACs, Corporate Unit Says," *Washington Post,* Apr. 12, 1983, p. A5. See also Alexander, *The Case for PACs,* pp. 29–30.
41. Jones and Miller, "Financing Campaigns," pp. 41–42.
42. From *The Federalist, No. 10.*
43. Alexis de Tocqueville, *Democracy in America* (New York: Schocken Books, 1970), 1:221.
44. As quoted in *Association Management* 35 (July 1983): 54.
45. See the example of the American Medical Association's successful attempt to seek exemption from Federal Trade Commission regulations in the House of Representatives, and its subsequent defeat in the Senate once the public spotlight was focused on the matter (Chapter 4, pp. 132–135).
46. Tocqueville, *Democracy in America,* 1:224.
47. As quoted in Elizabeth Drew, "Politics and Money, Part I," *The New Yorker* 58 (Dec. 6, 1982): 147.

48. Granted, certain PACs such as the dairy committees have an interest in food stamps and nutrition programs, but the point made here seems valid nonetheless.
49. See Sabato, *The Rise of Political Consultants,* pp. 284–85.
50. As quoted in *Political Finance/Lobby Reporter,* Nov. 18, 1981, p. 298.
51. The reader is referred to the Selected Bibliography, which contains a number of works on the subject. See especially Herbert E. Alexander, *Financing Politics: Money, Elections and Political Reform* (2nd ed.; Washington, D.C.: Congressional Quarterly, Inc., 1980); and Adamany and Agree, *Political Money.* See also Malbin, "Looking Back at the Future of Campaign Finance Reform," pp. 235–43; and Sorauf et al., *What Price PACs?,* pp. 3–25, 99–110.
52. H.R. 1377. See *PACs and Lobbies* 4 (Feb. 16, 1983): 6; and *Congressional Record,* Feb. 10, 1983, p. H511.
53. Center for Responsive Politics's poll of Congress, summer 1983, with 140 respondents. About 76% of the respondents favored changes in the laws, while 21% were satisfied with the current statutes, and 3% had no opinion.
54. Quoted in Associated Press dispatch, Jan. 6, 1984.
55. Prepared statement of John T. Dolan, national chairman, National Conservative Political Action Committee, in U.S., Congress, Senate, Committee on Rules and Administration, *Hearing on the Federal Election Campaign Act of 1971, as Amended, and on Various Measures to Amend the Act: S. 85, S. 151, S. 732, S. 810, S. 1185, S. 1350, and S. 1684,* 98th Cong., 1st sess., S. HRG 98–588, May 17, 1983, p. 377.
56. Quoted in Herbert E. Alexander and Brian A. Haggerty, *The Federal Election Campaign Act: After a Decade of Political Reform* (Washington, D.C.: Citizens' Research Foundation, 1981), p. 124.
57. For details of these bills, see Cantor, *Political Action Committees,* pp. 185–89; Malbin, "Looking Back at the Future of Campaign Finance Reform," pp. 235–38; *PACs and Lobbies* 4 (Apr. 6, 1983): 2; and ibid., May 18, 1983, p. 6. Some congressmen have also called for an outright ban on PAC contributions (ibid.).
58. Cited in Fred Wertheimer, "The PAC Phenomenon in American Politics," *Arizona Law Review* 22, no. 2 (1980): 611–12. The poll was released Apr. 3, 1980.
59. Cantor, *Political Action Committees,* p. 201; prepared statement of Herbert E. Alexander, director, Citizens' Research Foundation, and professor of political science, University of Southern California, in U.S., Congress, Senate, Committee on Rules and Administration, *Hearing on the Federal Election Campaign Act of 1971, as Amended, and on Various Measures to Amend the Act: S. 85, S. 151, S. 732, S. 810, S. 1185, S. 1350, and S. 1684,* 98th Cong., 1st sess., S. HRG 98–588, Jan. 26, 1983, p. 104.
60. See note 53, above.
61. See Malbin, "Looking Back at the Future of Campaign Finance Reform," pp. 240–41, on this point.
62. Prepared statement of John T. Dolan, *Hearing on the Federal Election Campaign Act of 1971,* p. 377.
63. This is precisely what has already happened to some degree in election cam-

paigns where public funding prevails. See Malbin, "Looking Back at the Future of Campaign Finance Reform," pp. 252–53.

64. This point is made by Robert J. Samuelson, "The Campaign Reform Failure," *The New Republic* 189 (Sept. 5, 1983): 35.
65. As quoted in Alexander and Haggerty, *The Federal Election Campaign Act,* p. 74.
66. See Sabato, *The Rise of Political Consultants,* pp. 272–84.
67. See *Political Finance/Lobby Report* 3 (Sept. 22, 1982): 252. The nonprofit rate of 5.2¢ per letter is used by political parties.
68. These two proposals were contained in recommendations made by the Campaign Finance Study Group of Harvard University's Institute of Politics. See U.S. Congress, Committee on House Administration, *An Analysis of the Impact of the Federal Election Campaign Act, 1972–1978,* Institute of Politics, John F. Kennedy School of Government, Harvard University (Washington, D.C.: U.S. Government Printing Office, 1979).
69. See Sabato, *The Rise of Political Consultants,* pp. 326–28. Incidentally, allocation of free time to parties rather than to individual candidates solves the problem of time availability in large metropolitan areas combining dozens of congressional districts and candidates.
70. As quoted in *First Monday* 13 (November/December 1983): 9.
71. Michael J. Malbin, in his testimony before the Committee on House Administration (Testimony of Dr. Michael J. Malbin, American Enterprise Institute for Public Policy Research, *Hearings Held before the Task Force on Elections,* in U.S., Congress, House, Committee on House Administration, 98th Cong., 1st sess., June 16, 1983, p. 259), offers another reason to oppose completely unlimited expenditures for national parties: "An incumbent president has too many levers he can still pull with national party organizations to make me feel comfortable with that. I believe the nation is well served by having a congressional party that can maintain some distance from the White House and I am concerned that this could weaken Congress's ability to do that. I look much more favorably, therefore, on unlimited expenditures that pass through state and local parties and require the use of volunteers." Malbin's suggestion is a plausible alternative that would basically accomplish the same goal, although his concern about White House control is more justified for the RNC and DNC than for the separate House and Senate campaign committees in each party. These latter groups, it can be argued, are more responsive to their congressional sponsors than to the White House even in a strong, centralized administration like Reagan's. They are certainly semi-autonomous bodies that have occasionally undertaken activities not entirely pleasing to the national committees or the incumbent administration, as the national party leaders are frank to admit in private.
72. See *Congressional Quarterly Almanac 1977* (Washington, D.C.: Congressional Quarterly, Inc., 1978), p. 798; *Congressional Quarterly Almanac 1978* (Washington, D.C.: Congressional Quarterly, Inc., 1979), p. 769; *Congressional Quarterly Almanac 1979* (Washington, D.C.: Congressional Quarterly, Inc., 1980), p. 551. See also Alexander, *Financing the 1980 Elections,* pp. 19–21; and a number of other sources listed in the Selected Bibliography. For a discussion

of more recent proposals on public financing, see Malbin, "Looking Back at the Future of Campaign Finance Reforms"; and Candice J. Nelson, "The Consequences of Campaign Finance Reform," *Election Politics* 1 (Winter 1983–1984): 25–28.

73. Prepared statement of Steven J. Uhlfelder, chairman, Special Committee on Election Law and Voter Participation on Behalf of the American Bar Association, in U.S., Congress, Senate, Committee on Rules and Administration, *Hearing on the Federal Election Campaign Act of 1971, as Amended, and on Various Measures to Amend the Act: S. 85, S. 151, S. 732, S. 810, S. 1185, S. 1350, and S. 1684,* 98th Cong., 1st sess., S. HRG 98–588, Jan. 27, 1983, p. 302.
74. *PACs and Lobbies* 3 (Dec. 15, 1982): 2.
75. See editorial, *Business Week,* Nov. 22, 1982, p. 132.
76. Center for Responsive Politics' poll of Congress. See note 53, above. The question read: "What is your view of some form of public financing of congressional elections?" While 51% were in favor, 43% were opposed, with 6% not sure. The Center's survey of 120 former congressmen produced a different result, however: only 39% were in favor of public financing, with 59% opposed. See *U.S. News and World Report,* Mar. 7, 1983, pp. 42–44.
77. Common Cause, in cooperation with congressional allies, designed just such a proposal in 1983.
78. *PACs and Lobbies* 4 (June 15, 1983): 6.
79. Prepared statement of John T. Dolan, *Hearing on the Federal Election Campaign Act of 1971,* p. 377.
80. See Schneider, "Campaign Financing"; Alexander, *Financing the 1980 Election,* p. 16–17; and Cantor, *Political Action Committees,* p. 210.
81. An in-person, random sample of 1,500 adults conducted in August 1982.
82. An in-person, random sample of 1,503 adults conducted in January and February 1983.
83. While just 4% *strongly* approved of public funding, 29% registered strong disapproval.
84. See *State Opinion Report* 2 (Summer 1983). For example, a Gannett News Service/Gordon Black poll, a random-sample telephone survey of 1,026 registered voters in New York state, conducted from June 23 to July 1, 1982, prior to the November 1982 gubernatorial election, asked its sample this question: "In the contest for Governor this Fall, both candidates are likely to raise and spend in excess of $10 million dollars on their campaigns. This means that the candidates will be forced to raise most of this money through appeals to wealthy private citizens and various interest groups. One alternative to this situation would be to have these campaigns financed out of public funds raised through taxes. In general, how do you feel about the public financing of statewide races? Are you strongly in favor, moderately in favor, moderately opposed, or strongly opposed?" Despite the question wording's slight bias *in favor* of public financing (because of the public's likely negative reaction to candidate solicitation of "fat cats" and special-interest groups), respondents were opposed to public financing by more than two to one (65% to 30%). And while only 8% "strongly favored" financing, fully 39% "strongly opposed" it, indicating that the intensity of feeling about the issue is almost monopolized

by the proposal's opponents. It may be that the key phrase in the question is "raised through taxes." In an age of diminishing resources and significant tax-increase pressures, voters are much more likely to nix measures they consider worthwhile once they see the pricetag—a pricetag they know will be reflected in their tax bill. Similarly, in the fifth annual Florida Policy Survey, a random-sample telephone poll of 923 adult Florida residents conducted from Jan. 24 to Feb. 21, 1983, respondents were asked whether the state or private contributors should provide campaign financing for statewide candidates. Only 14% favored state aid, while about 64% preferred private donations, and 19% expressed belief in a "middle position" between the two alternatives (about 4% had no opinion on the subject). It should be noted that the question's wording may have tilted the results somewhat against public financing. Had the phrase "special-interest money" been used instead of "private" contributions, for example, the proportion of respondents favoring public financing would undoubtedly have been higher.

85. See Cantor, *Political Action Committees,* p. 210; Schneider, "Campaign Financing," p. 473.
86. As quoted in *Newsweek,* July 18, 1983, p. 11.
87. The reform proposed here is similar in some but not all respects to a bill introduced in 1983 by Reps. Matthew McHugh (D–N.Y.) and Barber Conable (R–N.Y.).
88. Estimate of the Joint Tax Committee of Congress, provided by Common Cause.
89. See Chapter 3, p. 86. See also Alexander and Haggerty, *The Federal Election Campaign Act,* p. 57.
90. Samuelson, "The Campaign Reform Failure," p. 35.
91. Adamany and Agree, *Political Money,* p. 113; David Adamany, "PAC's and the Democratic Financing of Politics," *Arizona Law Review* 22, no. 2 (1980): 597–98.
92. See Sabato, *The Rise of Political Consultants,* pp. 220–67.
93. Robert Timberg, "The PAC Business," *Baltimore Sun,* a series of articles which ran during July 11–19, 1982.
94. See also the deceptive NCPAC letter described in Chapter 3, pp. 100–101.
95. See *Political Finance/Lobby Reporter* 24 (June 30, 1982): 173.
96. See Alexander, *Financing the 1980 Election,* pp. 412–15.
97. Testimony of Sen. Paul S. Sarbanes (R–Md.), in U.S., Congress, Senate, Committee on Rules and Administration, *Hearing on the Federal Election Campaign Act of 1971, as Amended, and on Various Measures to Amend the Act: S. 85, S. 151, S. 732, S. 810, S. 1185, S. 1350, and S. 1684,* 98th Cong., 1st sess., S. HRG 98–588, Jan. 27, 1983, p. 157.
98. As quoted in Alexander and Haggerty, *The Federal Election Campaign Act,* p. 86.
99. See Margaret Ann Latus, "Assessing Ideological PACs: From Outrage to Understanding," in *Money and Politics in the United States: Financing Elections in the 1980s,* edited by Michael J. Malbin (Washington, D.C.: American Enterprise Institute / Chatham House, 1984), p. 150.
100. See Alexander, *Financing the 1980 Election,* p. 388; and *National Journal* 15

Dec. 17, 1983): 2631. In March 1985 the Supreme Court upheld a lower court ruling that declared unconstitutional the $1,000 limitation on independent spending by any PAC in a presidential election. (FEC v. NCPAC, 105 Sup. Ct. 1459 [1985]). The FEC lost an earlier case on the same matter when the Supreme Court deadlocked with a split four-to-four vote, and since the Court did not decide the new case until well after the 1984 elections, PACs were in essence free to spend independently without limit in the 1984 presidential race. (*See Campaign Practices Reports* 11 [April 23, 1984]: 3.) The FEC has also been rebuffed in attempts to force some individuals using independent expenditures to comply with the disclosure requirements of FECA. For example, in 1983 a U.S. District Court judge in California refused to fine two businessmen for failing to disclose the $33,000 they spent on newspaper advertisements critical of President Carter shortly before the 1980 general election. Since the advertisements did not expressly advocate Carter's defeat in his reelection bid, they were deemed outside the FEC's jurisdiction–and thus outside the realm of FECA's disclosure and reporting requirements, as well as its contribution and spending limitations. See Steve Goldberg, "Big Hole Seen in Campaign Spending Law," *Richmond Times-Dispatch,* Feb. 26, 1984, pp. A1, A7.

101. 96 S. Ct. 612 (1976) or 424 U.S. 1 (1976).
102. See John P. Relman, "Making Campaign Finance Law Enforceable: Closing the Independent Expenditure Loophole," *Journal of Law Reform* 15 (Winter 1982): 370–72.
103. See Alexander, *Financing the 1980 Election,* pp. 464–65; *Political Finance/Lobby Reporter,* Nov. 11, 1981, p. 291; ibid., Dec. 9, 1981, p. 319; *PACs and Lobbies* 4 (July 6, 1983): 1; *Campaign Practices Reports* 10 (Mar. 18, 1983): 4, 8; *Washington Post,* Oct. 3, 1983, p. A3.
104. See Alexander, *Financing the 1980 Election,* pp. 474–75; and *PACs and Lobbies* 4 (Feb. 2, 1983): 4.
105. See testimony of Sen. Lloyd Bentsen (D–Tex.), in U.S., Congress, Senate, Committee on Rules and Administration, *Hearing on the Federal Election Campaign Act of 1971, as Amended, and on Various Measures to Amend the Act: S. 85, S. 151, S. 732, S. 810, S. 1185, S. 1350, and S. 1684,* 98th Cong., 1st sess., S. HRG 98–588, Jan. 26, 1983, p. 56.
106. Sen. Slade Gorton (R–Wash.) has introduced a bill to permit candidates to declare to the FEC that independent expenditures benefiting them *appear* to be coordinated, thus (says Gorton) subjecting the independent spending to regular contribution limits. The independent groups scoff at the proposal, calling it prior restraint on their free speech, and they pledge to fight it in the unlikely event it is enacted. See *PACs and Lobbies* 4 (Feb. 2, 1983): 4.
107. *Washington Post,* Oct. 3, 1983, p. A3.
108. This was one provision of Obey's "Clean Campaign Act of 1983," H.R. 2490.
109. See note 53, above. In the poll of 140 congressmen, 29% opposed the proposal and 11% had no opinion.
110. Malbin, "Looking Back at the Future of Campaign Finance Reform," p. 239.
111. See, for example, the prepared statement of John T. Dolan, *Hearing on the Federal Election Campaign Act of 1971,* p. 377.
112. Note especially the distinction between "honest" and "dishonest" graft in

William L. Riordan, *Plunkitt of Tammany Hall: A Series of Very Plain Talks on Very Practical Politics Delivered by Ex-Senator George Washington Plunkitt, the Tammany Hall Philosopher, From His Rostrum—the New York County Courthouse Boot Black Stand* (New York: McClure, Phillips and Co., 1905; reprinted New York: Dutton, 1963), p. 29.

113. "Cleaning Up Reform," *Wall Street Journal,* Nov. 10, 1983, p. 26.
114. Finley Peter Dunne, *The World of Mr. Dooley,* edited with an introduction by Louis Filler (New York: Collier Books, 1962), pp. 155–56.
115. From *Federalist No. 51.*

AFTERWORD. THE 1984 ELECTIONS

1. See Table 1–1, pp. 12–13. There were actually 4,345 PACs active at some time in the 1983–1984 election cycle, but only 4,009 remained in existence by December 31, 1984. Only 3,006 PACs actually made contributions to federal candidates in 1983 or 1984.
2. Nonconnected PACs recorded the largest gain (34 percent), followed by corporate PACs (28 percent), labor (27 percent), and trade (21 percent).
3. This compares with 16 percent in 1982 Senate contests and 29 percent in 1982 House races.
4. From 1980 to 1982 spending increased by 43 percent, and from 1978 to 1980 by 23 percent.
5. Spending in Senate races rose at a much higher rate of 23.1 percent.
6. Challengers received 10 percent of corporate PAC funds and 11 percent of the trade PAC money; open-seat candidates managed to secure 12 percent of the corporate PAC treasure and 10 percent of the trade PAC cash.
7. Labor PACs gave 23 percent of their money to challengers and 13 percent to open-seat candidates.
8. Nonconnecteds gave 50 percent of their money to incumbents, 34 percent to challengers, and 16 percent to open-seat candidates.
9. See Table 3–2, p. 75 for comparison.
10. In 1980 and 1982 House incumbents received 34 percent and 37 percent, respectively, of their campaign funds from PACs.
11. Common Cause campaign finance press release, April 12, 1985, pp. 4–5.
12. As counted here, an "unopposed" candidate had no general-election opponent and either no or only minor primary opposition.
13. These same reasons account, in part, for the tapering off of campaign spending mentioned earlier. In addition, the declining rate of increase in spending is a product of the lower inflation rate and the provision of more cut-rate campaign services by the political parties in 1984.
14. Michael J. Malbin and Thomas W. Skladony, "Campaign Finance, 1984: A Preliminary Analysis of House and Senate Receipts" (Washington, D.C.: American Enterprise Institute, December 2, 1984), p. 1.
15. Brooks Jackson, "GOP Group Uses Cash Creatively," *Wall Street Journal,* September 13, 1984, p. 58.

16. See Chapter 6. Even while the parties are indirectly limiting PACs, they increased the share of PAC money given to national party committees from $6 million in 1982 to $10.4 million in 1984.
17. About $3.4 million was spent independently on Senate races ($2.1 million positively, $1.3 million negatively); $1.5 million was spent independently on House contests ($1.3 million positively, $0.2 million negatively).
18. About $2 million was spent independently by PACs for pro-Democratic or anti-Republican purposes, compared to $2.9 million for pro-Republican or anti-Democratic campaigns. The edge for the GOP was actually somewhat less because of anti-Republican independent expenditures by individuals, mainly Michael Goland, a wealthy real estate developer from California who spent more than $400,000 to help defeat GOP Senator Charles Percy of Illinois.
19. George Lardner, Jr., "Outlays for Reagan Avoid Federal Ceiling," *Washington Post,* November 4, 1984, p. A8. The ASC mailing was technically not an independent expenditure, as determined by the group, and was apparently not reported to the FEC.
20. *The Political Report* 7 (August 24, 1984): 2.
21. See *Campaign Practices Reports* 11 (July 30, 1984): 1–3.
22. *New Republic* 190 (May 28, 1984): 9.
23. It could be convincingly argued that the FEC–intentionally starved and hamstrung by Congress to keep it relatively toothless–needs an infusion of funds even if no new responsibilities are added. Among other things, disclosure (particularly as election day approaches) needs to be more prompt and accessible, but the FEC currently lacks the resources to accomplish this.
24. See Richard P. Conlon, "A New Problem in Campaign Financing . . . and a *Simple* Legislative Solution," prepared for the annual meeting of the American Political Science Association, Washington, D.C., August 30–September 2, 1984. Conlon also provided the 1984 figure to the author. Individual contributions of all sizes have also declined as a proportion of money raised. Whereas House and Senate candidates secured 61 percent of their funds from individuals in 1978 and 57 percent in 1980, individuals provided only 53 percent in 1982 and 49 percent in 1984.
25. See p. 180.
26. See Edward Roeder, "House Campaign Borrowing is Corrupting Elections," *Washington Post,* April 14, 1985, p. B1; and "Banks and Political Lending," *Washington Post* editorial, April 16, 1985, p. A18. It is certainly true that fundraising pressure is a constant of life for all congressmen, whether they have debts or not. But personally secured loans are particularly worrisome, since they present the opportunity for the lending banks to assert undue influence–though they are strictly regulated on this score. Or, in the case of a loan from a candidate's personal monies, post-election PAC and individual gifts can go right into a congressman's pocket (as he repays the loan to himself).
27. The clause was contained in the 1979 amendments to the Federal Election Campaign Act.

28. See Kevin Chaffee, "Money Under the Mattress: What Congressmen Don't Spend," *Washington Monthly* 16 (September 1984): 32–38.
29. Congressmen must pay tax on any campaign money converted to personal use —but not on loans.
30. Chaffee, pp. 36–37.
31. As quoted in Chaffee, p. 37.
32. To reduce administrative costs, *pro rata* refunds of contributions could be limited to those who gave more than a nominal amount (perhaps $100).
33. Common Cause press release, April 12, 1985, p. 6.

Selected Bibliography

This very brief selective bibliography lists some major books, articles, and conference papers about PACs. The footnotes in this volume refer to many other works as well. Readers who would like a lengthier bibliography on the subject may obtain one from the author for a prepaid charge of $10.00 by writing to: Prof. Larry Sabato, Department of Government, University of Virginia, 232 Cabell Hall, Charlottesville, VA 22901.

BOOKS

Adamany, David W. *Campaign Finance in America.* North Scituate, Mass.: Duxbury Press, 1972.

———, and Agree, George E. *Political Money: A Strategy for Campaign Financing in America.* Baltimore, Md.: The Johns Hopkins University Press, 1975.

Alexander, Herbert E. (ed.). *Campaign Money: Reform and Reality in the United States.* New York: The Free Press, 1976.

———. *The Case for PACs.* Washington, D.C.: Public Affairs Council, 1983.

———. *Financing Politics: Money, Elections, and Political Reform,* 3rd ed. Washington, D.C.: Congressional Quarterly Press, 1984.

———. *Financing the 1980 Election.* Lexington, Mass.: D. C. Heath, 1983.

———, and Haggerty, Brian A. *The Federal Election Campaign Act: After a Decade of Political Reform.* Washington, D.C.: Citizens' Research Foundation, 1981.

Congressional Quarterly, Inc., *Dollar Politics,* 3rd ed. Washington, D.C.: Congressional Quarterly, Inc., 1982.

Drew, Elizabeth. *Politics and Money: The New Road to Corruption.* New York: Macmillan, 1983.

Edsall, Thomas B. *The New Politics of Inequality.* New York: W.W. Norton & Co., 1984.

Fraser Associates. *The PAC Handbook: Political Action for Business.* Cambridge, Mass.: Ballinger Publishing Company, 1980.

Handler, Edward, and Mulkern, John R. *Business in Politics: Campaign Strategies of Corporate Political Action Committees.* Lexington, Mass.: Lexington Books, 1982.

Heard, Alexander. *The Costs of Democracy.* Chapel Hill, N.C.: University of North Carolina Press, 1969.

Jacobson, Gary C. *Money in Congressional Elections.* New Haven, Conn.: Yale University Press, 1980.

———. *The Politics of Congressional Elections.* Boston: Little, Brown and Company, 1983.

———, and Kernell, Samuel. *Strategy and Choice in Congressional Elections,* 2nd ed. New Haven, Conn.: Yale University Press, 1983.

Kau, James B., and Rubin, Paul H. *Congressmen, Constituents and Contributions.* Boston: Studies in Public Choice Service, Martinus Nijhoff, 1982.

Malbin, Michael J. (ed.). *Money and Politics in the United States: Financing Elections in the 1980s.* Washington, D.C.: American Enterprise Institute / Chatham House, 1984.

——— (ed.). *Parties, Interest Groups and Campaign Finance Laws.* Washington, D.C.: American Enterprise Institute, 1980.

Ornstein, Norman J., and Elder, Shirley. *Interest Groups, Lobbying and Policymaking.* Washington, D.C.: Congressional Quarterly, Inc., 1978.

Overacker, Louise. *Money in Elections.* New York: Macmillan, 1972.

Roeder, Edward. *PACs Americana: A Directory of PACs and Their Interests.* Washington, D.C.: Sunshine Services, 1982.

Rothenberg, Stuart, and Rolden, Richard R. *Business PACs and Ideology: A Study of Contributions in the 1982 Elections.* Washington, D.C.: The Institute for Government and Politics of the Free Congress Research and Education Foundation, 1983.

Sabato, Larry. *The Rise of Political Consultants: New Ways of Winning Elections.* New York: Basic Books, 1981.

Sethi, S. Prakash, and Nemiki, Nobuaki. *Public Perception of and Attitude toward Political Action Committees (PACs): An Empirical Analysis of Nationwide Survey Data—Some Strategic Implications for the Corporate Community.* Richardson, Tex.: Center for Research in Business and Social Policy, School of Management and Administration, University of Texas at Dallas, 1982.

Sorauf, Frank J., and the Twentieth Century Fund Task Force on Political Action Committees. *What Price PACs?* New York: Twentieth Century Fund, 1984.

Thayer, George. *Who Shakes the Money Tree?* New York: Simon and Schuster, 1973.

Weinberger, Marvin, and Greevy, David U. *The PAC Directory.* Cambridge, Mass.: Ballinger Publishing Company, 1982.

ARTICLES

Adamany, David. "PAC's and the Democratic Financing of Politics." *Arizona Law Review* 22, no. 2 (1980): 569–602.

Arieff, Irwin B.; Cohodes, Nadine, and Whittle, Richard. "Senator Helms Builds a Machine of Interlinked Organizations to Shape Both Politics, Policy." *Congressional Quarterly Weekly* 40 (Mar. 6, 1982): 479–505.

Bolton, John R. "Constitutional Limitations on Restricting Corporate and Union PACs." *Arizona Law Review* 22, no. 2 (1980): 373–426.

Bonfede, Dom. "Some Things Don't Change—Cost of 1982 Congressional Races Higher Than Ever." *National Journal* 14 (Oct. 30, 1982): 1832–36.

Budde, Bernadette A. "The Practical Role of Corporate PACs in the Political Process." *Arizona Law Review* 22, no. 2 (1980), 555–67.

Chappell, Henry W., Jr. "Campaign Contributions and Congressional Voting." *Review of Economics and Statistics* 61 (1982): 77–83.

———. "Campaign Contributions and Voting on the Cargo Preference Bill: A Comparison of Simultaneous Models." *Public Choice* 36 (1981): 301–12.

Cohen, Richard. "Giving Till It Hurts: 1982 Campaign Prompts New Look at Financing Races." *National Journal* 14 (Dec. 18, 1982): 2144–53.

Edsall, Thomas B. "Economic Ills Strain Alliance of Oilmen, GOP." *Washington Post,* Apr. 25, 1983, pp. A1, A4.

Ehrenhalt, Alan. "The Natural Limitations of PAC Power." *Congressional Quarterly Weekly* 41 (Apr. 9, 1983): 723.

Elliott, Lee Ann. "Political Action Committees—Precincts of the 1980's." *Arizona Law Review* 22, no. 2 (1980), 539–54.

Epstein, Edwin M. "Business and Labor under the Federal Election Campaign Act of 1971." in *Parties, Interest Groups, and Campaign Finance Laws,* edited by Michael J. Malbin. Washington, D.C.: American Enterprise Institute, 1980.

———. "An Irony of Electoral Reform." *Regulation* 3 (May–June 1979): 35–44.

Glen, Maxwell, and Popkins, James K. "Liberal PACs Learning It Won't Be Easy to Stem the Conservative Tide." *National Journal* 14 (Mar. 20, 1982): 500–1.

Green, Mark. "Political PAC-Man." *The New Republic* 188 (Dec. 13, 1982): 18–25.

Hamburger, Tom. "How to Fleece the PACs." *Washington Monthly* 15 (July–August 1983): 27–31.

Herndon, James F. "Access, Record, and Competition as Influences on Interest Groups' Contributions to Congressional Campaigns." *Journal of Politics* 44, no. 4 (1982): 996–1019.

Hunt, Albert R. "An Inside Look at Politicians Hustling PACs." *Wall Street Journal,* Oct. 1, 1982, p. 43.

Kamenar, Paul D. "PACs, the Taxpayer, and Campaign Finance Reform." The Heritage Foundation *Backgrounder* 257 (Apr. 14, 1983): 1–19.

Light, Larry. "The Game of PAC Targeting: Friends, Foes and Guesswork." *Congressional Quarterly Weekly* 39 (Nov. 21, 1981): 2267–70.

Malbin, Michael J. "The Business PAC Phenomenon: Neither a Mountain Nor a Molehill." *Regulation* 3 (May–June 1979): 41–43.

———. "The Problem of PAC-Journalism." *Public Opinion* 5 (December/January 1983): 15–16, 59.

Maraniss, David. "In PAC Heaven, Contributions Flow Plentifully, All Year Long." *Washington Post,* Aug. 21, 1983, pp. A1, A6.

Perry, James M. "How Realtors' PAC Rewards Office Seekers Helpful to the Industry." *Wall Street Journal,* Aug. 2, 1982, pp. 1, 13.

Relman, John P. "Making Campaign Finance Law Enforceable: Closing the Independent Expenditure Loophole." *Journal of Law Reform* 15 (Winter 1982): 363–97.

Robinson, Gail. "Many Happy Returns." *Environmental Action* 12 (December 1980): 28–32.

Roeder, Edward. "Catalyzing Favorable Reactions: A Look at Chemical Industry PACs." *Sierra Club Bulletin* 66 (March/April 1981): 23–26.

Russakoff, Dale. "Getting Out 'Green Vote' for Friends of Nature." *Washington Post,* Oct. 5, 1982, p. A1.

Samuelson, Robert J. "The Campaign Reform Failure." *The New Republic* 189 (Sept. 5, 1983): 28–36.

Schneider, William. "Campaign Financing: Curb Special-Interest Giving but Don't Go Public." *National Journal* 15 (Feb. 26, 1983): 472–73.

Sorauf, Frank J. "Political Parties and Political Action Committees: Two Life Cycles." *Arizona Law Review* 22, no. 2 (1980): 445–63.

Sproul, Curtis C. "Corporations and Unions in Federal Politics: A Practical Approach to Federal Election Law Compliance." *Arizona Law Review* 22, no. 2 (1980): 465–518.

Taylor, Paul. "Efforts to Revise Campaign Laws Aim at PACs." *Washington Post,* Feb. 28, 1983, pp. A1, A5.

———. "Lobbyists Lose the Game, Not the Guccis," *Washington Post,* July 31, 1983, pp. A1, A12.

Thomas, Evan, and Issacson, Walter. "Running with the PACs." *Time,* Oct. 25, 1982, pp. 20–26.

Timberg, Robert. "The PAC Business." *Baltimore Sun,* July 11–19, 1982.

Welch, William P. "Campaign Contributions and Legislative Voting: Milk Money and Dairy Price Supports." *Western Political Quarterly* 35 (December 1982): 478–95.

———. "Money and Votes: A Simultaneous Equation Model." *Public Choice* 36, no. 2 (1981): 209–34.

Wertheimer, Fred. "The PAC Phenomenon in American Politics." *Arizona Law Review* 22, no. 2 (1980): 603–26.

Wright, J. Skelly. "Money and the Pollution of Politics: Is the First Amendment an Obstacle for Political Equality?" *Columbia Law Review* 82 (May 1982): 609–45.

Zuckerman, Ed. "Campaign Disclosure I: Money for What?" *Campaigns and Elections* 3 (Fall 1982): 36–39.

CONFERENCE PAPERS

Brown, Kirk F. "Campaign Contributions and Congressional Voting." Prepared for the annual meeting of the American Political Science Association, Chicago, Ill., Sept. 1–4, 1983.

Eismeier, Theodore J., and Pollock, Philip H. "Political Action Committees: The Shaping of Strategy and Influence." Prepared for the annual meeting of the Midwest Political Science Association, Chicago, Ill., Apr. 20–23, 1983.

Frendreis, John P., and Waterman, Richard W. "PAC Contributions and Legislative Behavior: Senate Voting on Trucking Deregulation." Prepared for the annual meeting of the Midwest Political Science Association, Chicago, Ill., Apr. 20–22, 1983.

Gais, Thomas L. "On the Scope and Bias of Interest Group Involvement in Elections." Prepared for the annual meeting of the American Political Science Association, Chicago, Ill., Sept. 1–4, 1983.

Green, John C. "Interest Group Campaign Contributions: Teaching Old Dogs New Tricks or Getting New Dogs?" Prepared for the annual meeting of the Southern Political Science Association, Atlanta, Ga., Oct. 28–30, 1982.

———, and Guth, James L. "Party, PAC, and Demonization: Religiosity among Political Contributors." Presented to the Caucus on Faith and Politics, at the annual meeting of the American Political Science Association, Chicago, Ill., Sept. 1–4, 1983.

Jones, Ruth S., and Miller, Warren E. "Financing Campaigns: Modes of Individual Contribution." Prepared for the annual meeting of the Midwest Political Science Association, Chicago, Ill., Apr. 21–23, 1983.

Latus, Margaret Ann. "Mobilizing Christians for Political Action: Campaigning with God on Your Side." Prepared for the annual meeting of the Society for the Scientific Study of Religion meeting jointly with the Religious Research Association and the Association for the Sociology of Religion, Providence, R.I., Oct. 22–24, 1982.

Nelson, Candice J. "Counting the Cash: PAC Contributions to Members of the House of Representatives." Prepared for the annual meeting of the American Political Science Association, Denver, Colo., Sept. 2–5, 1982.

Sorauf, Frank J. "Accountability in the Political Action Committees: Who's in Charge?" Prepared for the annual meeting of the American Political Science Association, Denver, Colo., Sept. 2–5, 1982.

Yiannakis, Diana Evans. "PAC Contributions and House Voting on Conflictual and Consensual Issues: The Windfall Profits Tax and the Chrysler Loan Guarantee." Prepared for the annual meeting of the American Political Science Association, Chicago, Ill., Sept. 1–4, 1983.

Index